D1566216

Making innovative use of Kierkegaard's later religious writings as well as his earlier philosophical works, David Gouwens explores this philosopher's religious and theological thought, focusing on human nature, Christ, and Christian discipleship. He helps the reader approach Kierkegaard as a religious thinker, since Kierkegaard regarded religion as fundamental to his enterprise, and sought to evoke religious dispositions in his audience. Gouwens discusses Kierkegaard's main concerns as an advocate of genuine Christianity; his treatment of religion using the dialectic of "becoming Christian"; and whether the common interpretation of Kiekegaard's religious thought as privatistic and asocial is correct. Gouwens appraises both the edifying discourses and the pseudonymous writings, and studies the particular problems posed by the latter. Situated between foundationalism and irrationalism, Kierkegaard's thought is seen to anticipate the end of "modernity," while standing at the center of the Christian tradition.

KIERKEGAARD AS RELIGIOUS THINKER

KIERKEGAARD AS
RELIGIOUS THINKER

DAVID J. GOUWENS

Associate Professor of Theology,
Brite Divinity School,
Texas Christian University

Published by the Press Syndicate of the University of Cambridge
The Pitt Building, Trumpington Street, Cambridge CB2 1RP
40 West 20th Street, New York, NY 10011–4211, USA
10 Stamford Road, Oakleigh, Melbourne 3166, Australia

© Cambridge University Press 1996

First published in 1996

Printed in Great Britain at Woolnough Bookbinders, Irthlingborough, Northants.

A catalogue record for this book is available from the British Library

Library of Congress cataloguing in publication data

Gouwens, David Jay.
Kierkegaard as religious thinker
David J. Gouwens.
p.   cm.
Includes bibliographical references and index.
ISBN 0 521 46031 X (hardback)   ISBN 0 521 55551 5 (paperback)
1. Kierkegaard, Søren, 1813–1855 – Religion. 1. Title.
B4378.R44G68 1996
230'.044'092 – dc20 95–11442 CIP

ISBN 0 521 46031 X hardback
ISBN 0 521 55551 5 paperback

CE

To Sharon
and
In Memoriam
Arthur H. Jentz, Jr.
(1934–1993)

Contents

Acknowledgements

A number of friends and institutions have supported me over the course of this endeavor. Paul L. Holmer and Don E. Saliers – both then of Yale – engendered and directed my early interest in Kierkegaard's thought; to them I owe the basic orientation of this study, and the wonderful example of their passion as teachers. I have also learned much from the scholarship and friendship of members of the Søren Kierkegaard Society, too many to name individually; their stimulation is evident throughout this study. Initial research on what Robert L. Perkins has dubbed Kierkegaard's "second literature" came from a summer research grant from Brite Divinity School, Texas Christian University. During that summer, the Howard V. Hong and Edna H. Hong Kierkegaard Library at St. Olaf College, Northfield, Minnesota, provided its remarkable resources, housing, and hospitality; Cynthia Lund was most helpful. A further semester's leave of absence from Texas Christian University enabled initial work on the manuscript; warm thanks are due to the Disciples Divinity House of the University of Chicago for its hospitality, and that university's library for its research facilities. Dr. David W. Johnson, colleague and friend, took time away from his own teaching and research to read a draft of early chapters. His comments and criticisms were most helpful, as were those of the readers for Cambridge University Press. I am indebted to Alex Wright of Cambridge University Press for his interest in this project and good counsel throughout. Thanks also to my research assistants, Don Bright, who creatively found his way through the intricacies of modern library computing in early stages of this study, and Ben Taylor, who checked citations prior to final publication. Lana Byrd's superb secretarial skills were invaluable. These colleagues and friends are, of course, not responsible for the views expressed in these pages.

This book is offered in memory of a teacher without parallel, Arthur H. Jentz, Jr., Professor of Philosophy at Hope College, Holland,

Michigan. No Kierkegaardian, he none the less embodied many of the passions discussed in this book – not least a truly Climacean humor. His premature death is a loss to many.

Without the support and love of my wife Sharon, this book could not have been written. Busy enough with her own writing projects in religion and the visual arts, she always gave of her time, attention, and support, and it is to her that I dedicate this book.

Abbreviations

References to Kierkegaard's writings in the footnotes use the sigla given below, followed by page number, for example, *SUD* 14. (Where possible, and with few exceptions, I employ the new Princeton University Press translations, *Kierkegaard's Writings*, 1978–   .) Immediately following this reference, and in parentheses, are the corresponding volume and page numbers in the first Danish edition, *Søren Kierkegaard's Samlede Værker* [*The Collected Works of Søren Kierkegaard*], ed. A. B. Drachmann, J. L. Heiberg, and H. O. Lange, 14 volumes (Copenhagen: Gyldendal, 1901-06). For example, *SUD* 14 (*SV* XI 127).

References to Kierkegaard's journals are from *Søren Kierkegaard's Journals and Papers*, ed. and trans. Howard V. Hong and Edna H. Hong, assisted by Gregor Malantschuk, 7 volumes. Bloomington and London: Indiana University Press, 1967–78. The abbreviation is *JP*, followed by the volume and entry numbers. For example, *JP* 1 400. This is immediately followed in parentheses by the location in *Søren Kierkegaards Papirer* [*Søren Kierkegaard's Papers*], I–XI³ and XII–XIII, ed. P. A. Heiberg, V. Kuhr, and E. Torsting, 16 volumes. 2nd edn., augmented, Niels Thulstrup. Copenhagen: Gyldendal, 1968-78. The abbreviation is *Pap.* followed by the volume, group, and entry numbers, and finally by the date. For example, *JP* 1 400 (*Pap.* X⁴ A 200, n.d., 1851). *JP* followed by a paginated number refers to an editor's note in that volume rather than an entry. For example, *JP* 1, p. 100.

OAR   *On Authority and Revelation: The Book on Adler, or a Cycle of Ethico-Religious Essays*, trans. Walter Lowrie, introduction to the Torchbook edition by Frederick Sontag. Harper Torchbooks. The Cloister Library. New York: Harper & Row, 1955; 1966.

CD	*Christian Discourses*, including *The Lilies of the Field and the Birds of the Air* and *Three Discourses at the Communion on Fridays*, trans. Walter Lowrie. Princeton University Press, 1940.
CA	*The Concept of Anxiety*, trans. Reidar Thomte in collaboration with Albert B. Anderson. Princeton University Press, 1980.
CI	*The Concept of Irony, together with "Notes on Schelling's Berlin Lectures,"* trans. Howard V. Hong and Edna H. Hong. Princeton University Press, 1989.
CUP	*Concluding Unscientific Postscript*, ed. and trans. Howard V. Hong and Edna H. Hong. 2 volumes. Princeton University Press, 1992.
COR	*The* Corsair *Affair, and Articles Related to the Writings*, ed. and trans. Howard V. Hong and Edna H. Hong. Princeton University Press, 1982.
EUD	*Eighteen Upbuilding Discourses*, trans. Howard V. Hong and Edna H. Hong. Princeton University Press, 1990.
EO	*Either/Or*, trans. Howard V. Hong and Edna H. Hong. 2 volumes. Princeton University Press, 1987.
FT	*Fear and Trembling*, in *Fear and Trembling* and *Repetition*, trans. Howard V. Hong and Edna H. Hong. Princeton University Press, 1983.
FSE	*For Self-Examination*, in *For Self-Examination* and *Judge for Yourself!*, trans. Howard V. Hong and Edna H. Hong. Princeton University Press, 1990.
JC	*Johannes Climacus, or De omnibus dubitandum est*, in *Philosophical Fragments* and *Johannes Climacus*, trans. Howard V. Hong and Edna H. Hong. Princeton University Press, 1985.
JP	*Journals and Papers*. See above.
JFY	*Judge for Yourself!*, in *For Self-Examination* and *Judge for Yourself!*, trans. Howard V. Hong and Edna H. Hong. Princeton University Press, 1990.
KAUC	*Kierkegaard's Attack Upon "Christendom" 1854–1855*, trans., with introduction, Walter Lowrie. Princeton University Press, 1944.
Pap.	*Papirer*. See above.
PF	*Philosophical Fragments*, in *Philosophical Fragments* and *Johannes Climacus*, trans. Howard V. Hong and Edna H. Hong. Princeton University Press, 1985.

PV   *The Point of View for My Work as an Author: A Report to History and Related Writings,* trans. Walter Lowrie, newly edited with a preface by Benjamin Nelson. New York: Harper & Row, 1962.

PC   *Practice in Christianity,* trans. Howard V. Hong and Edna H. Hong. Princeton University Press, 1991.

R   *Repetition,* in *Fear and Trembling* and *Repetition,* trans. Howard V. Hong and Edna H. Hong. Princeton University Press, 1983.

SV   *Samlede Værker.* See above.

SUD   *The Sickness Unto Death,* trans. Howard V. Hong and Edna H. Hong. Princeton University Press, 1980.

SUD   *The Sickness Unto Death,* trans. Alastair Hannay. London: Penguin Books, 1989.

SLW   *Stages on Life's Way,* ed. and trans. Howard V. Hong and Edna H. Hong. Princeton University Press, 1988.

TDIO   *Three Discourses on Imagined Occasions,* ed. and trans. Howard V. Hong and Edna H. Hong. Princeton University Press, 1993.

TA   *Two Ages: The Age of Revolution and the Present Age: A Literary Review,* trans. Howard V. Hong and Edna H. Hong. Princeton University Press, 1978.

UG   "The Unchangeableness of God," in *For Self-Examination and Judge for Yourselves! and Three Discourses 1851,* trans. with introduction and notes, Walter Lowrie. Princeton University Press, 1941.

UDVS   *Upbuilding Discourses in Various Spirits,* ed. and trans. Howard V. Hong and Edna H. Hong. Princeton University Press, 1993.

WL   *Works of Love: Some Christian Reflections in the Form of Discourses,* trans. Howard and Edna Hong, preface R. Gregor Smith. Harper Torchbooks. The Cloister Library. New York: Harper & Row, 1962.

Introduction

The writings of Søren Kierkegaard (1813–55) have undergone a fate that he himself foresaw: appropriation and interpretation by scholarship and the canons of the academy – whether theological, philosophical, historical, or literary. Hence arise the uses of Kierkegaard and the primary myths they engender: Kierkegaard as "the father of existentialism" or inspirer of Christian "neo-orthodoxy" (the early Karl Barth and Rudolf Bultmann) or, more recently, Kierkegaard as proto-deconstructionist (Mark C. Taylor, Christopher Norris). Appropriated into the "history of philosophy" or "the history of theology," with the historian's need for typologizing (hence, comparing and contrasting him with other thinkers) and the professor's need to cover a wide range of "material," Kierkegaard's writings ironically have often become what he himself feared – a "subsection" within the history of thought, to say nothing of grist for the mill of academic publication and the furtherance of academic careers.[1]

The irony is compounded by two facts: first, Kierkegaard's stated intention in his literature was for what he called a "primitive" reading that engendered reflection and self-reflection in the reader, rather than merely abstract reflection unrelated to an existing person's concerns. "Scholarship more and more turns away from a primitive impression of existence ... One does not love, does not have faith, does not act; but one knows what erotic love is, what faith is."[2] So too, as a writer he distinguishes between an "essential author" who is inwardly directed, with a distinctive life-view (*Livsanskuelse*), from a "premise author" who lacks inward direction.[3] Hence, Kierkegaard muses again and again on the difficulties of writing and reading, the uncertainties of communication between author and reader. Second, such primitive reading was

---

[1]   *CUP* 250 (*SV* VII 211).
[2]   *CUP* 344 (*SV* VII 298).
[3]   *OAR* 3–11 (*Pap.* VII² B 235, 6–16).

I

meant to outmaneuver the scholarly apparatus of high academic
culture that systematically places obstacles before such primitive
reading, obstacles that he thought revealed deep resistances that people
place before such reading and understanding. Judging by the profusion
of scholarly literature on Kierkegaard, even he has been swallowed up
into the "subsection-uniform."

All of this makes yet another book "about Kierkegaard" immediately suspect, as a basic misunderstanding and betrayal of his intent as
a writer and thinker. For more readers than care to admit it, there is
something deeply opaque and troubling in strategy and spirit about
Kierkegaard's thought, for he is a writer who calls attention to the
resistances against primitive reading, and he can make one ashamed of
one's own thoughts and passions. In this he resembles such reflective
interrogators as Socrates and Ludwig Wittgenstein; American philosopher O. K. Bouwsma, who knew Wittgenstein, said that he was "the
nearest to a prophet I have ever known," and that "he robbed me of a
lazy comfort in my own mediocrity."[4]

But Bouwsma's reactions to Wittgenstein also offer a clue as to how
one might write and read "about Kierkegaard" without betraying
Kierkegaard's intent. In his own writing on Wittgenstein, Bouwsma said
that he was "a helper" who might orient a reader to Wittgenstein's
thought.[5] "Helper" is perhaps unfortunate, for it is not that Kierkegaard
(or Wittgenstein) is somehow beyond summation, scrutiny, or dis-
agreement. But "helper" is apt if it means that the solution to
scholarly misunderstanding of Kierkegaard is not hagiography –
indeed, Kierkegaard would himself see hagiography as yet another
misreading. The solution to both scholarly misunderstanding and hero-
worship is, rather, engagement with his writing. What Kierkegaard
desired – and deserves – above all is readers (and writers) who attempt to
"think with" (and "against") him, to enter into the concerns and issues
he raises with philosophical *eros* and passion.[6]

The present study is intended as an attempt to "think with"
Kierkegaard, specifically to help one approach Kierkegaard as a

[4]   O. K. Bouwsma, *Wittgenstein: Conversations 1949–1951*, ed. with an introduction by J. L. Craft
      and Ronald E. Hustwit (Indianapolis: Hackett Publishing Company, 1986), xv–xvi.
[5]   O.K. Bouwsma, "The Blue Book," in *Philosophical Essays* (Lincoln: The University of
      Nebraska Press, 1965), 177. Cited also in Robert C. Roberts, *Faith, Reason, and History:
      Rethinking Kierkegaard's* Philosophical Fragments (Macon, GA: Mercer University Press,
      1986), 4.
[6]   "Thinking with Kierkegaard" is the felicitous subtitle of a book of essays, Richard H. Bell,
      ed., *The Grammar of the Heart: Thinking with Kierkegaard and Wittgenstein: New Essays in Moral
      Philosophy and Theology* (San Francisco: Harper & Row, 1988).

religious thinker. By "religious thinker" I mean that his thought is *about* religion and at the same time is itself religious. Kierkegaard both analyzes religion and seeks to evoke religious dispositions in his readers. Indeed, one reason that Kierkegaard is a thinker to be reckoned with is that he has so many arrows in his quiver: as a religious thinker he at once presents profound and interesting philosophical and theological reflections *about* religion, but also presents his thoughts within a literary form that offers to an interested reader a "training" in religious ways of thinking and living. It is in this important sense that Kierkegaard wishes not only to describe what religion (and especially the Christian religion) are, but also to show it; his philosophy and theology are an introduction to, an exercise of, the practice of religious reflection. In this study, I will place him in dialogue with other religious thinkers, and I will disagree with him on certain theological matters, but throughout I attempt not simply to place him within either the history of thought or a typology of theologians, but to engage sympathetically with the questions and issues he raises as a religious thinker. In my view, this is what any work of commentary and criticism should do with any thinker of caliber.

Before elaborating on my approach more fully, it may help the reader to point out how this book differs from other approaches. Modern scholarship has devised a variety of ways to "read" Kierkegaard's authorship. This is due not only to the prolixity and inventiveness of scholars, but also to the fact that, as we have seen, Kierkegaard himself is many-sided as a thinker, at once a religious thinker, a philosopher, and a literary artist. Add to this his self-proclaimed irony and the pseudonymity of much of his authorship, to say nothing of its dialectical complexity, and Kierkegaard's writings appear to be a vast field awaiting the tools of competing schools of thought.

First, some scholars, like Josiah Thompson and Walter Lowrie, read Kierkegaard's literature biographically, as an account – veiled and cryptic though it be – of Kierkegaard's own struggles and turmoils, in particular the broken engagement with Regine Olsen and his troubled, ambivalent relationship with his father.[7] The assumption here is that the primary "meaning" of Kierkegaard's literature is a

---

[7]   See Josiah Thompson, *The Lonely Labyrinth: Kierkegaard's Pseudonymous Works* (Carbondale, IL: Southern Illinois University Press, 1967), and *Kierkegaard* (New York: Alfred A. Knopf, 1973); Walter Lowrie, *Kierkegaard* (New York: Oxford University Press, 1938) and *A Short Life of Kierkegaard* (Princeton University Press, 1942; 1965); Naomi Lebowitz, *Kierkegaard: A Life of Allegory* (Baton Rouge and London: Louisiana State University Press, 1985).

veiled communication of his personal experiences. On this reading, the literary devices he employed were designed primarily to disguise, yet indirectly reveal, the hidden secret meaning of his life. In more interesting vein is the approach that explores the literature with biographical methods aimed at showing the interplay between the author's various textual and empirical "I's," and the ambiguities of those various authorial masks.[8] Kierkegaard's use of pseudonymity – the device of publishing some of his books under pseudonyms – and the "secrets" that literature can simultaneously reveal and conceal have all understandably led many scholars to read the literature biographically. There is ample room for this kind of reading, for Kierkegaard himself acknowledged these deeply personal relationships as the fountainhead of his own productivity, and he speaks in his journals of the "secret note" that interprets his literature.[9] If the literature was, as he said, the product of his own struggles, are there not clues to these struggles to be unearthed in the texts, just as they are clearly spelled out in the journals? To take only one example: surely, this approach concludes, the meaning of Abraham's sacrifice of Isaac in *Fear and Trembling* is Søren's sacrifice of his engagement to Regine Olsen. At its extreme, this view holds the Kierkegaardian literature to be simply material for psychological diagnosis.

The biographical approaches nonetheless have limitations. As Mark C. Taylor has noted, Kierkegaard is not interested in his own existence, but in the existence of the reader; Kierkegaard deliberately withdraws behind the pseudonymous authors he creates.[10] He was adept at employing masks for the purposes of self-concealment and self-revelation, but he also maintained that the poet deals not with personal experience as such, but with the "possibilities" and "idealities" that experience generates. One's own "personal actuality" is not legitimate literary property.[11] In short, many things engaged Kierkegaard's concern as a writer, and not just his own struggles. His concern is with the "idealities," the "possibilities," of existence.

A second strategy of reading is to approach Kierkegaard primarily as a philosopher, a thinker who presents philosophical arguments and

---

8 Joakim Garff, "The Eyes of Argus: The Point of View and Points of View with Respect to Kierkegaard's 'Activity as an Author,'" *Kierkegaardiana* 15 (1991): 29–54.
9 *JP* v 5645 (*Pap.* IVA 85, n.d., 1843).
10 Mark C. Taylor, *Kierkegaard's Pseudonymous Authorship: A Study of Time and the Self* (Princeton University Press, 1975), 29–30.
11 *TA* 98–99 (*SV* VIII 91–92).

takes positions on certain classic issues in Western thought.[12] C. Stephen Evans, for example, rightly defends seeing at least the major Climacean writings (*Philosophical Fragments* and *Concluding Unscientific Postscript*) not only as philosophy, but much of it as good philosophy, and Kierkegaard as a philosopher who entertains ideas and presents philosophical arguments.[13] None the less, Kierkegaard is a philosopher with a difference. His concerns are often outside the mainstream of the philosophical tradition. As Richard H. Bell has noted, whereas philosophers of religion are often concerned with the justification of religious belief, or the range of epistemic credentials, that is, with presenting philosophical arguments, Kierkegaard, while concerned with these matters too, is equally interested in curing diseases of thought and life.[14] This contributes to the peculiar elusiveness of his thinking. Stanley Cavell's reflections on Wittgenstein and Freud characterize Kierkegaard's religious thought as well: it aims at preventing understanding unaccompanied by inner change.[15] And James Conant warns against seeing Kierkegaard as concerned primarily with "evidences" for religious or Christian belief.[16] *Pace* Conant Kierkegaard is concerned with such epistemological questions, yet Conant rightly sees that Kierkegaard's epistemological interests are in the service of another concern: allowing the religious context of the use of such concepts to stand forth. Hence, the therapy involved in Kierkegaard's philosophy too is not conducted only by marshaling arguments, but by unlearning old patterns and habits of thought, asking ourselves what we understand and do not understand, and by turning our attention as much to ourselves as "thinkers" and "questioners" as to the "issues." This therapy confronts illusions, disentangles meanings, weighs what we say and how we live.[17]

A third approach, sometimes in response to the philosophic appro-

---

[12] For Kierkegaard as "paraphilosopher," see Alastair Hannay, *Kierkegaard. The Arguments of the Philosophers*, ed. Ted Honderich (London and New York: Routledge & Kegan Paul, 1982), 8–18.

[13] C. Stephen Evans, *Kierkegaard's* Fragments *and* Postscript: *The Religious Philosophy of Johannes Climacus* (Atlantic Highlands, NJ: Humanities Press International, 1983), 4.

[14] Bell, *The Grammar of the Heart*, xii.

[15] Stanley Cavell, "The Availability of Wittgenstein's Later Philosophy," in George Pitcher, ed., *Wittgenstein: The "Philosophical Investigations." Modern Studies in Philosophy*, ed. Amelie Rorty. Anchor Books. (Garden City, NY: Doubleday & Co., 1966), 184.

[16] James Conant, "Kierkegaard, Wittgenstein, and Nonsense," in Ted Cohen, Paul Guyer, and Hilary Putnam eds., *Pursuits of Reason: Essays in Honor of Stanley Cavell* (Lubbock, TX: Texas Tech University Press, 1993), 209.

[17] See again O. K. Bouwsma, "The Blue Book," in *Philosophical Essays*, 183–87, on the therapy in Wittgenstein's philosophy of dispelling illusions.

priations of Kierkegaard, insists that Kierkegaard cannot be understood apart from his literary artistry. Louis Mackey's *Kierkegaard: A Kind
of Poet* has been the primary advocate of this position. He claims not
only that Kierkegaard's writings are literary – this has been long
recognized and studied in works such as Aage Henriksen's *Kierkegaards
Romaner (Kierkegaard's Novels)* – but that an understanding of his
literature is possible *only* through the use of literary critical approaches
to the literature. For Mackey, only attending to the literary aspects of
this literature can reveal its true shape and character.[18] The strength
of this approach is that it is sensitive to the qualities of Kierkegaard's
literature as literature. Helpful as Mackey's study is, however, one
must wonder whether such an extensive claim for literary study is
warranted. A primary difficulty with this approach is that it too tends
to misconstrue the intent of the writings. As Robert C. Roberts has
put it, Mackey's concern, as he himself admits, is to understand
Kierkegaard as Kierkegaard; Roberts judiciously counters that Kierkegaard's concern is rather with the reader's coming to understand other
matters.[19]

Related to this are varieties of deconstructionist readings of Kierkegaard's writing that undermine the illusion of an authoritative reading
of a text. They find in Kierkegaard's practice of indirect communication, duplicity, irony, and his uses of multiple pseudonymous masks
ample warrant for an approach that rejects a single authoritative
reading of the literature, allowing for multiple, indeed contradictory,
readings.[20] The undoubted strength of this approach is that it takes
seriously the possibility of multiple readings of his literature, that one
may, for example, read the aesthetic writings of *Either/Or* I and opt for
a life of pleasure, what Kierkegaard describes as an aesthetic existence,
and that there is not an internal necessity to the progression of the
"stages on life's way." This approach also serves notice that one
should not (and need not) make claims concerning Kierkegaard's
authorial intentions as the key to "understanding the meaning" of his

---

[18]   Louis Mackey, *Kierkegaard: A Kind of Poet* (Philadelphia: University of Pennsylvania Press, 1971);
       Aage Henriksen, *Kierkegaards Romaner* (Copenhagen: Gyldendal, 1954).
[19]   Robert C. Roberts, *Faith, Reason, and History*, 6.
[20]   Examples are found in the series *Kierkegaard and Postmodernism*, ed. Mark C. Taylor, including
       Louis Mackey, *Points of View: Readings of Kierkegaard* (Tallahassee: Florida State University
       Press, 1986); John Vignaux Smyth, *A Question of Eros: Irony in Sterne, Kierkegaard, and Barthes*
       (Tallahassee: Florida State University Press, 1986); Sylviane Agacinski, *Aparté: Conceptions and
       Deaths of Søren Kierkegaard* (Tallahassee: Florida State University Press, 1988). See also John
       Caputo, *Radical Hermeneutics: Repetition, Deconstruction, and the Hermeneutic Project* (Bloomington:
       Indiana University Press, 1987).

writing.[21] However, one restrained practitioner of deconstructive read-ings, Christopher Norris, has cautioned that, even without resorting to authorial intention, there are limits to this deconstructive reading of Kierkegaard. Instead of dissolving the texts into an ironic play of tropes, Kierkegaard's decentering texts employ irony to another end, made clear already in his dissertation *The Concept of Irony*: they drive the reader to a self-irony that may lead to a decisiveness that affirms "an undeconstructible bedrock of authenticated truth" in the choice of a way of life, be it aesthetic or ethical or religious existence.[22]

Falling broadly within the literary category, and informed by postmodern and theological concerns, is George Pattison's provocative study, *Kierkegaard: The Aesthetic and the Religious: From the Magic Theatre to the Crucifixion of the Image*. Pattison explores an escalating tension in Kierkegaard's literature between the distancing of aesthetic and narra-tive imaging and the requirements of communication and Christian discipleship. The limits of the aesthetic image and the dogmatic theological heritages are revealed finally as violence; the poet who tries to depict the crucified is a torturer. In contrast to poetic idealization, the image of the crucified One, as a crucifixion of the image, gives a much truer portrayal of Christian discipleship.[23]

Pattison's work engages a number of the same issues and concerns of this study, especially in chapters 4-7, exploring Christ as Pattern. Where my approach differs is in reflecting upon positive *uses* of the imagination, not solely in providing ideals of perfection giving comfort to pilgrims, but as learned imaginative capabilities that, in the words of another recent study, provide a "transforming vision" within concrete human existence.[24] Kierkegaard's "inverted dialectic," or what I have

---

[21]   Henning Fenger's historical analysis of Kierkegaard is allied in result if not in method to deconstructionist readings. He calls into question Kierkegaard's stated religious intent in *The Point of View*, yet still locates the meaning of the texts in authorial intention. Henning Fenger, *Kierkegaard: The Myths and Their Origins: Studies in the Kierkegaardian Papers and Letters*, trans. George C. Schoolfield (New Haven: Yale University Press, 1980).

[22]   Christopher Norris, *The Deconstructive Turn: Essays in the Rhetoric of Philosophy* (London and New York: Methuen, 1983), 87; see also his "The Ethics of Reading and the Limits of Irony: Kierkegaard Among the Postmodernists," *Southern Humanities Review* 23:1 (Winter 1989):1–35; and "De Man Unfair to Kierkegaard?: An Allegory of (Non)-Reading," in Birgit Bertung, ed., *Kierkegaard – Poet of Existence. Kierkegaard Conferences 1* (Copenhagen: C. A. Reitzel, 1989), 89–107.

[23]   George Pattison, *Kierkegaard: The Aesthetic and the Religious: From the Magic Theatre to the Crucifixion of the Image* (New York: St. Martin's Press, 1992), xi. Pattison generously reviews, and disagrees with, my own work.

[24]   M. Jamie Ferreira, *Transforming Vision: Imagination and Will in Kierkegaardian Faith* (Oxford: Clarendon Press, 1992).

called elsewhere the "reversal" involved *in* "repetition," is the key to
seeing this positive role for the imagination.[25] In ethical upbuilding, in
religious repentance, and in faith, hope, and love as imitation of Christ
as Pattern, the imagination breaks through the limitations of aesthetics
into the harshest concrete realities of life, including, as we will see in
the last chapter, the political realm.

Pattison's work partakes of another method, with a lengthy history
behind it, of reading Kierkegaard as a *religious author*. The present study
too naturally falls into this category, but we might pause to consider
what is involved in making this claim. The approach is in one sense
self-evident; even if questions arise about whether, and if so in what
sense, Kierkegaard is a philosopher, he is certainly a religious thinker
of the first rank. He described himself in *The Point of View for My Work as
an Author* as a "religious author," one who did not begin as an aesthetic
author and then became a religious writer, but whose production had a
religious teleology from the outset.[26] Even if, with Henning Fenger,
one does not accept Kierkegaard's later account of his authorship, one
can still read the literature on its own as religious. The difference, then,
from biographical religious readings of Kierkegaard's literature noted
earlier, is that one can simply turn to the writings as *writings* and
investigate their content. In short, there is much to be said for reading
Kierkegaard as a religious and Christian author.[27]

If Kierkegaard can be read as a religious author, is he therefore a
theologian? After all, he was a student of Christian theology, especially
familiar with Lutheran dogmatic theology and Schleiermacher's *The
Christian Faith*.[28] Further, he by and large accepted the established
dogmas of the Christian faith, and, apart from some notable exceptions
that we will consider along the way, he did not believe that the

[25]   On "inverted dialectic," see Sylvia Walsh, "Kierkegaard: Poet of the Religious," in George
       Pattison, ed., *Kierkegaard on Art and Communication* (New York: St. Martin's Press, 1992), 6–8.
       Walsh develops this positive understanding of the imagination in her fine recent study *Living
       Poetically: Kierkegaard's Existential Aesthetics* (University Park, PA: The Pennsylvania State
       University Press, 1994). On "repetition in reversal," see my *Kierkegaard's Dialectic of the
       Imagination* (New York: Peter Lang, 1989).
[26]   *PV* 5–6 (*SV* xiii 517–18).
[27]   C. Stephen Evans, *Søren Kierkegaard's Christian Psychology: Insight for Counseling and Pastoral Care*
       (Grand Rapids, MI: Zondervan, 1990), 9.
[28]   On Kierkegaard's early studies in theology, see, for example, Niels Thulstrup, "Theological
       and Philosophical Studies," in *Kierkegaard's View of Christianity*, ed. Niels Thulstrup and Marie
       Mikulová Thulstrup, *Bibliotheca Kierkegaardiana*, 16 vols. (Copenhagen: C. A. Reitzel, 1978), i,
       38–60, and Niels Thulstrup, *Kierkegaard's Relation to Hegel*, trans. George L. Stengren (Princeton
       University Press, 1980), 41–45. Kierkegaard studied under the rationalist theologian H. N.
       Clausen and read Schleiermacher with H. L. Martensen. He was also familiar with the range
       of theological manuals.

established dogmas called for revision: "The doctrine in the established Church and its organization are very good. But the lives, our lives – believe me, they are mediocre."[29] Because Kierkegaard's writings reveal not only profound literary creativity and philosophical acuity, but also a detailed knowledge of the history of theology and of dogmatics, it is possible and even instructive to trace out Kierkegaard's understanding of Christian doctrinal issues and the positions that he occupied theologically. I will treat these issues in due course.

A common way of studying Kierkegaard as a "theologian" is the descriptive or comparative approach. This has a long history in Kierkegaard scholarship, including such classic studies as Torsten Bohlin's *Kierkegaards dogmatiska åskådning* (*Kierkegaard's Dogmatic Views*).[30] Bohlin's works, as described by one commentator, do indeed establish a series of "points of contact between SK and theological positions of the past."[31] Another example of a descriptive account of "Kierkegaard as theologian" is Louis Dupré, who in his study of that title locates Kierkegaard historically and systematically as an intermediary figure between Reformation Protestantism and Roman Catholic theology. Kierkegaard's dialectic of existence is, for Dupré, the most consistent application of Reformation principles, especially the principle of subjectivity and the importance of the individual conscience. Yet Kierkegaard also relates to the Catholic tradition in his understanding of freedom's role in faith and grace and reintegrating Christian asceticism with Reformation solafideism.[32]

Nonetheless, as Dupré notes, there are limitations in approaching Kierkegaard as a theologian. Kierkegaard's religious and Christian thought is misrepresented if it is overly systematized, or if the Socratic nature of his "dialectical probings" is neglected in the interest of simply stating his "positions" on theological issues.[33]

Finally, mention should be made of the common interpretation of Kierkegaard as an *existentialist*, a label that carries both philosophical and theological weight. The standard portrait, arrived at by placing Kierkegaard as a progenitor of later philosophical existentialists such as

[29] *JP* vi 6727 (*Pap.* x⁴ A 33, n.d. 1851).

[30] Torsten Bohlin, *Kierkegaards dogmatiska åskådning* (*Kierkegaard's Dogmatic Views*) (Stockholm: Svenska Kyrkans Diakonistyrelses, 1925); in German: *Kierkegaards dogmatische Anschauung*, trans. Ilse Meyer-Lüne (Gütersloh: Bertelsmann, 1927).

[31] Per Lønning, "Kierkegaard as a Christian Thinker," in Thulstrup and Thulstrup, eds., *Bibliotheca Kierkegaardiana*, i, 165.

[32] Louis Dupré, *Kierkegaard as Theologian: The Dialectic of Christian Existence* (New York: Sheed and Ward, 1963), x–xi.

[33] Dupré, *Kierkegaard as Theologian*, xii.

Jean-Paul Sartre and Martin Heidegger, and theological existentialists such as Rudolf Bultmann and Paul Tillich, leads to a number of longstanding, persistent characterizations of Kierkegaard, some accurate, others less so.

According to this picture, as a philosophical existentialist, Kierkegaard is praised or blamed as an "irrationalist," "subjectivist," or "relativist." Epistemologically, his attacks on Hegelian rationalism and foundationalism, his reflections on the "leap," the "absurd," and "subjectivity," are taken as attacks on reason and advocacy of "groundless choice" as the only possible basis for ethical and religious commitment.[34] So too, Kierkegaard is charged with being the primary creator of a modern myth of the self as the "solitary individual," unmoored from history or tradition, a permutation of the Cartesian ego or the self-creating individual of Romanticism, a myth that many see in need of radical deconstruction. To take only one aspect of this picture, Kierkegaard is seen to hold a concept of the person that locates the will as the center of selfhood; for existentialism, in Iris Murdoch's memorable image, the agent, "thin as a needle, appears in the quick flash of the choosing will."[35] As another commentator has recently put it, under Sartre's influence, existentialists have focused on notions of an anxious, directionless freedom from which the self creates itself from nothing.[36] But, as we will see, Kierkegaard has a very different understanding than Sartre or for that matter Bultmann of human freedom and of the self. To be a "self" ethically and religiously includes the will for Kierkegaard, but the self is hardly self-created by daily exercise of the will.[37] The task

34   Peter J. Mehl includes Leo Shestov, Walter Kaufmann, Alasdair MacIntyre, and Robert C. Solomon among those who bring these charges against Kierkegaard; see Peter J. Mehl, "Kierkegaard and the Relativist Challenge to Practical Philosophy," *Journal of Religious Ethics* 14 (1987): 247–78, especially 265, 274n. For example, the charge of "subjectivism" and "relativism" is made by Alasdair MacIntyre, *After Virtue* (University of Notre Dame Press, 1981). Some recent studies that challenge such views include: Edward F. Mooney, *Knights of Faith and Resignation: Reading Kierkegaard's* Fear and Trembling (Albany, NY: State University of New York Press, 1991), especially 7–11 (against "relativism") and 73–78 (on "objectivity"); Edward F. Mooney, "Kierkegaard Our Contemporary: Reason, Subjectivity and the Self," *Southern Journal of Philosophy* (Fall 1989): 381–97; C. Stephen Evans, *Kierkegaard's* Fragments and Postscript, 115, 126–27 (against epistemological relativism), 126–31 (against subjectivism), and ch. 11 (against irrationalism); C. Stephen Evans, *Passionate Reason: Making Sense of Kierkegaard's Philosophical Fragments.* The Indiana Series in the Philosophy of Religion, general ed., Merold Westphal (Bloomington and Indianapolis: Indiana University Press, 1992).
35   Iris Murdoch, *The Sovereignty of Good* (New York: Schocken Books, 1971), 53.
36   Mehl, "Kierkegaard and the Relativist Challenge to Practical Philosophy," 248.
37   Two recent critiques of volitionalism, to which we will return in chapter 4, are found in M. Jamie Ferreira, *Transforming Vision,* and C. Stephen Evans, *Passionate Reason.* I will return to the theme of the narrative understanding of the self in chapter 2.

of becoming a self in the eminent sense is, for Kierkegaard, much more a matter of developing longterm habits or dispositions. He is much closer to the classical virtue tradition than to existentialist volitionalism, and, indeed, closer to current discussions of a "narrative" understanding of the self than has been appreciated. So too, the picture of Kierkegaard's "solitary self," cut off in azure isolation from community and history, is a caricature in need of critique.[38]

The "existentialist" label applied to Kierkegaard's theological thought is also misleading, for it places him in theological company with whom he would have as many disagreements as agreements. An illustration of this is how Kierkegaard, in this standard picture, is often seen as a precursor to such "existentialist theologians" as Bultmann and Tillich, who are, in fact, quite different from Kierkegaard.

In chapter 4, we will contrast in particular the Christologies of Bultmann and Tillich, and their understandings of faith, with Kierkegaard's reflections on these matters. But we can illustrate the differences between them here by noting briefly how "existentialists" such as Tillich and Bultmann differ from Kierkegaard in a more "methodological" matter: their understanding of the theological enterprise.

In their reflections on the theological enterprise Tillich and Bultmann (and here the debt to Hegel is obvious) both see the theological task as one that provides or uncovers meanings for faith, and that either correlates (Tillich) or translates (Bultmann) the conceptual content of Christian belief into other conceptualities that are functionally equivalent, but more "modern."

For Tillich, theology is the methodical interpretation of Christian faith's content.[39] In the method of correlation, the Christian message is, and must be, adapted to the situation of the culture one addresses.[40] In other words, theology must interpret the content of religious symbols into forms that address modern culture; indeed, this is the responsibility of each generation. Tillich exercised that responsibility for his own generation in the form of an existential ontology that attempted to correlate with the concepts and language of biblical faith: each biblical symbol leads inescapably to an ontological question, while theology's answers necessarily contain ontology.[41] For the

38 We will turn to this in chapter 7.
39 Paul Tillich, *Systematic Theology.* Three volumes in one. (University of Chicago Press; New York and Evanston: Harper & Row, 1967), I, 15.
40 Paul Tillich, *Systematic Theology*, I, 6.
41 Paul Tillich, *Biblical Religion and the Search for Ultimate Reality* (University of Chicago Press, 1955), VII.

later Bultmann, this interpretive task is just as urgent, but also more philosophically specific, since one must hermeneutically translate the mythological language of the New Testament into terms of Heideggerian existentialism in order for that language to be understood by moderns. Philosophy is required to discover the appropriate conceptions for such a translation.[42] For Kierkegaard, by contrast, theology is anything but correlation or translation of Christian concepts into a philosophical terminology. Indeed, some of his most strenuous criticisms of Hegel in such books as *Philosophical Fragments* and *Concluding Unscientific Postscript* are aimed precisely against speculative philosophy's claim that theological terminology can be translated into another conceptuality. For Kierkegaard, translation is treason, and the basic task of the theologian is not to make Christianity understandable to moderns, but to train moderns in the capabilities that can allow them to understand the gospel.

If Kierkegaard's writings, then, are not quite "theological," perhaps it is better to say that Kierkegaard is a "kind of theologian."[43] Calling Kierkegaard "a kind of theologian" points to how he envisioned his task to be different from that of most theology: instead of focusing on the doctrinal content of Christian faith, the "what" of the faith (which he believed in any event to be essentially a completed task within the Christian tradition) or reinterpeting or translating Christian belief into other conceptual categories, Kierkegaard's concern is to direct attention to the "how" of the appropriation of Christian faith. Although I will argue for an important place for the "what" of faith in his thought, his interest is primarily (in Hans Frei's phrase) with "the logic of coming to belief," with "how" Christianity can in the eminent sense be "reduplicated" in existence. As a religious and Christian writer, then, Kierkegaard is a "theologian" with a difference.[44]

---

[42]   See, for example, Rudolf Bultmann, *Jesus Christ and Mythology* (New York: Charles Scribner's Sons, 1958), 54. For a detailed and sophisticated critique of Bultmann, see Robert C. Roberts, *Rudolf Bultmann's Theology: A Critical Interpretation* (Grand Rapids, MI: William B. Eerdmans, 1976).

[43]   Louis Mackey's earlier study of Kierkegaard calls him "a kind of poet," and Robert L. Perkins speaks of him as "a kind of epistemologist," see "Kierkegaard, A Kind of Epistemologist," *Journal of the History of European Ideas* 12:1 (1990): 7–18.

[44]   Hans Frei, *Types of Christian Theology*, ed. by George Hunsinger and William C. Placher (New Haven: Yale University Press, 1992), 54. Frei uses the phrase "the logic of coming to belief" to describe D. Z. Phillips' understanding of theology, which according to Frei combines Christian self-description with appeals to prereligious and non-religious life attitudes. In some ways this fits Kierkegaard's understanding of the "stages on life's way," yet I will also argue later that Kierkegaard has a place for what Frei calls "the logic of belief," distinct from "the logic of coming to belief." I will return to these matters in chapters 2 and 4.

Because the "how" is central to Kierkegaard, we must attend closely not only to the pseudonymous literature that has received the bulk of scholarly attention, but also to the series of upbuilding or edifying discourses published concurrently with the pseudonymous literature, and to what Robert L. Perkins has helpfully termed Kierkegaard's "second authorship," the straightforwardly religious literature published (with some exceptions) under Kierkegaard's own name after *Concluding Unscientific Postscript* (1846).[45] It was the edifying writing that Kierkegaard considered in some ways most important, even more important than the pseudonymous literature; he said, for example, that, while he offered his little edifying discourses in his right hand and his pseudonymous writings in his left, the public accepted with its right hand the pseudonymous literature in his left, and in its left hand the edifying literature in his right.[46] Although there have been a number of fine studies in recent years that attend to the second literature,[47] there is room for further reflection on the inner logic and character of the upbuilding and "second literature." This study is an attempt to contribute to that reflection. What lies behind this is a conviction that finally the *audience* Kierkegaard's literature addresses consists of not simply, or even first of all, philosophers or literati (whether of nineteenth-century Denmark or today), but persons attempting to be human beings and, perhaps, Christians.[48] This is why, at the end of *Concluding Unscientific Postscript*, Kierkegaard, in his own voice, says that the value of his pseudonymous literature

> does not consist in making any new proposal, some unheard-of discovery, or in founding a new party and wanting ... to go further, but precisely in the opposite, in wanting once again to read through solo, if possible in a more inward way, the original text of individual human existence-relationships, the old familiar text handed down from the fathers.[49]

Given the religious and Christian teleology of Kierkegaard's writings, it is no surprise that the literary form of his productivity was

---

[45] John W. Elrod, *Kierkegaard and Christendom* (Princeton University Press, 1981), xi. Elrod credits this term to Robert L. Perkins.

[46] *PV* 20 (*SV* XIII 527).

[47] Examples of studies focusing on the second literature include Bradley Dewey, *The New Obedience: Kierkegaard on Imitating Christ*. Foreword by Paul L. Holmer (Washington, Cleveland: Corpus, 1968); John W. Elrod, *Kierkegaard and Christendom*; Bruce H. Kirmmse, *Kierkegaard in Golden Age Denmark* (Bloomington and Indianapolis: Indiana University Press, 1990).

[48] On this question of Kierkegaard's audience, see the spirited interchange between Robert C. Roberts and Alastair Hannay: Roberts, "A Critique of Alastair Hannay's Interpretation of the *Philosophical Fragments*," *Kierkegaardiana* 13 (1984): 149–54 and Alastair Hannay, "Reply to Roberts' Critique," *Kierkegaardiana* 14 (1988): 114–21.

[49] *CUP* 629 (*SV* VII 548–49).

crucial to him. The literary approach to Kierkegaard, discussed above, while in itself too limiting, is not only appropriate, but of central significance. His sustained reflections on the "how" in addition to the "what" of Christianity, led him not only to reflect upon, but also to practice, rhetorical devices designed to invite (never force) the reader to what he called "redoubling," the kind of appropriation that not only assents to religious belief, but that practices ethical, religious or Christian concepts in the formation of the self. The technique of pseudonymity, for example, is designed to remove the reader from any false "authorial tyranny." As a "religious poet," Kierkegaard insists that he possesses no authority, but simply presents the qualifications of religious and Christian existence to the reader. Pseudonymity raises questions, not about the author's religiosity or lack of religiosity, but about the reader.

In saying that Kierkegaard as religious author claimed no authority, he took on another role, that of the maieutic, the role of Socrates as ironic "midwife," who himself did not claim to know the truth, but raised the question of truth and brought the truth to birth for those with whom he engaged in dialogue. Here too for Kierkegaard, the stress again is on the reader, not on the author. Indeed, a religious author respects the distance between author and reader; success in communicating religious capacities is not measured by the success of any "result" or the use of what Johannes Climacus terms a "rhetorical shower bath" that bypasses the decision of the reader for or against the religious, since religious capacities cannot be directly communicated.[50]

The literary form of pseudonymity and the role of the maieutic are summed up in Kierkegaard's understanding of "indirect communication." In lectures outlined in 1847 but never delivered, Kierkegaard distinguishes between the communication of knowledge and the communication of a capability. The first is a "direct communication," as in the communication of scientific information. Appropriation of knowledge is direct in the sense that one can demonstrate that one "understands" or "possesses the knowledge" by what Kierkegaard calls "immediacy": "when one person states something and another acknowledges the same thing verbatim, they are assumed to be in agreement and to have understood each other."[51] A peculiarity of ethics and religion, however, a peculiarity he believed was system-

---

[50] *CUP* 48 (*SV* vii 36).
[51] *CUP* 74 (*SV* vii 57).

atically forgotten in the modern age, is that ethics and religion cannot be adequately communicated "directly," but only "indirectly." This is because ethics and religion involve the communication of a capability, even if (as in Christianity), there is an element of knowledge that needs to be communicated as well.

An example of the misunderstanding through conceiving instruction aimed at capability as instruction in knowledge. A sergeant in the National Guard says to a recruit, "You, there, stand up straight." Recruit: "Sure enough." Sergeant: "Yes, and don't talk during drill." Recruit: "All right, I won't if you'll just tell me." Sergeant: "What the devil! You are not supposed to talk during drill!" Recruit: "Well, don't get so mad. If I know I'm not supposed to, I'll quit talking during drill."[52]

One aspect of indirect communication, which applies especially to the aesthetic works from *Either/Or* to *Stages on Life's Way* and goes to the heart of Kierkegaard's concern with the "how" of becoming a Christian – is that indirect communication involves deceiving the reader. Ironically, Kierkegaard suggests, if one is interested in communicating Christianity in a hyperintellectualized age, one cannot rest with simply summarizing Christian teachings. Rather, one must confront a fact about one's audience, the "frightful illusion" that pervaded his time: that all are Christians in Christendom. Given this situation, direct communication, he writes, is not enough, since direct communication assumes merely the receiver's ignorance combined with a willingness to be taught. But what if persons are subject to an illusion – the illusion that "all are Christians" when in fact they live in aesthetic categories or at most in aesthetic-ethical categories and are thus unwilling to be taught? In that case, ironically, the author concerned to communicate Christianity must "not begin thus: I am a Christian; you are not a Christian. Nor does one begin thus: It is Christianity I am proclaiming; and you are living in purely aesthetic categories. No, one begins thus: Let us talk about aesthetics."[53]

The task that confronted Kierkegaard as a religious and Christian writer was that of communicating religious and Christian capabilities to persons surfeited with "knowledge about" religious and Christian matters, but who nonetheless lived in "aesthetic" categories (living for

---

[52]   *JP* I 649, paragraph 14 (*Pap.* VIII[2] B 81, n.d. 1847). See the entire series of Kierkegaard's lecture notes on indirect communication in *JP* I 648–57; compare also *PV* 39–41 (*SV* XIII 540–42); *CUP* 72–80 (*SV* VII 55–62); *Practice in Christianity* relates indirect communication extensively to Christ.

[53]   *PV* 41 (*SV* XIII 541).

pleasure), committing the intellectualist error of confusing their "knowledge about" Christianity with faith. This is why, for Kierkegaard, the need of his age was not for more knowledge about Christianity, but rather for persons to learn to hear religiously and Christianly.

Kierkegaard believed that encouraging this hearing was a difficult and multilayered task. Just how difficult it was can be gauged by the levels of confusion he felt he had to circumvent in his task of Christian communication. First, in a culture that was self-deceived in thinking it was Christian, what was needed was training, not in knowledge alone, but in a range of *capacities* that were forgotten – such capacities as "being faithful," "fearing for one's happiness," "repenting," "being expectant for the future." Second, this situation was complicated by the root of the illusion, that, while the capacities were forgotten, the language of faith was still used, but in different contexts: people would continue to use such words as "faith," but see faith as an inferior or uncertain kind of "knowledge." This meant, ironically, that not only did his culture lack religious capacities, but people did not even notice the lack of these capacities or even feel a need for them. As the pseudonym Anti-Climacus puts it in *The Sickness Unto Death*, in speaking of what it might mean to "lack a self,"

such things do not create much of a stir in the world, for a self is the last thing the world cares about and the most dangerous thing of all for a person to show signs of having. The greatest hazard of all, losing the self, can occur very quietly in the world, as if it were nothing at all. No other loss can occur so quietly; any other loss – an arm, a leg, five dollars, a wife, etc. – is sure to be noticed.[54]

Third, given the ease with which ethical and religious concepts are not even missed, the task was not only to communicate discursively about "ethics" or "faith," but to communicate also a *context in life* for the exercise of these capacities. It was this nuanced task that required of Kierkegaard the "poetic" strategies he deployed.

Discerning how Kierkegaard is a "religious thinker" and author is then partly a matter of discerning "style." Stanley Cavell has written that philosophy, like theology, employs a variety of styles: against intellectual challenge, dogmatics; against dogmatics, confession; and in both, dialogue.[55] If Kierkegaard is not a theologian in the sense of one

[54] *SUD* 32–33 (*SV* xi 146).
[55] Stanley Cavell, "The Availability of Wittgenstein's Later Philosophy," in Pitcher, ed., *Wittgenstein: The "Philosophical Investigations,"* 183.

whose *primary* concern is with the correct statement of Christian belief (Dogmatics), he is a religious and Christian author who employs a multitude of styles, including (at times) the style of Confession, with the aim of Dialogue with the reader: written "without authority," by a "poet of the religious," the goal is not to dictate correct belief to the reader, but rather to present to the reader, in sharpened form, basic options in human existence to which the reader can respond.

Yet it is not that "indirect communication" alone cultivates religious capacities. In *The Point of View*, Kierkegaard writes that the pseudonymous literature (*Either/Or* through *Postscript*) is maieutic in indirectly, even deceptively, leading one to the religious, yet the strand of upbuilding discourses paralleling it is direct communication, and both strands end in the direct religious communication of the later literature. The tactics differ, but the directly religious literature early and late is also "indirect" in the sense of being aimed at eliciting capabilities, and the goal of the entire movement of direct and indirect literature is broadly maieutic, to bring the reader to "simplicity," "to make aware of the essentially Christian."[56]

Central to this multilayered process is the philosophical, descriptive goal of *clarification of religious and Christian concepts*, understood as reintroducing religious and Christian capabilities for the reader. As a clarifier of concepts Kierkegaard's intellectual affinities are thus less with Sartre and Heidegger or Tillich and Bultmann than with philosophical "grammarians" like Ludwig Wittgenstein. The extent of Wittgenstein's deep regard for religious belief and for Kierkegaard as a religious thinker has become increasingly known in recent years; he said that Kierkegaard was easily the most profound thinker of the nineteenth century, and that he was a saint.[57] In spirit they are markedly similar: both share a suspicion of discursive or intellectualistic solutions to problems of the spirit; both oppose traditional philosophical justifications of religious belief as irrelevant and misleading. In place of philosophy or theology providing general structures of meaning (in the style of Bultmann or Tillich), or philosophy providing foundational accounts of religious or Christian belief, whether metaphysical, historical, rational, or experiential (in the tradition of "philo-

---

[56] *PV*, "My Activity as a Writer," 141–51 (*SV* XIII 489–501).

[57] M. O'C. Drury, "Some Notes on Conversations with Wittgenstein," in Rush Rhees, ed., *Recollections of Wittgenstein* (Oxford University Press, 1984), 87. Wittgenstein also said to Drury that there was a sense in which he thought they both were Christians; see Drury, "Conversations with Wittgenstein," in *ibid.*, 114.

sophy of religion"),[58] both thinkers recognized the limits of philosophy
with regard to ethics and religious belief. Yet both also saw philosophy
as having another, more positive role to play in clarifying the "logic" of
concepts, in particular locating the point and sense of religious
concepts, not in a philosophical justification, but in the practices and
concerns of religious belief and faith. Philosophy, in other words, has
an instrumental value; it does not "deliver meanings," but assists a
person to clarity of thought.[59]

A large part of this task is critical, or as Kierkegaard would say,
"dialectical." Dialectic specifies the particular confusions that lead one
to see "faith," for example, as an inferior sort of knowledge. Kierkegaard
saw philosophy as a matter of making distinctions between apparently
similar concepts. Here a comparison between Kierkegaard and Ludwig
Wittgenstein is particularly instructive. Just as Kierkegaard in his
"qualitative dialectic" sought distinctions in the definition of apparently
similar concepts, Wittgenstein likewise said – in the context of remarks
to M. O'C. Drury on Hegel and Kierkegaard – that "Hegel seems to
me to be always wanting to say that things which look different are
really the same. Whereas my interest is in showing that things which
look the same are really different. I was thinking of using as a motto for
my book (*Philosophical Investigations*) a quotation from *King Lear*: 'I'll teach
you differences.'"[60] For Kierkegaard, the task of such logical clarification focused on such concepts as "God," the "self," "sin," "truth," and
"faith" – as they actually function in religious language and life.

To identify, as some have suggested, Kierkegaard's "stage on life's
way" with Wittgenstein's "form of life" is probably incautious, since
"form of life" is not applicable to something as global as "religion."[61]
Kierkegaard's reflections on religion and on Christianity as "stages on
life's way," in their concern to show the connections between concepts

58 Fergus Kerr, citing Donald MacKinnon's phrase that in place of natural theology we need
many more practitioners of the philosophy of theology (*Theology after Wittgenstein* [Oxford and
New York: Basil Blackwell, 1986], 171).
59 I am indebted in my understanding of this approach to Paul L. Holmer, who first fruitfully
explored the connections between Kierkegaard and Wittgenstein in numerous essays
(published and unpublished) and in his teaching. See especially Paul L. Holmer, *The Grammar
of Faith* (San Francisco: Harper & Row, 1978).
60 Drury, "Conversations with Wittgenstein," in Rhees, ed., *Recollections of Wittgenstein*, 157.
61 Stanley Cavell, "Kierkegaard's *On Authority and Revelation*," in Josiah Thompson, ed.,
Kierkegaard: A Collection of Critical Essays. Modern Studies in Philosophy, ed. Amelie Oksenberg
Rorty (Garden City, NY: Doubleday-Anchor, 1972), 384. See the cautions by Kerr, *Theology
after Wittgenstein*, 29; Kerr argues against identifying "religion" as an example of Wittgenstein's
"form of life," and against the claim that "form of life" can be used to support
"Wittgensteinian fideism."

and existence, are comparable rather to Wittgenstein's notion of "theology as grammar," pointing to the connections between language and how language is used, what can and cannot be said.[62] Kierkegaard's writings attempt to clarify the connections between what we say about "God," the "self," "sin," "truth," "belief," and "faith" with the contexts of this language. To speak of "God" is not simply to employ the term, but to have a place for the word, to use it appropriately within a range of applications. For both thinkers, the "meanings" of religious language are grounded in the uses of the language of the faith and the activities of that faith. So too, the interconnections between beliefs, emotions, and language dominate each thinker's reflections on religion. Finally, for both of them the issues of ethics and the religious life are closely involved with the need for clarity and for health – a theme we will pursue further in chapter 1.[63]

Another benefit of seeing the connections between Kierkegaard and Wittgenstein is that it can help cure a longstanding dichotomy that stands behind the common existentialist views of Kierkegaard: the dichotomy, philosophical and theological, between "subjectivism" and "objectivism." Constructively, I want to explore how Kierkegaard's careful reflections on "subjectivity" and "objectivity" allow him to steer a path between the shoals of both philosophical *and* theological "objectivism" and "subjectivism" that continue to afflict modern Christian theological discourse. I have already noted some recent studies that counteract past portrayals of Kierkegaard's concern with "subjectivity," the "leap," and the "absurd" as "irrationalism," "relativism," and "subjectivism." The focus of these studies have been largely philosophical: attempts to clarify the kinds of "objectivism" or "rationalism" that Kierkegaard opposes, while outlining carefully his more nuanced reflections. Or else these discussions have focused on such central Kierkegaardian theological concepts as "faith," "belief," and "will." I will have recourse to these discussions, especially in

[62] For "theology as grammar," see Ludwig Wittgenstein, *Philosophical Investigations*, trans. G. E. M. Anscombe (New York: The Macmillan Company, 1953), 1, 373; compare *Wittgenstein's Lectures Cambridge 1932–1935*, ed. Alice Ambrose (Oxford: Basil Blackwell, 1979), 32. See also Kerr, *Theology after Wittgenstein*, 145–46.

[63] In addition to Holmer's work, and the Cavell and Conant essays on Kierkegaard, other studies that creatively develop the links between Kierkegaard and Wittgenstein include Bell, ed., *The Grammar of the Heart* and Richard H. Bell and Ronald E. Hustwit, eds., *Essays on Kierkegaard and Wittgenstein: On Understanding the Self* (Wooster, OH: The College of Wooster, 1978). See also Charles L. Creegan, *Wittgenstein and Kierkegaard: Religion, Individuality, and Philosophical Method* (London and New York: Routledge & Kegan Paul, 1989) and Patrick Sherry, *Religion, Truth and Language-Games* (London: Macmillan, 1977).

chapter 4 on Kierkegaard's understanding of belief, faith, and object-ivity/subjectivity. But, while relying upon these studies, I will attempt to draw out some related constructive *theological* implications of Kierke-gaard's thought. More specifically, I want to reflect carefully on Kierkegaard's understanding of the "person," "God," "Christ," and "salvation" as they relate to the tasks of becoming religious and becoming Christian. In place of the usual portrait of the existentialist Kierkegaard, my argument will be that he gives a carefully nuanced picture of religious and Christian existence that can constructively avoid a common dichotomy in contemporary Christian *theology* (as well as in Western philosophy): a seemingly forced option between some form of "theological subjectivism" and "theological objectivism."

In the standard picture, Kierkegaard is linked with, or even seen as, the prime progenitor of, not only existentialism, but also a broader "theological subjectivism": the anthropocentric "turn to the self" typical of post-Kantian thought (Schleiermacher); the appeal to "ex-perience" as the basis for the intelligibility and (possibly) truthfulness of religious language (and hence the importance of apologetic theology); the principle of immanence, "that the divine is already within the individual, who is essentially grounded in God, whether God be understood personally or impersonally";[64] the symbolic as opposed to referential functions of religious language (including "God" and "Christ"); the lack of "objective" criteria for religious judgments; and the importance of such "nonrational" factors as will and emotion in religion.

In contrast to this, a "theological objectivism" (Barth is a classic example) seeks to be theocentric (and sometimes Christocentric); frees itself from a methodological tie to the self's experience (and hence frees dogmatics from apologetics); affirms the referentiality of language about "God," "Christ," etc.; outlines "objective" criteria in theology, allowing theology again to be a kind of "science"; and emphasizes the rationality of faith and of theology.[65]

My argument will be that, while Kierkegaard shares *some* of the concerns of theological subjectivism (such as a tempered apologetics), his religious and Christian theological thinking actually steers a path between theological subjectivism and objectivism, and, more impor-

---

[64] As defined by Evans, *Kierkegaard's* Fragments *and* Postscript, 25.
[65] While Barth is a classic example of theological objectivism, he can also be seen closer to Kierkegaard's and Wittgenstein's "grammatical" investigations, grounded as Barth's theology is in the primary language of Christian faith and liturgy. See Don E. Saliers' recent investigations of this side of Barth in *Worship as Theology: Foretaste of Glory Divine* (Nashville: Abingdon, 1994), ch. 4.

tantly, that Kierkegaard's religious and theological thought has constructive theological possibilities. In a manner similar to Fergus Kerr's discussion of how Wittgenstein's thought, in its critique of "realism," does not lead to "subjective idealism," so too Kierkegaard's thought, in its critique of "objectivism," does not lead to a reductionistic "theological subjectivism."[66]

To anticipate, against "theological subjectivism," Kierkegaard, despite his stress on "subjectivity," emphasizes the "objectivity" of Christ *extra nos* and so avoids reducing Christology to anthropological or soteriological-subjective categories (a continuing problem from Schleiermacher to Bultmann to pragmatism and relativism). Yet, against "theological objectivism," Kierkegaard – in using the rich "subjective" virtue language of faith, hope, and love to discuss salvation *pro nobis* and *pro me* – avoids the opposite danger of subordinating soteriology to "objective" Christological categories in such a way that description of Christian existence is placed under some severe strictures. Rather, I will argue, Kierkegaard's understanding of the mutual correlations between Christ and the dispositions of the specifically Christian virtues of faith, hope, and love is logically complex: Christ is the logical and actual basis of Christian existence and virtues; at the same time, the virtues are the necessary subjective means for apprehending Christ.

Most importantly, I want to suggest that Kierkegaard's thought allows us to move beyond the terms of this dispute, for finally that dispute also misses what Kierkegaard thought most crucial: turning away *from* the temptations of "objectivism" *and* "subjectivism" *to* a close-textured and careful description of the context of Christian faith, not only the "clarification" of concepts, but also the painstaking account of how and why religious persons and Christians do speak of "God" and "Christ."[67] Constructively, Kierkegaard's religious and Christian thought can contribute to a more finely textured 'grammar," not only of what is said in Christian faith, but also what is shown. In such a project, "grammar" has regard, not only for the concepts of the faith ("dogma"), but also for "rhetoric," not in the sense of "oratory" alone unrelated to conviction, but the language of faith as it is used in the situations of existence.[68] Thus Kierkegaard wrote of Socrates

---

[66] Kerr, *Theology after Wittgenstein*, chs. 5–6. See also Rowan Williams' insightful essay, "'Religious Realism': On Not Quite Agreeing with Don Cupitt," *Modern Theology* 1:1 (1984): 3–24.
[67] Kerr, *Theology after Wittgenstein*, 147–48.
[68] *JP* III 3715 (*Pap.* x⁴ A 525, n.d., 1852.)

refusing the speech offered him for his defense that "the person in whom a point of view is a life, an existentiality, a presence, will also have enough well-considered remarks to give at any time."[69]

In other words, I want to argue that Kierkegaard is best seen as a person standing at the center of the Christian tradition rather than at its fringe, deeply informed by the church's thought and its spirituality, that he is, as one commentator has put it, "a theologian in the classical, catholic, and orthodox sense," not on the model of the "academic theologian," but rather one whose "work was not merely to describe or analyze doctrine but rather to proclaim God's relationship with us and point out the way of following Christ, of imitation as the pattern of the baptized life."[70]

If I am right that Kierkegaard should be seen as a "grammarian" of religious and Christian belief, one who, as a religious thinker, gives voice to a particularly Christian vision and the specifics of its concepts and language, it is important to see something else that has been relatively neglected: the extent to which Kierkegaard is a *biblical* thinker. For Kierkegaard, a large part of the task of relearning the capacities attending faith means relearning the language of the Bible. Here too, his use of Scripture, not only in works like *Fear and Trembling* and the *Upbuilding Discourses*, but also in the philosophical literature, such as *Philosophical Fragments*, is both profound and distinctive. Kierkegaard's practice reveals a particularly reflective understanding of how one reads Scripture. Like his pseudonym Johannes de Silentio in *Fear and Trembling*, who writes of "a man" who immersed himself in the story of Abraham and Isaac, Kierkegaard *immersed* himself in the biblical world, seeing in Scripture, not an object of scholarly investigation, but the source for the primary categories of the Christian faith.[71] Here too, rather than adapting the biblical world *to* modernity, Kierkegaard allowed himself to be shaped *by* the biblical world. Well

[69] *JP* iv 4283 (*Pap.* x⁴ A 314, n.d., 1851).

[70] Michael Plekon, "Kierkegaard the Theologian: The Roots of His Theology in *Works of Love*," in George B. Connell and C. Stephen Evans, eds., *Foundations of Kierkegaard's Vision of Community: Religion, Ethics, and Politics in Kierkegaard* (Atlantic Highlands, NJ, and London: Humanities Press, 1992), 4.

[71] *FT* 9 (*SV* iii 61–62). See also O. K. Bouwsma, "Notes on 'The Monstrous Illusion,'" *Perkins Journal* 24 (Spring 1971): 12; cited in D. Z. Phillips, *Belief, Change and Forms of Life* (Atlantic Highlands, NJ: Humanities Press International, 1986), 43. On Kierkegaard as student of Scripture, see L. Joseph Rosas, III, *Scripture in the Thought of Søren Kierkegaard* (Nashville: Broadman and Holman, 1994); Timothy Polk, "'Heart Enough To Be Confident': Kierkegaard on Reading James," in Bell, ed., *The Grammar of the Heart*, 206–33; and the still instructive "Preface" to Paul Minear and Paul S. Morimoto, *Kierkegaard and the Bible: An Index* (Princeton Theological Seminary, 1953).

aware of the contributions of critical biblical scholarship, he was also aware of the inherent limits of scholarship. To read Scripture with a scholarly eye is at best a preparation, he thought, for another kind of reading of Scripture. That is to see the Scripture on analogy with a "letter from one's beloved."[72] Kierkegaard's recommended reading is not to be ignored, as scholars often ignore it, as pietistic, or as "merely edifying" and thus inferior to the alleged true task of the student of the Bible: critical reflection. Neither should such a reading be assumed to be easily accomplished (as not requiring scholarly equipment and training) after one has by scholarly means "discerned the meaning" of the text. Both of these diminutions of reading "the letter from one's beloved" assume that an edifying reading is somehow simple, either an "emotional" (and perhaps non-cognitive) reading or an easy "application" of the meaning of the text to one's life, all of this by contrast to the real scholarly reading that is supposedly more difficult and therefore the more to be valued.

For Kierkegaard, however, the simple task, comparatively speaking, is the scholarly task. The truly difficult task in reading, one that requires both "the heart" and the mind, is that of attending to the text by placing oneself *within* it, or, to vary the image, to *meditate* upon the text and *apply* the text to the shaping of the reader's beliefs, emotions, judgments, policies, and affections.[73] This immersion within the biblical texts that Kierkegaard exemplifies, and also calls his readers to engage in with him, is strenuous and difficult, for it entails a painful baptism of the imagination. To give only one example: imagining Abraham journeying to Mount Moriah with Isaac is, as Johannes de Silentio puts it, not simply imagining the local setting and "color" of the trek, but also imagining Abraham's dialectical dilemma and his consequent terror: that God calls him to sacrifice the child of promise. Imagining that terror includes even more: placing oneself on such a trek. Although the imagination is not the sole medium for reflecting on Abraham, much less executing the movements of faith oneself, nonetheless, attempting to imagine Abraham is essential to such understanding.[74] Imaginative, empathetic engagement with the Scriptural

---

[72] See "What Is Required in Order to Look at Oneself with True Blessing in the Mirror of the Word?" in *FSE* 26–28 (*SV* xii 316–17)

[73] There is something akin here to Karl Barth's discussion of the traditional distinction among *explicatio*, *meditatio*, and *applicatio* as three movements in biblical interpretation; see *Church Dogmatics*, i, part 2, ed. G. W. Bromiley and T. F. Torrance, trans. G. T. Thomson and Harold Knight (Edinburgh: T. &. T. Clark, 1956), 722–40.

[74] *FT* 33–34 (*SV* iii 84–85).

text is central to Kierkegaard's work as philosopher and theologian, for two reasons. First, it is here that Kierkegaard learned and discerned the "grammar" of faith, hope, and love, that is, the exercise of these virtues as capacities called forth and given in Christian existence. Second, it was precisely because he took this education of Christian capacities so seriously that he was able to discern the *intellectual* contrast between the world of Scripture and the remodeling of that world by modernity (most notably, but not solely, in Hegelianized philosophy and theology).

In short, the proposal of this book is that the works of Kierkegaard as a religious thinker can be fruitfully investigated as extended grammatical exercises, attempts to re-present ethicoreligious and Christian concepts in an imaginative and fulsome manner. My attempt, therefore, is to place Kierkegaard again more firmly within the broad Christian tradition. Further, the book is written with the hope that it will be helpful not only for scholars of theology and religion, but also for someone who simply wishes to think seriously about – or even enter into – Christian discipleship.

Something now needs to be said about some standard questions on how I am approaching Kierkegaard's writings. Unlike other studies, this book does not focus on a particular Kierkegaardian work or set of works, whether philosophical, pseudonymous, upbuilding, or aesthetic.[75] Neither is this a study of a particular theme in Kierkegaard's thought. Rather, the attempt is broader: to provide an entrée and introduction to reading Kierkegaard as a religious and particularly Christian thinker, in order to help the reader avoid some initial misunderstandings when she or he turns to Kierkegaard's pages.

This immediately raises several further questions about how I am approaching Kierkegaard's texts, particularly his use of pseudonymity. Since I am drawing upon both the pseudonymous *and* upbuilding literature (the latter published in Kierkegaard's own name), three critical questions arise: first, does seeing the literature *as a "whole,"* tend to suppress the differences within the literature, especially the differences among the various pseudonyms? Second, does seeing a "Chris-

[75] Recent examples of studies focusing on a particular Kierkegaardian work or works are: Robert C. Roberts, *Faith, Reason, and History: Rethinking Kierkegaard's* Philosophical Fragments; C. Stephen Evans, *Kierkegaard's* Fragments *and* Postscript; C. Stephen Evans, *Passionate Reason: Making Sense of Kierkegaard's* Philosophical Fragments; H. A. Nielsen, *Where the Passion Is: A Reading of Kierkegaard's* Philosophical Fragments (Tallahassee: University Presses of Florida, 1983); Edward F. Mooney, *Knights of Faith and Resignation: Reading Kierkegaard's* Fear and Trembling.

tian" conclusion to the literature fall into the trap of taking the "author's" assertions as determinative, and ignoring other options for reading these texts? Third, does speaking of "Kierkegaard's position" ignore Kierkegaard's own ironic presentation, which he acknowledges by saying that none of the pseudonyms represents his own position?[76]

I would respond, however, that my approach is warranted, if it is aware of these dangers and follows some interpretive guidelines: first, Kierkegaard's literature can be *read as a whole* as long as one is sensitive to the ways in which the various characters and pseudonyms speak for themselves alone, and does not homogenize them.

Second, seeing the literature as having a *Christian "conclusion,"* is, as I have argued, borne out by Kierkegaard himself in *The Point of View.* In what he himself admits to be a retrospective view, he recommends that the literature be read with the purpose of addressing the question of how one can become a Christian. Again, such a reading is not dependent upon Kierkegaard's authorial assertion, since finally a "religious" or "Christian" reading needs as its only defense that it *can* be read in such a way, not that it is necessarily the *only* way to read it.[77]

Third, on *attributing positions to Kierkegaard himself,* it is plainly a mistake to attribute to Kierkegaard everything that a pseudonym says. The same problems apply to the journals.[78] Patrick Goold suggests (following Mackey) that the criterion for discerning "Kierkegaard" within the literature is to locate him in the internal relations of the works and the reciprocal reinforcement they provide.[79]

The structure of this study is as follows:

Chapters 1–3 form an introduction to some of Kierkegaard's central concerns as a religious and Christian thinker. In chapter 1, I will examine Kierkegaard's diagnosis of certain diseases of reflection, especially those characteristic of the Western philosophical and theological tradition, and outline Kierkegaard's understanding of an alternative "style" of "subjective thinking" in philosophy and religion. Chapter 2 will examine how Kierkegaard proposes and practices this alternative kind of "reflection" that addresses these diseases, an anthro-

[76] *CUP* 625–30 (*SV* vii 545–49).
[77] For a defense of Kierkegaard's "retrospective" understanding of his literature as religious, see N. J. Cappelørn, "The Retrospective Understanding of Kierkegaard's Total Production," in Alastair McKinnon, ed. and Introduction, *Kierkegaard: Resources and Results* (Waterloo, ON: Wilfrid Laurier University Press, 1982), 18–38.
[78] Patrick Goold, "Reading Kierkegaard: Two Pitfalls and a Strategy for Avoiding Them," *Faith and Philosophy*, 7:3 (July 1990): 311.
[79] Mackey, *Kierkegaard: A Kind of Poet*, 261, quoted in Goold, "Reading Kierkegaard," 311.

pological reflection that interweaves psychological analysis and specifically Christian dogmatic concepts in a religious understanding of the
self. This in turn will allow a closer look at Kierkegaard's religious
understanding of the self, including his analysis of moods and emotions,
the "stages on life's way," and finally his Christian narrative understanding of the self. Chapter 3 will discuss Kierkegaard's understanding
of "becoming religious," which he sees in terms of "upbuilding" and
"forming the heart." Here we need to examine Kierkegaard's vision of
becoming religious, not in terms of mere "feeling" or a sheer decision
of the will, but in the development of personal emotional and
ethicoreligious capacities. This will link Kierkegaard much more
strongly with the virtue tradition in moral philosophy and theology
than the stereotype of "the existentialist Kierkegaard" will allow.

Chapters 4–6 will focus Kierkegaard's treatment of religion by
turning to the dialectic of "becoming Christian." Here the governing
image is the relation between Christ and the believer, and in particular
the relation between Christ and each of the three Christian virtues of
faith, hope, and love. Within this overall aim in chapters 4–6, chapter 4
will examine Kierkegaard's anatomy of Christian faith as a "disposition." In connection with this, we will examine the Kierkegaardian
conception of grace and freedom, and Christology and soteriology.
Chapter 5 will continue the "dispositional" analysis of Christian
existence by turning to the Christian response to Christ in suffering and
hope. Chapter 6 will complete the analysis of Christ and the Christian
virtues by examining Christian works of love.

Finally, chapter 7 will take up a theme of recent current interest in
Kierkegaard scholarship, the question of whether the common interpretation of Kierkegaard's religious thought as privatistic and asocial is
correct. In particular, we will need to examine the later Kierkegaard's
conception of how the dispositional virtue language of faith, hope, and
love is altered in the public role for Christian discipleship Kierkegaard
develops in his last years: the "witness to the truth."

CHAPTER I

Diseases of reflection

In this chapter I want to approach Kierkegaard as religious thinker by beginning with some of his diagnostic reflections on the self, in particular what he sees as diseases of "reflection," including those that he feels afflict the practice of philosophy and theology. To begin here is to begin with the polemical side of Kierkegaard. I do so deliberately, since polemic is of the essence of his religious thought.

We can begin with a quotation from *The Sickness Unto Death*. Anti-Climacus, the Christian pseudonym, writes:

From the Christian point of view, everything, indeed everything, ought to serve for upbuilding. The kind of scholarliness and scienticity that ultimately does not build up is precisely thereby unchristian. Everything essentially Christian must have in its presentation a resemblance to the way a physician speaks at the sickbed; even if only medical experts understand it, it must never be forgotten that the situation is the bedside of a sick person. [1]

Kierkegaard is part of a long tradition in the West of seeing human life, including the philosophical and religious understanding of life, in terms of illness and health, the diagnosis of a disease and deliverance from it. The diagnosis may be relatively mild (a person lives in misunderstanding or error) or it may be of a deeper spiritual malady (sin). In either case, this tradition postulates that the prior condition of "ill health" includes, as Kierkegaard puts it, diseases of "reflection." "Reflection" is a broad term for Kierkegaard, indicating not only one's thought and intellectual activity, but also the character or tone of one's imaginative and affective life. It includes the ways in which people dream and project images of themselves, how they think – with or without hope – about their prospects and possibilities, and how they relate – or fail to relate – to those images. It points to such matters as

[1] *SUD* 5 (*SV* xi 117).

27

living in self-deception as opposed to living "truthfully." It includes too *how* a person exercises his or her intellective capacities in whatever endeavor, whether "passionately" or "at a distance."

For this tradition, salvation as a search for truth becomes then a search for wholeness and unity over time.[2] It involves self-analysis and self-examination as a necessary part of "coming to the truth," and recognizes that this kind of thinking is both a clarification of intellectual confusion and (more painful and purgative) a passion desiring a better way of life. In the task of cleansing the glass of vision, philosophy is a way of wisdom and even spiritual rebirth.

For this reason, Kierkegaard saw philosophy, especially in its Greek origins, not as a subject, but as a way.[3] As Johannes Climacus writes in *Philosophical Fragments*, the pathos of Socratic philosophy is to strip away illusions and discover or "recollect" the truth "within" that one had forgotten.[4] Philosophical and religious reflection in this tradition are not, then, the specialties of some, or arcane realms of knowledge, or matters of technical expertise alone, but exercises in a discipline aimed at coming to wisdom, a spiritual as well as an intellectual *via disciplinae*.

For Kierkegaard, writing at the culmination of modernity, this tradition of philosophy and religious reflection as a spiritual discipline, a tradition stemming from Socrates and continued in Christianity, was in danger of being undermined in two ways. First, lost is the assumption that one lacks truth or wholeness, that one's present state is ignorance (Socrates) or sin (Christianity). This has been replaced by a confidence that, when one begins to reflect, one is not essentially in error, much less illness, but that the "truth" is easily grasped. At first glance, this too appears Socratic-Platonic, for did not Socrates posit an "inner truth" regained by "recollection"? But Kierkegaard's concern is that, in contrast to the Socratic tradition, self-identity was in his day being assumed as a given; one simply discovered one's unique identity (as in Romanticism) or discovered intellectually the unfolding self-revelation of the Absolute Spirit (Hegel), without self-purification or self-critique. A vocabulary of self-examination and self-purification was being replaced by a vocabulary of expressive self-fulfillment or a vocabulary

---

2   This is explored in George Connell, *To Be One Thing: Personal Unity in Kierkegaard's Thought* (Macon, GA: Mercer University Press, 1985).

3   I owe this phrase to C. S. Lewis, but it aptly fits Kierkegaard. See C. S. Lewis, *Surprised by Joy: The Shape of My Early Life* (New York: Harcourt, Brace & World, 1955), 225. Lewis writes that he once frivolously referred to philosophy as a "subject." Owen Barfield replied that for Plato philosophy was not a "subject," but a way.

4   *PF* 9–10 (*SV* IV 179–80).

of rational contemplation.[5] Second, since the prior condition of ignorance (or sin) is given up, the pathos of the quest for truth (or salvation) is sabotaged, for there is no need to *pursue* a truth one already has.

With these two developments, Kierkegaard thought, the personal and human element in philosophical reflection and in ethicoreligious existence is necessarily sacrificed. As early as *The Concept of Irony*, his dissertation, Kierkegaard may have located this shift from "Socratic ignorance" to Platonic speculation.[6] But the historical moment of the transition from the Socratic to the Platonic mode in philosophy also indicates for Kierkegaard a continuous struggle between two different types of reflection. On the one hand is the Socratic mode, seen in other thinkers admired by Kierkegaard, such as Hamann and Lessing. On the other hand are the speculative thinkers who exemplify the second Platonic movement, epitomized above all in his own day by Hegel and Danish Hegelianism.[7] The problem with such thinking, for Kierkegaard, is twofold, related to (1) dangers inherent in thinking and (2) the particular institutionalization and professionalization of philosophy and theology in the modern age. Kierkegaard's diagnosis of the diseases of philosophical and theological reflection is therefore both a general critique of reflection's dangers and a social critique of how philosophy and theology are done in the modern age.

A useful approach to Kierkegaard as religious thinker is to begin with his diagnosis of some diseases of reflection. The overall diagnostic

---

[5] On the development of a vocabulary of self-fulfillment in modernity and its conflicts with a "disengaged reason" of instrumentalism, see Charles Taylor, *Sources of the Self: The Making of the Modern Identity* (Cambridge, MA: Harvard University Press, 1989). Kierkegaard's attack on disengaged objectivity and concern for human wholeness and unity do not commit him to Romantic expressivism and "self-fulfillment." He stands rather in a quite different philosophical and theological tradition, one more concerned with "self-purification" than with "self-fulfillment."

[6] *The Concept of Irony* in this regard may, on the other hand, reflect a Platonic moment in the young Kierkegaard's thought, in which Socrates' "negativity" gives way to Plato's "positivity." See *CI* 259–71 (*SV* XIII 333–44); compare Johannes Climacus' criticism of "Magister Kierkegaard's dissertation" in *CUP* 90n (*SV* VII 71n).

[7] For Hegel, Socrates was a surpassed moment in the history of philosophy, a negative moment in the dialectical advance to the positivity of Plato. Kierkegaard's repeated and nuanced use of Socrates as the model of philosophical reflection (in both its strengths and limitations) is a protest against Hegelian judgment on Socrates, as well as Kierkegaard's continuous protest at the lack of ethics in the Hegelian system. Whether this is fair to Hegel is another story, since Hegel too can be seen as a philosopher primarily engaged in education, a *Bildung* or upbuilding of the self. See Mark C. Taylor, *Journeys to Selfhood: Hegel and Kierkegaard* (Berkeley: University of California Press, 1980). On (perhaps unconscious) Hegelian elements in Kierkegaard's thought, see Stephen N. Dunning, *Kierkegaard's Dialectic of Inwardness* (Princeton University Press, 1985).

category that Kierkegaard uses for these related diseases of reflection is that of a misapplied "objectivity." This will be discussed in the first part, on the dangers inherent in thinking, which include two kinds of self-deception: not living "within" the concepts one entertains, and "self-forgetfulness." The second part will present a second diagnostic critique, aimed at the professionalization of philosophy and religion. The third part will then begin to outline Kierkegaard's understanding of the cure for these diseases of reflection, an alternative reflection he called "subjective thinking." We will approach this by looking briefly at the characteristics of some philosophical and religious thinkers Kierkegaard believed modeled subjective thinking. We can conclude this last part by examining briefly Kierkegaard's "anti-intellectualism" and his "intellectualism."

FIRST DIAGNOSTIC CRITIQUE OF OBJECTIVITY: DANGERS INHERENT IN THINKING

The first critique, of the dangers of reflection as such, centers around the inherent distancing from the self involved in the act of reflection. As we have seen, for Kierkegaard, "reflection" is a broad term; it includes thinking but also more than cognition or meditation. It involves rather any capacity for entertaining a possibility or idea. It is the capacity to "negate immediacy," that is, to stand back from experience; it thus also entails the use of language.[8] The metaphor of "distancing" here is important, and requires a bit more elaboration. *Johannes Climacus, or De omnibus dubitandum est*, never published in Kierkegaard's lifetime, centers on questions of thinking, consciousness, and reflection. The pseudonym Johannes writes that consciousness is an activity that is trichotomous, not dichotomous, for if I am conscious of something, there are three terms: the self, the object of which one is conscious, and consciousness. Presupposed by consciousness is "reflection" as "the possibility of the relation" that sets out categories, "For example, ideality and reality, soul and body, to know the true, to will the good, to love the beautiful, God and the world, etc. are categories of reflection. In reflection, they touch each other in such a way that a relation becomes possible."[9] The role of consciousness is to relate the categories given by reflection.

The problem, however, is that a person relates to the deliverances of reflection in various ways. In consciousness, there is an interest, a

8   Mark C. Taylor, *Kierkegaard's Pseudonymous Authorship*, 157.
9   *JC* 169 (*SV* IV B 1 147).

relation to an object; hence, objective thought arises. The point to emphasize is the *direction* of the thinker's interest. The thinker's concern, for example, is with the careful formulation of an argument, or the correct way to interpret a text, or the proper way of describing a set of phenomena. Attention, even absorption, is directed outward, toward the object being contemplated. Hence, one can speak of such thinking as being concerned with "objectivity," with the "what" of thought.

Now it is important to see that Kierkegaard is not critical of objective thinking in itself. Objective thinking is quite within its rights within its own domain – as in the sciences or in history. But the difficulty is that objective thought with its interest does not *by itself* touch the state of the thinker; in other words, there is an "externality" to objective thinking. If one contemplates the starry heavens above or the moral courage of Socrates, attention is still directed away from oneself.

But is this fair to objectivity? Certainly it is a mistake to think of "objective thinking" pejoratively as "cold." And Kierkegaard would agree; he would admit that objective thought may be, and often is, passionately inspired by a sense of awe, wonder, or admiration. In *Concluding Unscientific Postscript*, Johannes Climacus praises the scientist for being "erotically preoccupied in his noble pursuit."[10] More than that, Kierkegaard would also grant that it is only by the projection of reflection "outside" oneself that human beings engender images of who they are and who they may become. Finally – and this point is often lost in discussions of Kierkegaard's stress on subjectivity and objectivity – he admits that a disengaged reason can be ethically and spiritually valuable: if I am to see myself clearly, I must see myself "objectively."[11] With all of these qualifications, what then is Kierkegaard's point in criticizing "objectivity"? His point is that even if a person is seized with passion in objective thinking, he or she still is directed outwardly; a philosophically inclined scientist contemplates the heavens with awe, an Alcibiades ethically admires Socrates. Such enthusiasm is in no way to be criticized for what it is. The difficulty arises, however, when human beings rest content with objective thinking or when it is put to purposes beyond its scope.

At the heart of Kierkegaard's reflection on the distinction between objectivity and subjectivity, however, is another matter: his concern to

[10] *CUP* 152 (*SV* vii 125).
[11] *JP* iv 4542 (*Pap.* viii¹ A 165, n.d., 1847): "Most men are subjective toward themselves and objective toward all others, frightfully objective sometimes – but the task is precisely to be objective toward oneself and subjective toward all others."

delineate the distinction between thought and logic on the one hand, and existence and movement on the other. For Kierkegaard, influenced by Aristotle and Trendelenburg, the categories and concepts of thought and of logic are, contrary to Hegel's belief, not concerned with "movement," with transitions from one quality to another, or with contingency. Logic deals with universals and essences; movement has to do with the world of action and contingency. Confusing the two realms, those of static logic and dynamic existence, leads to the mistake of believing that by thinking, that is by reflection upon concepts, one is thereby also engaged in the movements of existing.[12] Again, it is important to emphasize that, for Kierkegaard, there is no inherent problem with the objectivity and timelessness of concepts. The indispensable tool of thought necessary to any person is simply clarity concerning the distinctions. Objective thinking by itself is innocent; confusion between thinking and existing is not innocent.

Beyond such innocent uses of objective reflection, we now come to a true disease of reflection that Kierkegaard believes does plague the philosophical enterprise and thinking in general. The difficulty with Western philosophical thought, for Kierkegaard, is that the model of objective reflection, which is, again, quite within its rights in certain realms such as science, is inappropriately applied to the realm of subjectivity (particularly ethics and religion). In place of the "quest for wholeness" that animated Socrates and drove him to ethics rather than to science, objectivity as a model of reflection rules also in reflection on the human.[13]

The result, for Kierkegaard, is a whole range of self-deception, apparent especially in modern philosophy and theology. We can look more closely at two types of self-deception: first, that of not living seriously within the concepts entertained, and, second, forgetting that one is an existing human being.

Self-deception of not living within the concepts entertained

With regard to the first self-deception, not living seriously within the concepts entertained, Kierkegaard was, for example, intrigued and

---

[12] See the important sections on the possibility of a logical system and the impossibility of an existential system, *CUP* 109–25 (*SV* vii 88–103). See also David F. Swenson, "The Anti-Intellectualism of Kierkegaard," *Something About Kierkegaard* (Minneapolis: Augsburg, 1941), 95–118; Paul L. Holmer, "Kierkegaard and Logic," *Kierkegaardiana* 2 (1957): 25–42.

[13] On Socrates' turning from astronomy to ethics, see *CUP* 83 (*SV* vii 64).

astounded at the ease with which modern philosophy in the style of Hegel began by "doubting everything," but then quickly overcame this doubt to go on "positively" to assert all manner of things. "Doubt" appeared, therefore, to be less a matter of personal concern, and became a "methodological moment" that was swallowed up in positive "results." Kierkegaard thought that this failed on two counts: first, it did not take seriously the honesty of methodological doubt in a thinker such as Descartes, for whom the questions of deception,·doubt, and knowledge were genuine; and second, it failed to take up seriously the kinds of doubt that do trouble human beings. In *Johannes Climacus* Kierkegaard satirizes this by portraying this young thinker who takes seriously that initial moment of "doubting everything," and ends up in despair. The satire is not so much upon Johannes for taking doubt seriously, as upon the age that believes that "doubt" as a human passion attending the philosophical quest for truth and wholeness can be done lightly, or by rote, that it is merely a surpassed moment in thought, rather than something that can afflict a human being deeply and painfully.

This failure to live within the concepts of one's thinking is especially apparent when one turns from the abstraction of Hegelian methodo-logical doubt to the "human studies," for example, "ethics." In this disease of reflection, "seeking to live ethically" becomes reduced to the study of "ethics," which may no longer be a Socratic quest for the good, or a striving for virtue, but merely an "objective" enterprise. Again, this "objectivity" must not be interpreted necessarily to mean disinterestedness, but rather a direction of thought away from the self. In *Philosophical Fragments* Johannes Climacus cites Socrates' chiding of Alcibiades for enthusiastically admiring and loving Socrates; Alci-biades' erotic and philosophic awe is admirable, and even "seductive," but Alcibiades' awe misses the point if it does not lead him beyond his love for Socrates to the development of his own soul.[14]

Alcibiades' almost innocent mistake – confusing his enthusiasm for the good with his enthusiasm for his teacher – is, however, a clue to a more serious disease of reflection in ethics. That is when a person's enthusiasm for ethics may be more accurately described as an enthu-siasm for an argument, or for clarity of thought, or for fame; in other words, it may be a passion for other goods, but without ever reflecting

---

[14] *PF* 24 (*SV* IV 193). Of course, Socrates' jesting about Alcibiades' erotic admiration is not meant to discourage that admiration, but to redirect it from Socrates toward Alcibiades' own growth in wisdom.

back into the self. One becomes absorbed in an ethical "ideal" or "issue," rather than the question of "how then shall I live?" The gap then is between contemplation and actualization. Hence arises the spectacle of the person who can rehearse the theories of the good and of justice, but who in his or her own life does not love the good or live justly.

Another related mistake in ethics is to focus upon an ethical ideal from the past (say, the figure of Socrates), but to distance that ideal, not only in thought, but into the safety of the past. By contemplating this past ideal, a person thinks that he or she has *become* that ideal. But this reveals a twofold misunderstanding: I misunderstand Socrates by forgetting that he faces his ethical choices in his own present and future, and I further misunderstand him when I forget that using Socrates as an ideal requires that I face my present and future. The humor is that I then treat *myself* as if I were locked into the past – as one who, like Socrates, is dead.[15]

This failure to live within the concepts on which one reflects is especially serious within the Christian religious tradition, for presumably the religious realm would be one in which this failure would be repeatedly warned against as a spiritual danger. For Kierkegaard, this failure ironically occurs in the religious realm just as much as in the philosophical realm. It takes, however, another form, and that is the form of "doctrinizing," by which Kierkegaard means that Christian faith is taken to *be* the doctrines or teachings of the church. The picture, then, is that Christianity is to be understood by means of appropriating it through theological or philosophical reflection.

Johannes Climacus insists, however, that "Christianity is not a doctrine but an existence communication [*Existents-Meddelse*]."[16] Or elsewhere, "Christianity is not doctrine; it is an existence [*Existents*], an existing [*Existeren*]."[17] By this he means that it is fundamentally an error to think that "Christianity," a phenomenon that is after all describable according to its beliefs, *is* therefore simply those beliefs. Climacus does say, it should be noted, that Christianity has beliefs. But it is precisely because those beliefs can be stated, analyzed, weighed,

15 *CUP* 146 (*SV* vii 119).
16 *JP* i 1060 (*Pap.* x² A 606, n.d., 1850). Compare *CUP* 379–80 (*SV* vii 328–29).
17 *JP* i 1061 (*Pap.* x³ A 150, n.d., 1850). Recent essays on this theme, with somewhat differing interpretations, are found in my "Kierkegaard's Understanding of Doctrine," *Modern Theology* 5:1 (October 1988): 13–22; John H. Whittaker, "Christianity Is Not a Doctrine," in Richard H. Bell, ed., *The Grammar of the Heart*, 54–74; and Steven M. Emmanuel, "Kierkegaard on Doctrine: A Post-Modern Interpretation," *Religious Studies* 25:3 (September 1989): 363–78.

and otherwise examined in a dispassionate manner that one must say that Christianity is not simply those beliefs. By saying that Christianity is, rather, an "existence-communication," Climacus means that those beliefs have their home within a particular context of life, or existence, and that this context is further defined as a "communication," not only of beliefs, but of "capabilities." In communicating those beliefs, the point of the communication is not to propose a hypothesis to be entertained, but to address and summon a person to examine his or her life in light of those beliefs, and to engender the abilities necessary to accept (or reject) those beliefs.[18]

In short, for Kierkegaard, just as it is a mistake to think that I "understand ethics" when I contemplate an ethical maxim or a figure from the past, so too it is a mistake of reflection to think that one "understands Christianity" simply by learning the teachings or doctrines (i.e., by theology, in the usual sense of theology as "studying doctrines"). When it comes to "understanding Christianity," a knowledge of the basic doctrines or teachings of the faith is a necessary, but not a sufficient, condition. The student of theology must be continually aware of the dangers of treating the increase in theological knowledge as an increase in faith. One may become adept at "moving the counters" of religious and theological concepts without actually living within those concepts.

Despite his admiration for Augustine, Kierkegaard finds in him the source of this "incalculable harm" of confusing "faith" for "knowledge."

Quite simply, Augustine has reinstated the Platonic–Aristotelian definition, the whole Greek philosophical pagan definition of faith . . .

In the Greek view, faith is a concept which belongs in the sphere of the intellectual (it is all splendidly presented, especially in Plato's *Republic*; however, Aristotle's *Rhetoric* also deserves notice). Thus faith is related to probability, and we get the progression: faith – knowledge.[19]

As Jeremy Walker puts it, at the bottom of this mistake of subsuming "faith" to "knowledge" is the classical picture of the relation between understanding and belief, in which understanding is considered to be prior to belief, and believing is viewed as assenting to an already understood proposition.[20] For Kierkegaard, however, Christianity is

---

[18] We will examine later what this means for the entire procedure of "giving reasons" for one's belief; suffice it to say here that Kierkegaard is not advocating an irrationalism in any crude sense, nor is he a volitionalist.

[19] *JP* 1 180 (*Pap.* xi¹ A 237, n.d., 1854).

[20] Jeremy Walker, *Kierkegaard: The Descent into God* (Kingston and Montreal: McGill-Queen's University Press, 1985), 43.

not first "understood" discursively and then believed, but rather the "understanding" includes personality requirements in addition to the intellectual: capacities such as "obedience," "trust," and "hope." The problem with the Augustinian appropriation of "faith" to "knowledge" is that it ignores the context of "understanding" involved in ethico-religious and Christian faith.

For "understanding Christianity" (and ethics as well), the common assumption is that the difficult achievement is obtaining a discursive clarity on ethicoreligious concepts, whereas it is then easy to "apply" or "appropriate" the concepts into one's existence. In other words, the passion of the thinker is directed to the "object" – be it a theory of justice or religion as an object of social-scientific investigation or a dogmatic analysis of Christology – and the assumption is that once the concept is correctly defined or analyzed there is either no further activity for the thinker, or the task of "appropriation" of the concept is then easily accomplished. On the contrary, Climacus affirms, "the ethical is not only a knowing; it is also a doing that is related to a knowing, and a doing of such a nature that the repetition of it can at times and in more ways than one become more difficult than the first doing."[21] The true task, it appears, is translating the ethical into one's life; the ethical gives "a person plenty to do as long as he lives."[22] But self-deception minimizes or ignores completely the necessity and difficulty of this task.

There is another way of "understanding Christianity" that mistakes it for a "doctrine," but in a different sense: this is the rendition of Christianity into what Kierkegaard considered to be alien philosophical categories, which in his day took the form of Hegelianizing Christian and religious concepts. (As noted in the introduction, the irony is that "existentialist theology" has become yet another conceptual scheme for this rendition of Christianity. Kierkegaard is quite different.) Because Christianity is an existence-communication rather than a doctrine, Kierkegaard finds supremely ironic the Hegelian claim that the beliefs or doctrines of the "faith" – the religious language, or in Hegel's terms, the representations (*Vorstellungen*) of religion – can be translated into philosophical concepts and categories and subsumed within "knowledge." He also finds fantastic the claim that these beliefs are now better comprehended within the context of speculative metaphysics, and can even be "understood" apart from faith; for precisely in that realm (the

---

21　*CUP* 160–61 (*SV* vii 132).
22　*CUP* 163 (*SV* vii 135).

religious and Christian) where one might expect clarity on the distinction between objective and subjective understanding, the beliefs that summarize this faith have been fundamentally misconstrued in an objectivizing manner.[23]

Self-deception as self-forgetfulness

The failure to live within ethicoreligious concepts signals for Kierkegaard a lack of "earnestness" in life. But there is also a second and in some ways more serious disease of reflection, which has its own tragicomic dimensions; this disease is that of *self-forgetfulness*. Kierkegaard diagnoses this especially with regard to philosophy in the modern age, but he also sees its more general relevance. Based upon this distinction between objective and subjective thinking, a person can live so much within the contemplation of ideas or external realities that a person comically–tragically "forgets" that he or she is an existing individual. In other words, "objective thinking" when it is beyond its rights reflexively affects the thinker.

It is a strange thing to "forget" that one is an existing human being; this is at once something very easy to understand, but also very elusive, which is why Kierkegaard explores it in such depth in *Concluding Unscientific Postscript*. He also treats it with great irony and humor – for diseases of reflection, and especially pompous reflection, sometimes are best exorcized with laughter. The results may be comic, since forgetting that one is a human being includes a loss of proportion between thinking and living. In one sense "forgetting that one is an existing human being" is as absurd as forgetting one's own name. Satirizing "the professor," Johannes Climacus writes, "Alas, while the speculating, honorable Herr Professor is explaining all existence, he has in sheer absentmindedness forgotten what he himself is called, namely, that he is a human being ... and not a fantastical three-eighths of a paragraph."[24] Yet in another sense this "forgetting that one is an existing human being" is less obvious and more common than the absurdity of forgetting one's own name, for the professor to all appearances still functions, still *seems* to be a human being.

"Forgetting that one is an existing human being" as a type of

---

[23] We will return to "understanding" in chapter 2, where we consider the other side of the question: whether an objective discursive understanding of Christianity is possible without faith.

[24] *CUP* 145 (*SV* vii 118).

self-deception is a complex and apparently paradoxical phenomenon; how can I forget that I exist? But this forgetfulness is not innocent; it is flight, ignoring what one is – an existing human being – in favor of an illusion called "pure thought." The results are by the same token tragic as well as fantastic, for the thinker lives abstractly, never relating the object of reflection to his or her own subjective, concrete existence.

For Kierkegaard, the paradox is only apparent. And it is here that he stands within the Augustinian tradition of seeing sin as a "willful ignorance." What is corrupted in self-deception is one's knowledge of oneself as well as one's will; one wills to be ignorant of what one is doing. This is also a temporal process of corruption, in particular, a strategy of delay; time elapses, allowing knowing to become ever more obscure.[25]

Not surprisingly, it is the Christian pseudonym, Anti-Climacus, who gives the most penetrating of analyses of self-deception, grounding it in a theological as well as psychological account. We will return to this self-deception in the next chapter (and see it described as a variety of despair). For now, however, it is important to see how self-deception emerges as a primary (but not a sole) disease of reflection.

Indeed, *The Sickness Unto Death*, as well as the entire earlier pseudonymous literature of Kierkegaard, can be seen as an "anatomy" of self-deception, as an escape from the self, a denial of the self. In this literature, Kierkegaard maps the territory of self-deception, the various strategies by which people attempt to remove themselves from the demands of being "an existing human being." Kierkegaard's own understanding of his authorship was to begin with the "illusions" of others, particularly, the illusion that in Christendom all are Christians, and then maieutically exhibit how they actually live in aesthetic categories, categories of seeking pleasure and avoiding pain, pursuing good fortune and lamenting evil fortune.[26] It is that gap between self-image and reality – and the fact that most people do not see the gap at all – that he probes empathetically as a physician of the spirit. If he focuses on the "dark" emotions, it is because he finds there important clues concerning what it is to be a human being, as well as the criterion of the spiritual health that identifies illness as illness.

Kierkegaard's analysis of self-deception sees it as a well-nigh universal human phenomenon, linked as it is with despair, and it takes on

---

[25]   *SUD* 94 (*SV* xi 205). See the helpful comments in Evans, *Søren Kierkegaard's Christian Psychology*, 86.

[26]   *PV* 22–43 (*SV* xiii 529–43).

a wide variety of forms. In *The Sickness Unto Death* Anti-Climacus discusses how self-deception and self-forgetfulness accompany even the narrowest of human lives, the lives of people who lack all "primitivity" by disappearing into the crowd. This self-deceptive "narrowness" is actually not simply lack of what Kierkegaard calls "spirit," but a defensive flight from spirit:

> surrounded by hordes of men, absorbed in all sorts of secular matters, more and more shrewd about the ways of the world – such a person forgets himself, forgets his name divinely understood, does not dare to believe in himself, finds it too hazardous to be himself and far easier and safer to be like the others, to become a copy, a number, a mass man.[27]

On the other hand, there is also a kind of self-deception that arises from a lack of "finitude," seen in the "fantastic" person who loses herself or himself in abstractions – such as loving "humanity" in the abstract while hating all particular persons.[28] Again, what Kierkegaard points out is the gap between self-image and reality.

In what I have called Kierkegaard's "anatomy of self-deception" there is, then, marked breadth of application. Human beings universally attempt to escape from themselves, and it is in describing the extent and variety of these diseases of reflection that one can find a diagnostic starting-point for thinking about religion and Christian faith. In the many roles that people play – as aesthetes, as "objective thinkers," as narrow members of the group, as "fantastic" lovers of humanity – there is a kind of perverse logic of self-deception, a disease of recoil from the need people have for self-knowledge.

SECOND DIAGNOSTIC CRITIQUE OF OBJECTIVITY: THE PROFESSIONALIZATION OF PHILOSOPHY AND RELIGION

We can give a concrete example of thought's recoil from self-knowledge by turning to another of Kierkegaard's diagnostic critiques, which focused more sharply on the modern Western philosophical and theological tradition: the professionalization of philosophy and religion in the university and clerical contexts. In place of the passion for philosophic truth and wisdom that animated Socrates, philosophy and theology have now become corrupted by money and have degenerated into a matter of livelihood rather than vocation.[29] In *Philosophical*

---

[27] *SUD* 33–34 (*SV* XI 147).
[28] *SUD* 30–33 (*SV* XI 143–46).
[29] See Stephen D. Crites' interesting contrast between Hegel's domesticity and Kierkegaard as

Fragments, Johannes Climacus contrasts Socrates to modern sophistical teachers. Socrates

refused to accept honor or honorific appointments or money for his teaching, because he formed his judgments with the unbribability of one who is dead. What rare contentment – how rare today, when no amount of money can be large enough and no laurels splendid enough to be sufficient reward for the gloriousness of teaching, but all the world's gold and honors are the express reward for teaching, since they are equal in value.[30]

Kierkegaard held a similar critique of the professionalization of the theological tradition, both in church and academy. To the scandal of taking money for philosophical teaching is added, among the theologians and pastors, the scandal that money is earned precisely because a man was executed.[31] Kierkegaard's critique of the theological professors and the clergy – to be examined in more detail in the final chapter on the late Kierkegaard's "attack" on the church – is especially pointed because he believed that the demands of religious and Christian existence are so trivialized in the professionalization of professorial and clerical life.

Beyond corruption by money and honors, the professionalization of philosophy and theology transforms them into "subject matter" to be "covered objectively" within a set curriculum, rather than as a passion in which one confronts one's own self-confusions in the desire for self-knowledge and self-clarity: "Take the paradox away from a thinker – and you have a professor. A professor has at his disposal a whole line of thinkers from Greece to modern times; it appears as if the professor stood above all of them. Well, many thanks – he is, of course, the infinitely inferior."[32] Kierkegaard comments on textbooks that see Socrates' philosophy "*as yet merely* a life" in contrast to Plato, where philosophy becomes scientific scholarship and doctrine. So too, in Christianity, Christ, the apostles and the first Christians are seen *as yet merely* lives, but now have become doctrine and scientific scholarship.[33]

This is why Kierkegaard commented so caustically upon Hans

one of the last of the "bachelor philosophers." *The Twilight of Christendom: Kierkegaard v. Hegel on Faith and History.* AAR Studies in Religion (Chambersburg, PA: American Academy of Religion, 1972), 4–15.

[30] *PF* 23 (*SV* IV 192).

[31] This theme occupied Kierkegaard in his last years, culminating in his "attack upon 'Christendom.'" *JP* III 3585 (*Pap.* XI¹ A 202, n.d., 1854): "It seems to me that to turn Jesus into money this way is worse than what Judas did." Compare *JP* III 3571 (*Pap.* X³ A 122, n.d., 1850); *JP* III 3578 (*Pap.* X⁴ A 532, n.d., 1852).

[32] *JP* III 3566 (*Pap.* X¹ A 609, n.d., 1849); quoted in *PF* 287n3.

[33] *JP* III 3317 (*Pap.* X⁵ A 113, n.d., 1853).

Lassen Martensen's 1849 *Christian Dogmatics*, which Kierkegaard called "a luxury item" in an age in which the basic abilities even to entertain a religious passion were lost. In this situation, the attempt at a new dogmatics that treats Christian faith as a "subject matter" – and comprehended in an Hegelian manner to boot – is beside the point.[34] What his abstract and super-reflective age required, Kierkegaard thought, was not to represent the teachings of Christian faith in new form, since, he believed, the "what" of Christianity was no longer at stake, but to attend to "how" Christianity is expressed in one's life.[35]

In our present age of "post-Christendom," I doubt whether we can share Kierkegaard's confidence that the concepts of Christian faith are so widely known as they still were in nineteenth-century Denmark, and so agree that dogmatics is "a luxury item." In contrast to his time, when Christian theological concepts were at least discursively well known even if misconstrued, many in twentieth-century Western culture lack even a modicum of discursive conceptual familiarity with the Christian faith.[36] But Kierkegaard's reminder is still pertinent that simply presenting the "what" of Christian faith positively invites misunderstandings and resistances, the same misunderstandings and resistances that Kierkegaard diagnosed, viz., that Christianity is a doctrine and hence "a subject matter" to which one can essentially relate in an objective manner. Crucial to Kierkegaard's thought here is how "objectivity" ironically removes one from the very "interested-ness" that characterizes ethics and religion. "Objectivity" as "disinter-estedness" subverts and betrays the heart of ethics and religion in the interests of distancing the uncomfortable demands of Christian faith.[37]

Again, and especially in relation to Christianity, for Kierkegaard the issue is one of self-deception: that persons do not want to understand

---

[34] *JP* III 3564 (*Pap.* x¹ A 561, n.d., 1849). Martensen's original title was *Speculative Dogmatics*; see Kirmmse, *Kierkegaard in Golden Age Denmark*, 175.

[35] *JP* I 627 (*Pap.* VI A 17, n.d., 1845): "A new science must be introduced: the Christian art of speaking, to be constructed *admodum* Aristotle's *Rhetoric*. Dogmatics as a whole is a misunderstanding, especially as it now has been developed."

[36] Here Karl Barth was prescient; he understood that the situation of the twentieth-century church demanded a clear statement of the doctrine, the "what" of Christian faith. Yet, like Kierkegaard, Barth did not rest content with presenting only the "what" of Christian faith; as Hans Frei states, he also attempted to recreate a universe of discourse and to instruct the reader in the use, principles, and rules of that Christian language. Hans Frei, "An Afterword: Eberhard Busch's Biography of Karl Barth," in H.-Martin Rumscheidt, ed., *Karl Barth in Re-View: Posthumous Works Reviewed and Assessed* (Pittsburgh, PA: The Pickwick Press, 1981), 111.

[37] As Merold Westphal succinctly puts it, "The entry into objectivity is through *disinterestedness*. The goal is *certainty*. The reward is *security*." Kierkegaard's analysis of objectivity sees it as one of "the noetic effects of sin," and one of its expressions is orthodoxy. Merold Westphal, *Kierkegaard's Critique of Reason and Society* (Macon, GA: Mercer University Press, 1987), 121.

what is only too easy to understand. The ranks of scholars and the volumes of commentaries on Scripture make the matter of Christian belief something intellectually difficult rather than personally difficult.

The difficulty lies somewhere else, in its not pleasing us – and therefore, therefore, therefore we must have commentaries and professors and commentaries. We are not "running the risk" of its becoming ambiguous – no, that is precisely what we want, and we hope that little by little, with the cooperation of commentaries, it will become ambiguous.[38]

For Kierkegaard the *context* of philosophizing and theologizing is not accidental; indeed, it is a mistake to think that philosophy and theology somehow can simply be translated from agora or cloister into the professional university or clerical contexts without being altered in the process and perhaps even destroyed. It is his judgment that, despite the belief that one "engages in" philosophy or theology in the academic or clerical setting, the passions that animate the life of academic setting and clerical life in the modern age are often astoundingly at odds with anything resembling either philosophical *paideia* or Christian faith, hope, and love.

SUBJECTIVE THINKING

I suggested at the beginning of this chapter that Kierkegaard as a religious thinker is helpfully seen as part of a long tradition in the West in which the life of reflection is viewed as diagnosis of a disease and a cure or deliverance from that disease. Further, Kierkegaard is convinced that this tradition was in his own day in jeopardy, partly for reasons that are inherent in reflection, but also for reasons having to do with conditions and institutions in the modern world.

If these are the diagnoses of the diseases of reflection, what then is their remedy? Kierkegaard's entire authorship can be seen not only as a diagnosis, but also as a cure for these illnesses. But, as a Christian "therapist," Kierkegaard knows that just as the disease is not easy to diagnose, so too the cure is not easily or quickly taken, for the problem is one of deep-going habits or dispositions of thought, feeling, and imagining. There is, he suggests, powerful resistance against the kind of philosophical and religious therapy that he proposes.

In elaborating on such concepts as the "individual," the "self," and "subjectivity," Kierkegaard seeks to give shape and substance to a

[38]   *JP* III 3597 (*Pap.* XI² A 376, n.d., 1854–55).

practice of philosophy and religion that brings reflection back from inhuman abstraction and forgetfulness to the concrete concerns of existence. His suggestion is that the concern of the thinker is not only with the object of thought (for example, contemplating a duty or one's devotion to God), but with how he or she relates to the object of thought. There is, in other words, a further kind of reflection needed beyond the reflection that "entertains an idea." By "subjectivity," Kierkegaard means not "subjectivism," the claim that a belief is true *because* one believes it to be true. Rather, the question is whether, and if so to what degree, the thinking person "lives within" the idea entertained or the belief that is held, despite the "objective uncertainty" of the belief. This "living within" a belief is what Kierkegaard calls "the double reflection." One not only reflects upon, say, a theological doctrine or teaching *qua* teaching, but one then also reflects that category of thought back upon oneself, or better, reflects one's own life into the category. For example, Kierkegaard criticizes Julius Müller's theological treatise on sin, for, whereas he correctly speaks about sin being experienced, he "now ... should have swung directly into the ethical-religious, into the existential, to the *you* and *I*. Earnestness is that I myself become conscious of being a sinner and apply everything in this respect to myself. But instead of that he goes into the ordinary problems about the universality of sin, etc."[39] There is, for Kierkegaard, something comic and absurd about a theologian who reflects upon the concepts of discipleship, taking up one's cross, and suffering, while living a life of bourgeois comfort. "Reduplication" is rather to exist within the concepts one understands.[40]

In *Concluding Unscientific Postscript*, Johannes Climacus treats in a few pages the topic of the subjective thinker's "task, form, and style." In these pages one finds the heart of Kierkegaard's own vision of the matter of "style" in philosophical and religious thinking and living – and here the question of the style of one's thinking is inseparable from the cure.[41] Climacus' concern here is to outline a manner of reflection that does not forget that one is an existing human being: "In all his thinking ... he has to include the thought that he himself is an existing person. But then in turn he also will always have enough to think about."[42] The task is to understand oneself in existence, which means

39 *JP* IV 4037 (*Pap.* x² A 482, n.d., 1850). Quoted also in *PF* 227.
40 *PC* 133 (*SV* XII 125); compare *JP* III, p. 910.
41 *CUP* 349–60 (*SV* VII 303–12).
42 *CUP* 351 (*SV* VII 305).

seeking to understand the abstract concretely.[43] In terms of self-reflection, this means that the passion of one's thinking is directed toward the problem of one's own existing. Rather than "admire" another person's ethical reality, one must rather live oneself within the ethical requirement.[44]

We can give closer definition to Climacus' understanding of the subjective thinker's task, form, and style by placing him in philosophical and theological company in which he himself felt most comfortable, not only with Socrates,[45] but also philosophers such as Lessing and Hamann, and religious figures such as Luther and Pascal, and the Pietist and Patristic traditions. Some disclaimers are in order. First, it is not that Kierkegaard limited himself in his study or learning to certain figures. Neither is it that he is uncritical of these figures; nor is it that they necessarily influenced him as greatly as has been argued (or as he himself leads one to believe); finally, the issue is not even whether Kierkegaard rightly understood their thought.[46] The purpose here is more modest: a reflection on matters of a thinker's style that can cast light on Kierkegaard's endeavor by comparison. By looking at the characteristics of these thinkers, it is possible to amplify the tradition of Western philosophical and religious thought that he felt was threatened in his own day.

In Lessing and Hamann, Kierkegaard admired some common characteristics: each possessed philosophic *eros* as a passion for truth; each saw his own edification as a central concern of thinking (thus recalling the Socratic pathos for self-knowledge, the desire to move from ignorance to truth); each was an institutionally "marginal" thinker and scholar; finally, each possessed what Kierkegaard considered to be an appropriate focus on particular problems of deep concern, this in marked contrast to the ambition of being a thinker on an objective "world-historical" scale.

---

43   *CUP* 352 (*SV* vii 305).
44   *CUP* 358–60 (*SV* vii 311–12).
45   On Kierkegaard's changing views of Socrates, see Winfield E. Nagley, "Kierkegaard's Early and Later View of Socratic Irony," *Thought* 55:218 (September 1980): 271–82. Nagley argues that in contrast to his early somewhat negative assessment of Socrates in *The Concept of Irony*, Kierkegaard came to appreciate Socrates as a model of existential thinking, ethics, and religious thinking.
46   As Kierkegaard notes in an early journal entry, "great geniuses are essentially unable to read a book. While they are reading, their own development will always be greater than their understanding of the author" (*JP* ii 1288 [*Pap.* ii A 26, n.d., 1837]). Kierkegaard had his own issues and is not a good guide to Lessing's own thought; see Gordon E. Michalson, Jr., "Kierkegaard's Debt to Lessing: Response to Whisenant," *Modern Theology* 6:4 (July 1990): 382.

Of the two, perhaps G. E. Lessing (1729–81) served Kierkegaard most as a model of a thinker. It is not that Kierkegaard was uncritical of Lessing; even if Johannes Climacus praises Lessing, Kierkegaard himself found fault. Indeed, it is curious that Lessing, who embodied so many of the ideals of the Enlightenment, served as a model for a post-Enlightenment thinker such as Kierkegaard. In some ways no greater dissimilarity could be found between the Christian Kierkegaard and the Deistically inclined Lessing, who championed natural religion over against the exclusive claims of any revealed religion. Yet on particular issues Lessing's influence is great. In "On the Proof of the Spirit and of Power," Lessing draws the famous distinction between necessary truths of reason and accidental truths of history.[47] Lessing's logical distinction manifests early Enlightenment awareness of history as creating a "ditch" across which a modern Christian believer must jump in order to bring about faith, a theme central to Kierkegaard's Climacean writings. But it was also the style of Lessing's thinking that attracts Climacus so forcefully.

Kierkegaard prized Lessing's striving for self-clarity as a primary philosophic aim, his conviction that religious truth cannot be communicated directly, and that for human beings the truth is found in striving for the truth rather than in any final system of thought.[48] In addition, there is modesty in Lessing: he is content to hold onto a few thoughts, but to think them through with consistency. In *Concluding Unscientific Postscript* Johannes Climacus praises Lessing for this modesty; Lessing "did not allow himself to be tricked into becoming world-historical or systematic with regard to the religious, but he understood and knew how to maintain, that the religious pertained to Lessing and Lessing alone, just as it pertains to every human being in the same way."[49]

Lessing's style as a thinker is Lessing's irony. He does not instruct the reader or build a system of thought, Johannes Climacus points out, but rather Socratically invites self-reflection by means of polemic and wit. His writings, in the form of the brief essay and aphorism, maintain the pitch of indirection that contributes to such self-reflection.[50] The irony and indirection explain why Climacus so relishes the story of Lessing's

---

[47]   G. E. Lessing, "On the Proof of the Spirit and of Power," in Henry Chadwick, ed., *Lessing's Theological Writings* (Stanford University Press, 1956), 51–56.

[48]   *JP* III, p. 798.

[49]   *CUP* 65 (*SV* VII 49); cf. *JP* III 2371 (*Pap.* VI B 35:7, n.d., 1845).

[50]   *CUP* 68–69 (*SV* VII 52).

"last word" to F. H. Jacobi; the true state of Lessing's beliefs troubled
Jacobi, who pressed him on the matter. Lessing's refusal to ease Jacobi's
mind serves to bolster one of Climacus' main concerns: that the
question of religious belief is not aided by testimony that a particular
person believes – a question strictly irrelevant to the truth of the belief
– but rather that the question of religious belief is one that a person
must decide for himself or herself. Lessing refused to make matters
easier for Jacobi, for Lessing recognized that the state of his own soul
was not Jacobi's essential concern, and indeed was a matter of
distraction from dealing with the issues oneself.[51]

Like Lessing, Johann Georg Hamann (1730–88) is also a thinker
whom Kierkegaard admires, albeit with distinct reservations.[52] But
how different Hamann is from Lessing, for while Lessing's indirection,
his refusal to commit himself with regard to his own faith or lack
thereof, is at the heart of Climacus' admiration, Hamann is much more
"directly" Christian. Despite Hamann's Christian directness, what
strikes Climacus is how Hamann is able (and in this he does resemble
Lessing) to make distinctions between matters of reason and matters of
faith. In contrast to Enlightenment rationalism, Hamann uses the
distinction between reason and faith not to the detriment of faith, but
rather to outline the distinctive realms of reason and faith by showing
reason's inability to prove matters of religious belief.[53] In *Philosophical
Fragments*, Hamann is quoted approvingly (twice) in connection with
Climacus' assertion of the offensiveness to the understanding of the
Absolute Paradox of Christian faith; Climacus' paraphrase of Hamann
runs: "Comedies and novels and lies must be probable, but how could
I [the Absolute Paradox] be probable?"[54] So too, Hamann, like
Climacus, emulates Socrates in pursuit of the truth, but combines that
with Christian confession, being known as "the Magus of the North"
for his following of Bethlehem's star.

---

51 *CUP* 70 (*SV* VII 53–54), 100–04 (*SV* VII 80–85). See also Niels Thulstrup, *Commentary on
    Kierkegaard's* Concluding Unscientific Postscript, *with a New Introduction*, trans. Robert J.
    Widenmann (Princeton University Press, 1984), 204, 216.
52 To what extent did Hamann influence Kierkegaard? Close study reveals less similarity than
    appears at first glance. Stephen N. Dunning claims rightly that Kierkegaard is more a distant
    admirer and critic than disciple of Hamann, and that ironically Kierkegaard's critique of
    Hamann echoes Hegel's. Stephen N. Dunning, "Kierkegaard's 'Hegelian' Response to
    Hamann," *Thought* 55:218 (September 1980): 259–70.
53 As Richard H. Popkin argues, Kierkegaard, like Hamann in his positive comments upon
    Hume's skepticism, came to see that precisely the skepticism that undermines belief provides
    the basis for belief, "Kierkegaard and Scepticism," in Josiah Thompson, ed., *Kierkegaard: A
    Collection of Critical Essays*, 360.
54 *PF* 52 (*SV* IV 219).

But most important is that Hamann, even more than Lessing, understood and practiced Socratic indirection; his *Socratic Memorabilia*, as one Hamann scholar puts it, presents Socrates on several levels at once (reminiscent of Climacus' own philosophic use of Socrates): it represents the historical Socrates, sees him also typologically as a forerunner of Christ, and finally serves as a mask for Hamann over against the Athenians of his own day, the Enlighteners.[55] In this last role, Hamann self-consciously uses Socrates in an indirect mode in criticizing the Enlightenment, revealing how fruitless it is to engage in direct conversation with rationalism: it is like a waking person and a sleepwalker talking past each other, and what is needed is for the sleepwalker to be stabbed awake.[56]

Turning now to Christian theologians and traditions, Kierkegaard was, as we saw in the Introduction, deeply schooled in Christian dogmatic theology, and had marked preferences for people such as Martin Luther and Blaise Pascal, as well as writers in the Pietist and Patristic traditions. These writers, he believed, grasped better than did contemporary academic theologians the context in life of religious and Christian faith; they were thinkers who possessed a "knowledge of the heart" and insight into the human condition. Further, they were not ashamed to address the individual struggling with such concerns, and they took seriously the discipline of "becoming a Christian." As Jeremy Walker has aptly put it, if we approach Kierkegaard theologically, "becoming a Christian" and "what it is to be a Christian" are at heart about prayer and worship.[57] The writers that Kierkegaard found nourishing for his own work and reflection were those especially concerned with the life of prayer and worship. This is why Kierkegaard is less interested in the dogmatic theological task than with the question of how one becomes disposed to religious and Christian issues. In contemporary terms, the *primary* discourse of religious and Christian language and concepts – especially as exemplified in prayer and worship – is also the primary descriptive and critical concern of the person who reflects deeply about religion.[58]

---

[55]   James C. O'Flaherty, *Johann Georg Hamann* (Boston: Twayne, 1979), 46.

[56]   O'Flaherty, *Johann Georg Hamann*, 46, citing and translating from *Johann Georg Hamann. Briefwechsel*, ed. Walther Ziesemer and Arthur Henkel, 6 vols. (Wiesbaden: Insel, 1955–75), I, 369–70.

[57]   Jeremy Walker, *Kierkegaard: Descent into God*, 13. Walker sees Kierkegaard as having strong connections with the classics of Catholic and Orthodox thought in their concern with moral and mystical theology (218).

[58]   See Holmer, *The Grammar of Faith*.

Although Kierkegaard came to him quite late, Martin Luther (1483–1546) was the object of his appreciation for the fact that his life exemplified his theology. Kierkegaard especially appreciated Luther's sermons, which exhibited so clearly how Luther's belief was not a matter of an opinion, but of life and death. Luther "certainly possessed the inward truth to dare to venture," and was "severely tried."[59] Kierkegaard was critical of Luther's (or rather, later Lutherans') stress on justification by faith, but this too was a matter of the change in *context* between Luther's own life and the very different conditions of Lutheranism in nineteenth-century bourgeois culture. In Luther's own life, Kierkegaard writes, the word of justification was addressed to one who knew the demands of the law and the pangs of conscience; the word of grace comforted because there was a prior need for comfort. But, in nineteenth-century Lutheranism, the context has shifted; the attempt to live before God (*coram Deo*) that so characterized Luther's life and thought is gone, and hence the word of justification by faith is cheapened and irrelevant.[60] The "anguished conscience" of Luther is more than a biographical fact about the Reformer, now dispensable; it is rather a necessary Christian concept, a prior condition for anyone confronting the Christian offer of salvation.[61]

Kierkegaard's admiration for Blaise Pascal (1623–62) and his writings is similarly based on the latter's concern for the context of religious existence. For Kierkegaard, the strength of Pascal's reflections is that he did not allow his scientific and mathematical expertise to swallow up his concern for the questions of existence. He recognized rather the limits of discursive reason in dealing with issues of religious belief. So too, his understanding of Christian existence was correctly focused upon the manner in which he personally appropriated Christian discipleship. In a journal entry, Kierkegaard cites Pascal's famous remark in the *Pensées* that few speak humbly about humility, few modestly about modesty, few doubtfully about doubt; Kierkegaard then comments that "this expresses what I advance in a still higher relation – reduplication. With Pascal it is still almost esthetic; I press it farther in the direction of existence."[62] Yet Kierkegaard appreciated

59 *JP* III 2518 (*Pap.* x³ A 153, n.d., 1850). On Kierkegaard's reading of Luther, see also Niels Thulstrup, "Theological and Philosophical Studies," in Thulstrup and Thulstrup, eds., *Bibliotheca Kierkegaardiana*, I, 38–60, especially 46–47.

60 *FSE* 16–19 (*SV* XII 307–10).

61 *JP* I, p. 521 (*Pap.* VII¹ A 192).

62 *JP* III 3107 (*Pap.* x³ A 544, n.d., 1850).

too that Pascal was no aesthete, but saw that Christian existence entails risk and suffering.[63]

The Pietist tradition of the seventeenth and eighteenth centuries was also influential on Kierkegaard, beginning with his exposure to Herrnhuter Pietism in his father's home, but developed also in his own reading and reflection. Thus, Kierkegaard evaluated highly the writings of Johann Arndt, Johann Gerhard, Philipp Spener, A. H. Francke, and Gerhard Tersteegen. He found encouragement in his own understanding of religious and Christian existence in the Pietists' demand that Christianity be seen as a way of life and not simply belief. And they shaped his understanding of the identification of the believer with Christ's sufferings in the imitation of Christ. Kierkegaard's regard for Johann Arndt (1555–1621) is especially evident in his journals; he owned both German and Danish editions of Arndt's *True Christianity*, and comments upon the simplicity and directness of Arndt's discussions of prayer, and the psychological insight shown in his treatment of the dangers of pride that lurk in renunciation and self-denial.[64] Yet Kierkegaard was also critical of Pietism, especially the tendency in Pietism toward moralism and external strictures. In a journal entry from 1850 Kierkegaard writes: "Yes, indeed, pietism (properly understood, not simply in the sense of abstaining from dancing and such externals, no, in the sense of witnessing for the truth and suffering for it . . .) is the one and only consequence of Christianity."[65]

As Marie Mikulová Thulstrup suggests, Pietists, like Arndt, introduced Kierkegaard to the Christian mystical tradition and most importantly to the Patristic writings. Especially in the ante-Nicene writers, before the Constantinian establishment, Kierkegaard found support for his own conviction of the centrality to Christian existence of witnessing to the truth, including witnessing to the truth in suffering.[66] He was especially partial to Tertullian (*c*. 160–*c*. 225), not least for his stress on obedience to God and suffering, and for his differentiation of faith from philosophic understanding, cited by Johannes Climacus in *Philosophical Fragments*.[67] Kierkegaard's attitude

---

[63]   See *JP*III, pp. 849–50.

[64]   See, for example, *JP*III 3446 (*Pap.* x² A 496, n.d., 1850) on prayer and *JP*III 3771 (*Pap.* x⁵ A 53, n.d., 1852) on self-denial. On Arndt, see Johann Arndt, *True Christianity*, trans. and Introduction Peter Erb. Preface by Heiko A. Oberman (New York, NY; Ramsey, NJ; Toronto, ON: Paulist Press, 1979).

[65]   *JP*III 3318 (*Pap.* x³ A 437, n.d., 1850).

[66]   See Marie Mikulová Thulstrup, "Studies of Pietists, Mystics, and Church Fathers," in Thulstrup and Thulstrup, eds., *Bibliotheca Kierkegaardiana*, 1, 60–80, especially 62–64, 71.

[67]   *PF* 52 (*SV* IV 218). See also M. M. Thulstrup, "Studies of Pietists," 74.

to later Patristic writers was more ambivalent, however, especially over two issues: the accommodation of faith with philosophy, which Kierkegaard calls the "intellectualizing of faith," and the parallel accommodation of the church to the surrounding culture in the birth of "Christendom." Augustine (354–430), for example, is a theologian who, despite his strong affinities with Kierkegaard, particularly in a work like the *Confessions*, has in Kierkegaard's view confused faith and philosophy; in his journal Kierkegaard links this accommodation of faith and philosophy to a second accommodation, that of the church to the surrounding culture: "But already at the time of Augustine, Christianity was much too much at rest, had leisure to enable the scientific or scholarly to rise – with its conceited and misunderstood importance – and then we get pagan philosophy – and this is supposed to be Christian progress ... "[68] Kierkegaard, especially late in his life, is particularly critical of the attempt of the post-Nicene fathers to translate the earlier Christian model of martyrdom into a post-Constantinian asceticism, as if the external political situation of the church determined the shape of Christian existence. For Kierkegaard, the Christian ideal is internally generated in Christ's call to the believer to discipleship, and writers such as Basil of Caesarea (*c.* 330–79) were deeply mistaken in accommodating this old ideal to the new conditions of the post-Constantinian settlement.[69]

Given this constellation of writers antedating Kierkegaard, one can suppose that he would find kinship with other philosophical and religious writers since his time (in addition to Wittgenstein), including figures as diverse as Simone Weil and Dietrich Bonhoeffer. The aphoristic style of Weil's *Gravity and Grace* as a means of self-reflection and communication parallels Kierkegaard, but beyond the form there is also a striking similarity, at least in some regards, in content. Her concern with "attention" resembles Kierkegaard's concern with "interest," her theme of "detachment" is mirrored in Kierkegaard's understanding of self-denial and affliction. Weil too, like Kierkegaard, holds to the centrality of the love of God (both God's love to human beings, seen especially in the crucifixion, and the person's reciprocated love to God) and love of neighbor – which is, as we will see in

[68] *JP*1 180 (*Pap.* xi¹ A 237, n.d., 1854). It is, of course, false that what Kierkegaard regards as an
accommodation between faith and philosophy only began with the accommodation of the
church to the surrounding culture in the Constantinian settlement. Kierkegaard over-
simplifies the history, and ignores the early Patristic concerns – going back to Justin Martyr –
to relate faith and philosophy. Cf. M. M. Thulstrup, "Studies of Pietists," 79–80.

[69] M. M. Thulstrup, "Studies of Pietists," 79.

chapter 6, the culmination of Kierkegaard's religious and Christian thought.[70] Finally, for Weil too, there is a suspicion of the dangers of theologizing as taking one away from the context of human life, for the gospels have a conception of human life rather than a theology.[71] Yet there are parallels between Kierkegaard and the more orthodox Dietrich Bonhoeffer as well, both the Lutheran heritage they share and in Bonhoeffer's serious theological reaffirmation of the "cost" of Christian discipleship and imitation of Christ, as a correction of a distorted Lutheran solafideism.[72]

Despite this diversity of Kierkegaard's affinities with other philosophical and religious thinkers, they share a certain "anti-intellectualism."[73] Philosophically, like Kant and Wittgenstein, Kierkegaard's intellect is at the service of delimiting the realm of thought in the service of existence; theologically, like Luther and Bonhoeffer, his passion points the reader to discipleship. Because of the misuses of thinking, as well as the social critique of the study of philosophy and theology in the academy, and the misuse of theology in the church, Kierkegaard's categories, such as "subjectivity," are intended to undermine the untoward excesses of hyperintellectualism and abstract thinking.

This "anti-intellectualism" of Kierkegaard can, however, be easily misunderstood, for an interesting aspect of Kierkegaard's thought is that, unlike Weil but like Bonhoeffer, he continues to have a great commitment to orthodox Christian teaching. As we saw in the Introduction, for all of his criticism of the dangers of intellectualizing Christian faith, he never rejects fundamental Christian teachings. It then appears to some that there is an inconsistency in Kierkegaard's religious and Christian thought. Some commentators, such as Torsten Bohlin, have alleged that Kierkegaard's concern with the "how" of Christianity is fundamentally at war with his Christian orthodoxy, that his interest in the subjective "how" leads to a deep split within his

---

[70] Simone Weil, *Gravity and Grace*, trans. Arthur Wills, Introduction Gustave Thibon (New York: G. P. Putnam's Sons, 1952). See also Simone Weil, *Waiting for God*, trans. Emma Craufurd, Introduction Leslie A. Fiedler (New York: G. P. Putnam's Sons, 1951).

[71] Simone Weil, *First and Last Notebooks*, trans. Richard Rees (Oxford University Press, 1970), 147; cited with comment in Peter Winch, *Simone Weil: "The Just Balance"* (Cambridge University Press, 1989), 199.

[72] Dietrich Bonhoeffer, *The Cost of Discipleship*, trans. R. H. Fuller, with some revision by Irmgard Booth (New York: Macmillan, 1963); see his critique of "cheap grace," 45–61.

[73] The phrase is used judiciously by David F. Swenson in his classic essay, "The Anti-Intellectualism of Kierkegaard," in *Something About Kierkegaard*, 95–118.

thought on Christianity.[74] But to allege such a split in his thought is a misunderstanding. Per Lønning correctly criticizes Bohlin's view of a basic opposition between traditional church orthodoxy and a strongly personalist experiential understanding of Christianity.[75] Lønning continues that other scholars, such as Eduard Geismar and Emanuel Hirsch, also see Kierkegaard as one who speaks from his personal experience to reject any intellectualizing of faith.[76] Scholars such as Bohlin, Geismar, and Hirsch have difficulty relating Kierkegaard's concerns for both traditional dogma and personal religious faith. They are reduced to speaking of a "tension" between orthodoxy and experience, with experience winning out in his thought. The vision is that of Kierkegaard as Pietist or Romantic against intellectualist orthodoxy.

Where these scholars are correct is that, as I have argued, an objective discussion of Kierkegaard's doctrinal and dogmatic beliefs (a *certain* sense of "Kierkegaard as theologian") inadequately characterizes his religious and Christian thought, and that Kierkegaard is concerned with the "how" of Christian faith. So too, he has links with Pietism in this concern, as we have seen. However, it misses the point to summarize this as a "tension" between intellect and experience, or between "theology" and "feeling." Kierkegaard never recommends a sacrifice of the intellect for the sake of "experience," and he has a central place for dogma.

The term "anti-intellectualist" as applied to Kierkegaard must thus be used with great caution. This is because, first, he cannot be associated with a thoughtless denigration of the mind or the rational capabilities in favor, say, of "choice" or "will" or "emotion." He has nothing in common with a mindless elevation of the "anti-rational"; and, as we will see in more detail in chapters 2 through 4, his thought is not in any way a recommendation of an anti-rational "leap of faith." Rather, as I will argue, emotion and belief are closely intertwined for him. In delimiting the areas of objectivity and subjectivity, Kierkegaard is not recommending that the realm of the objective is that of "reason"

[74] Bohlin, *Kierkegaards dogmatiska åskådning* [*Kierkegaard's Dogmatic Views*].
[75] Lønning, "Kierkegaard as a Christian Thinker," in Thulstrup and Thulstrup, eds., *Kierkegaard's View of Christianity*, 165. The original criticism of Bohlin on this issue is in Valter Lindström, *Stadiernas Teologie, en Kierkegaard Studie* (Lund: Haakon Ohlsons, 1943). Compare J. Heywood Thomas, *Subjectivity and Paradox* (Oxford: Basil Blackwell, 1957), 45–47; Mark C. Taylor, *Kierkegaard's Pseudonymous Authorship*, 22.
[76] Lønning, "Kierkegaard as a Christian Thinker," in Thulstrup and Thulstrup, eds., *Kierkegaard's View of Christianity*, 165.

and "the mind," with subjectivity excluding the mind and intellect. Rather, Kierkegaard is engaged in an intellectual and philosophical task of clarification of "subjectivity" that describes other functions of the mind that are not embraced in "objectivity."

Kierkegaard's thought is "intellectual" in a second sense, namely, that the realm of subjectivity is itself profoundly reflective and self-reflective; Christian faith in particular embodies what he calls a second "immediacy or spontaneity after reflection."[77] A person who is engaged in the subjective task does not abandon his or her mind, but engages in a particular kind of careful self-reflectiveness. The "sub-jective task" has ample room for intellectual labor.

There is finally a third sense in which Kierkegaard is not "anti-intellectual," namely, he believes that religion and Christianity are deeply conceptual. For example, while Christianity is not a doctrine but an "existence-communication,"[78] it still possesses doctrinal and conceptual content, such as revelation, Incarnation, consciousness of sin, and the possibility of offense. A student of Christianity needs to be familiar with these dogmatic concepts, not least, as we will see in more detail in the next chapter, because they "shape Christian emotion."[79] Hence, any analysis of religion and Christianity does them a disservice if it ignores the particular conceptual definitions they entail. For example, if someone says that "faith" is a matter of general or basic trust in another, Kierkegaard would respond that such an analysis lacks precision and rigor. What is necessary is to specify the particular conceptual determination of Christian "faith," especially its orientation to Christ, its relations to a failure in self-understanding (which Christians call "sin"), and so forth. Any analysis that does not take into account the particularities of the Christian concept of "faith" is then open to confusing that faith with all manner of other types of "faith." It is precisely Kierkegaard's "intellectualism" that insures against these common confusions.

Kierkegaard's anti-intellectualism, therefore, is in the interests not of an emotionalism or primitivism divorced from careful thought; it is rather aimed against an intellectualism that places obstacles before self-reflectiveness. This too places him firmly within the central orthodox Christian theological and spiritual tradition. "Edification," central to his entire endeavor, sees that the goal of thinking is to become clear on

[77] *JP* II 1123 (*Pap.* VIII¹ A 649, May 11, 1848).
[78] *CUP* 607–08 (*SV* VII 529–30).
[79] *OAR* 163–64 (*Pap.* VII² B 235, pp. 200–01).

the limits of pure thought, especially in the realm of ethics and religion, and hence to open a person to the need for the "upbuilding."[80] It is for Kierkegaard only by attending to the need for personal upbuilding that one can, first, root out the diseases of reflection that continually tempt one, and second, root out the diseases of the heart in which one is also mired. The two tasks are intimately connected.

In summary, Kierkegaard as a "diagnostic" thinker attempts to provide a therapy for persons who wish to reflect carefully upon the "diseases" of their own reflective lives, and in particular their ethical, religious, and, perhaps, Christian commitments. Having surveyed in the Introduction and in this chapter some of the general features of that reflection, we must now turn to the particular shape of that therapy: Kierkegaard's anthropological reflection.

---

[80]   In the new English translation of the "Edifying Discourses" (*EUD*), Howard and Edna Hong choose the term "Upbuilding" (in Danish, *opbyggelige*). For the Hongs' defense of the English translation "upbuilding," see *EUD*, 503–05n3.

CHAPTER 2

Anthropological reflection

Having focused in the first chapter on the diseases of reflection and his understanding of an alternative "style" of "subjective thinking," our task now is to look more carefully at the shape of Kierkegaard's alternative reflection. So, too, we need to broaden our analysis from the particular diseases of reflection analyzed in chapter 1 to his diagnosis of wider spiritual ills. We will see how he approaches the methods and tasks of understanding human existence that are part of what he calls "anthropological contemplation" and how this is central to his religious thought.[1] In particular, we will see how he interweaves the task of a general psychological analysis of the self with the dogmatic description of the self in terms of Christian concepts.

In the first part, we will look at how anthropological reflection relates analysis of the human – in particular, psychology – to religion and Christian belief. We will need to consider first how "psychological" investigations yield "objective" knowledge of the self; second, how psychology and religion (in particular Christian dogmatics) interact as separate yet related kinds of investigations; and third, the related question of whether Kierkegaard's anthropological and religious thought should be seen theologically as primarily "apologetic" or "dogmatic."

In the second part, we will turn from these methodological considerations to a fuller description of Kierkegaard's interweaving of psychology and Christian concepts in his religious understanding of the self. We will examine the fundamental orientation of the self to God in creation, his analysis of human emotions and moods and their relation

---

[1] Gregor Malantschuk, *Kierkegaard's Thought*, ed. and trans. Howard V. Hong and Edna H. Hong (Princeton University Press, 1971), ch. 1 stresses the unity and methodical nature of Kierkegaard's investigations of the human sphere. Kierkegaard notes that, while in Hegel the assumption is that there is "reality in thought," what "has not yet been undertaken" is "genuine anthropological contemplation" (*JP*1 37 [*Pap.* III A 3, July 5, 1840]).

to sin, the "stages on life's way" as a frame that accounts for moods and emotions, and, finally, Kierkegaard's Christian "narrative" understanding of the self.

"ANTHROPOLOGICAL REFLECTION" AS RELIGIOUS REFLECTION

Psychology

Against the diseases of reflection that arise from abstracting one's thinking from existence, Kierkegaard points his readers to the remedy of "anthropological reflection" as "self-reflection." Both phrases – "anthropological reflection" and "self-reflection" – are necessary for Kierkegaard, since he is engaged in a dual task, and, ironically, partly an "objective" task. First, anthropological reflection is an objective investigation, a "scientific" or "philosophical" study that descriptively defines the dynamics of the self. This study, however, need not be disinterested, but according to Kierkegaard must be a tool of thought preparatory for the second task: an individual's own self-reflection.

The first part of this task, the objective task of anthropological reflection, shows again what we saw at the conclusion of chapter 1, that Kierkegaard is by no means against careful reflection on the self; he does not see the self as inchoate and therefore inherently indescribable. Rather, a legitimate philosophical task is what in more modern terms we may call a "descriptive logic" of the self. While Kierkegaard is suspicious of the myth of the "observing self," nonetheless, "observation" is a legitimate philosophical tool applicable to subjectivity, for subjectivity exhibits patterns that are describable; generalizations are possible concerning what it is to be a human being.

This means that any picture of Kierkegaard's psychology as solipsistically centered on the individual – an essentially private, hidden, unknowable self – is false. For all of his stress on the "individual" and the particularity of a person's existence, and despite the influence on him of Romanticism, Kierkegaard is very far from any Romantic "expressivist" picture of the self, in which (a) the individual is allegedly "unique" and (b) this uniqueness is unknowably "hidden within." Kierkegaard does use the Romantic image of discovering and developing one's own given capacities to find the unique self; Judge William's understanding of ethics, for example, is a combination of the Romantic ideal of finding the unique self and the Kantian model of conforming to ethical imperatives. And Kierkegaard speaks much of psychological "hiddenness" and "secrecy," as well as, in *Postscript*, the "hidden inwardness" of the religious person.[2] Yet Kierkegaard does not find the uniqueness of the self to be either the Cartesian "ghost in the machine" or a given self discovered through introspection. This is because the self, for Kierkegaard, is acquired rather than given, formed rather than discovered; one is born as a human being, to be sure, but one *becomes* a "self" or an "individual" as one gains inwardness and subjectivity. Far from being an "aesthetic" examination of the immediate passing content of one's consciousness, for Kierkegaard "inwardness" is, as C. Stephen Evans nicely puts it, an examination of the larger patterns of action in a person's life that form a history.[3] Thus, inwardness and subjectivity are acquired not only in thought, but as one's actions and dispositions become increasingly apparent to oneself. Inwardness and subjectivity therefore have as much to do with the external actions and publicly observable dispositions of a person as with the alleged "contents" of private consciousness.[4]

Kierkegaard's anthropological reflection is then, despite superficial similarities, quite different from any notion of a given, unique individual self; it is rooted in the broad Christian tradition of self-reflection and self-knowledge as a spiritual discipline in which the self is not "expressed," but "developed." It is grounded, finally, in what we described in chapter I as the quest for self-knowledge from self-forgetfulness.[5]

Because of the "public" character of the self, Kierkegaard's psychological reflection is, as Kresten Nordentoft has argued, a combination of observation and involvement, or in Kierkegaard's terms "autopsy" and "engagement."[6] "Autopsy" assumes Kierkegaard's psychological premise that human subjectivity is "objectively" observable and describable. This can be seen especially in the pseudonymous literature, where important psychological-observational roles are played by Kierkegaard's "observer figures": Constantin Constantius in *Repetition*,

---

2 The pseudonym Anti-Climacus is later scathingly critical of this hidden inwardness, as we will see in chapter 7.

3 Evans, *Søren Kierkegaard's Christian Psychology*, 37.

4 Neither is Kierkegaard, for all of his interest in what it is to be a "genius," partial to the aristocratic Romantic notion that genius is necessary for self-knowledge. In contrast to this, he is stubbornly egalitarian in claiming that this self-reflection is a skill or capacity open to any person.

5 Jeremy Walker's *Kierkegaard: Descent into God* has seen most clearly this aspect of what we can call Kierkegaard's "spirituality."

6 Kresten Nordentoft, *Kierkegaard's Psychology*, trans. Bruce Kirmmse (Pittsburgh: Duquesne University Press, 1978), ch. I.

Johannes de Silentio in *Fear and Trembling*, Frater Taciturnus in *Stages on Life's Way*, and Johannes Climacus as an observer of religious existence in *Philosophical Fragments* and *Postscript*. These observer figures provide penetrating insights into the psychological and spiritual state of the persons they examine (such as the Young Man in *Repetition*, and Abraham – as well as the tragic figures – in *Fear and Trembling*). Indeed, at one level, the observer figures understand their subjects better than those subjects understand themselves. They are able to plot out the dilemmas their subjects face, and can even suggest possible solutions to those dilemmas.

Yet, as we saw in chapter 1, Kierkegaard does not see "understanding" as being exhausted in "objective description." How then do we reconcile the psychological observers' ability to understand with Kierkegaard's insistence that understanding depends upon existential capacities? The answer is, as both Vigilius Haufniensis in *The Concept of Anxiety* and Anti-Climacus in *The Sickness Unto Death* say, there is "understanding and understanding." While capable of great insight, the observers themselves are also aware of the limits of their own observational understanding. For example, Johannes de Silentio in *Fear and Trembling* says that he is able to "describe" the movements of faith like a person slung in a swimming belt can describe the motions of swimming, but he himself cannot make Abraham's movements of faith.[7] Actually, for Kierkegaard the observer figures can even be ranked according to the degree of their own participation or lack of participation in what they describe; Constantin as an ironist in some ways is limited in his understanding of the Young Man's religious crisis in *Repetition*, while Johannes Climacus, as a humorist, is much more capable of understanding the Christian sphere of existence that he himself does not occupy. Finally, for Kierkegaard, the second kind of understanding is given only by participating in the sphere of existence.

For these reasons, objective psychological analysis, apart from participation in the way of life being analyzed, is both valuable and limited. The issue is relevant to current discussions of the extent to which, say, a non-religious person can understand religion, and also the degree to which an objective analysis of religion is possible. Kierkegaard is often portrayed as a "fideist" on such issues, as one claiming a "hard perspectival" position, viz., that only a person participating in a religion can understand it and that criticism by a

---

[7]   *CA* 142 (*SV* IV 408), *SUD* 90 (*SV* XI 202), *FT* 37–38 (*SV* III 88–89), *FT* 50 (*SV* III 100).

non-participant is impossible. Actually, his position is more complex and more interesting; in modern terms it is closer to a "soft perspectival" position, i.e., that a person who does not participate within a religious way of life can understand it and even make perceptive critical judgments concerning it that are closed to the participant, although there will also be elements that are opaque to such a person's understanding.

Hence, one can discriminate various levels of understanding and failure to understand: first, there is the understanding gained by observational analysis, an understanding open to anyone with the requisite analytic skills; second, there is the understanding gained only by participation in a way of life – in Kierkegaard's terms, by a passional sympathy. There is yet a third kind of understanding, often missed by commentators on Kierkegaard's thought, which is a combination of the two: one can gain an understanding of a person or a religion by way of a passional antipathy. For example, in *Postscript*, Climacus praises the scoffer who "attacks Christianity and at the same time expounds it so creditably that it is a delight to read him, and the person who is really having a hard time getting it definitely presented almost has to resort to him."[8] Such a knowledge is both observational, open to a person not participating in Christian existence, and passional, and thus akin to the understanding gained only by one passionally engaged in Christian existence.

What applies to the "understanding" of religion applies also to psychological understanding by an observer, and illuminates the extent and the limits of a psychologist's understanding of another person. "Insight" as a capability, in other words, includes analytic and imaginative skills that do not depend on participating in the psychological dynamics of the subject; at the same time, Kierkegaard is also acutely aware that such "insight" can fail, that one can finally find another person "opaque" in a way that is very difficult to overcome.[9]

There is another element of Kierkegaard's psychological method in addition to observation, and that is what Kierkegaard calls "experimentation." Like observation, experimentation occurs when one re-creates imaginatively the psychological situation of another person

---

8   *CUP* 614 (*SV* vii 535). The likely reference is Ludwig Feuerbach.

9   Even so perceptive a Kierkegaard commentator as Merold Westphal misses the nuances of Kierkegaard's third kind of understanding of religion; see *God, Guilt, and Death: An Existential Phenomenology of Religion* (Bloomington: Indiana University Press, 1984), 15. For an account that does not attribute "fideistic insulation" to Kierkegaard, see M. Jamie Ferreira, *Transforming Vision*, 137–44.

without participating in it; thus, experimentation too will not guarantee understanding. Nonetheless, experimentation is a tool for gaining closer *empathetic* as well as critical psychological insight. As an imaginative recreation of a person's psychological characteristics it includes a good deal of identification with the subject.[10] The young Kierkegaard with his vivid imagination steeped himself in such experimentation, in both seeking out the "secret" behind his father's melancholy, and in his use of literature and mythology as a source for psychological insight. Literature and mythology function, for Kierkegaard, "typologically" and even (but without Jungian overtones) "archetypically," providing illustrations of particular psychological stances. The virtuosity of this use of literature and mythology is quite astounding, and is not limited to the "aesthetic" writings: in "The Immediate Erotic Stages" in *Either/Or* I, the figures of the Page in Mozart's *Figaro*, Papageno, and Don Juan exemplify those three immediate stages; but, in *Fear and Trembling*, Abraham is contrasted to tragic figures like Agamemnon, Brutus, and Jephthah to illuminate, not simply ethical, but also psychological issues; perhaps centrally, Kierkegaard's writings compare and contrast Socrates and Christ.

Although Kierkegaard's psychological analyses can appear architectonic at times (as in *The Sickness Unto Death*, where despair is discussed according to such elements as the infinite/finite, eternal/temporal, and possibility/necessity), what enlivens these discussions is the imaginative projection, the "engagement," with which Kierkegaard as an observer of the human condition enters into the state of mind of the figures he discusses. Even his "types," though not "realistic," are presented with verisimilitude and a penetrating treatment of psychological dynamics. His *imaginative sympathy* as experimenter locates the hidden despair and pain. It is precisely his experimental *empathy* that can *identify with* that pain and thus help *explain* behavior he portrays, where normally an observer would see only the exterior behavior. Second, these psychological portrayals are best presented in narrative frameworks, the fruit of his poetic invention. A narrative is necessary because people exist within time. Hence, Kierkegaard's psychology does not simply present static "types" or awkward "marionettes," as is often asserted. Even in his most architectonic and "algebraic" presentations, the reader is

---

[10]   Kierkegaard's term for this is "*Tanke-Experiment*," which Howard and Edna Hong translate as "imaginative construction." See Howard Hong's "*Tanke-Experiment* in Kierkegaard" and Robert L. Perkins' response, "Comment on Hong," in McKinnon, ed., *Kierkegaard: Resources and Results*, 39–55.

invited to engage in an imaginative and empathetic response in which even Kierkegaard's most abstract psychological descriptive categories are rendered into narrative form, required exactly by the dynamics of the outworking of psychological conflicts.[11]

We will return to this "narrative" aspect of Kierkegaard's psychology at the end of this chapter, in order to criticize a common misunderstanding of his thought. The point to be stressed for the moment is how (like Freud after him) Kierkegaard's use of literary, mythological, and even operatic sources for psychological analysis contributes to an imaginative "experimental" empathy that in turn demands the discursive talents of the writer ("the poet") to provide sympathetic portrayals of psychological conflicts and resolutions.

Psychology and dogmatics

Given both Kierkegaard's interest in psychology and the overall religious teleology of his writings, how do psychology and specifically Christian concepts relate to one another? As Gregor Malantschuk notes, Kierkegaard was concerned with this issue from early in his career, and maintains that Kierkegaard wished to hold together two apparently incompatible factors: the human position and Christianity's claim upon the whole person.[12] To see just how Kierkegaard relates the human and the Christian – without incompatibility – is the goal of this and the following section. We can begin by examining how he came to regard the relation between psychology and dogmatics.

Kierkegaard, like a number of his contemporaries, reflected carefully upon the relations between various ways of understanding human beings, including the relations between psychology and dogmatics. The "encyclopedia" of knowledge, especially knowledge of the human, called for careful discriminations. As Niels Thulstrup comments, Kierkegaard developed in contrast to Hegel his own encyclopedia of the sciences in the spirit of Schleiermacher.[13]

Kierkegaard's primary aim, against Hegel, was to resist attempts to develop a general metaphysical system that claims to provide a system of meanings that will embrace various fields of inquiry, such as art, ethics, psychology, and religion. In contrast to this claim, Kierkegaard

[11]   For the term "algebraic," see, for example, *CA* 113n (*SV* IV 382), 128 (*SV* IV 395), 137 (*SV* IV 403).
[12]   Malantschuk, *Kierkegaard's Thought*, 19.
[13]   Niels Thulstrup, *Kierkegaard's Relation to Hegel*, 351–52.

sought to preserve the differences among the "sciences," and he felt
that nothing but conceptual confusion would result from blurring the
distinctions. In his important methodological reflections at the beginning of *The Concept of Anxiety*, the pseudonym Vigilius Haufniensis
criticizes the tendency in speculative philosophy and theology to
obscure linguistically the distinctions between fields of study by interpreting particular concepts into such an all-embracing meta-logical or
speculative field. If this interpretation is made, the language and
concepts of particular fields become confused with one another. For
example, in Hegel's meta-logical scheme, "faith" becomes confused
with a preconceptual "immediacy," and then is seen as prior to, and
surpassed by, knowledge.[14]

For Kierkegaard, anyone concerned with the respective domains,
say, of ethics, psychology, philosophy, and dogmatics, needs to be
sensitive to what concepts belong to that particular field of inquiry,
especially what concepts act as "presuppositions," or logically basic
concepts for that field. For example, "original sin" is a logically basic
concept in Christian dogmatics, but not in psychology. "Anxiety" is a
psychological concept, but not strictly a dogmatic concept. Furthermore, such concepts are irreducible to concepts in other domains. As
Lee Barrett has convincingly argued, Kierkegaard's reflections about
presuppositional concepts resemble certain analytic philosophers'
remarks on the epistemic autonomy of distinctive language-games.[15] At
the same time, Barrett continues, Kierkegaard recognizes that while
ethics, psychology, or dogmatics cannot be reduced to one another,
they do relate to each other in significant ways.[16]

Kierkegaard's suspicion of reducing various disciplines into one
another, or into a metaphysical scheme, explains why, as we saw in the
Introduction, religion and especially dogmatic theological concepts
need not be "interpreted," either by correlating theological concepts to
philosophical or psychological phenomena (in the manner of Tillich's
theology), or translating them into another vocabulary (in the manner
of Bultmann). The student of psychology and religion should aim

[14] *CA* 10 (*SV* IV 282).
[15] Lee Barrett, "Kierkegaard's 'Anxiety' and the Augustinian Doctrine of Original Sin," in
Robert L. Perkins, ed., *International Kierkegaard Commentary, Volume 8:* The Concept of Anxiety
(Macon, GA: Mercer University Press, 1985), 43. Barrett's fine article argues that
Kierkegaard's distinction between psychology and dogmatics allows him without contradiction to speak of sin both as an act and as a state. Only if one ignores the logical distinction
between the language of psychology and dogmatics does it appear (to many commentators)
that Kierkegaard contradicts himself.
[16] Barrett, "Kierkegaard's 'Anxiety'," 48.

rather at obtaining clarity concerning the basic concepts in the respective "sciences," and exercise care in relating them to one another.

Yet these respective domains can fruitfully interact. Psychology can illuminate, even correct, distinctively religious and Christian concerns; this is clear in Vigilius' criticism of how dogmatics fantastically places Adam outside the human family, in either Catholic or Protestant federal theology, a situation psychology can remedy.[17] On the other hand, religious or dogmatic concepts can illuminate psychological concerns. This duality between the independence and interaction of psychology and dogmatics in Kierkegaard's thought is not, I would argue, ambivalence or ambiguity. On the contrary, I think it is a consistent and distinctive understanding of the relation between psychology and dogmatics that is relevant to current discussions. Because it goes to the heart of his understanding of human nature, psychology, and of religious existence and the task of Christian theology, we should pause to consider his "methodological" reflections on these matters more carefully.[18]

In order to clarify the character of Kierkegaard's anthropological reflection as both psychological and theological – and how those two elements are at once independent and related – we will need to see more clearly the particular distinctions he makes between psychology and religious concepts.

The fact of the matter is that Kierkegaard's careful distinctions between psychology and religion establish at once their logical independence as separate disciplines, yet also witnesses to the religious and specifically Christian orientation of Kierkegaard's psychological account of human nature. The classic Kierkegaardian texts that deal with these concerns are *The Concept of Anxiety* and *The Sickness Unto Death*, pseudonymously written by Vigilius Haufniensis and Anti-Climacus respectively. Despite the differences between the two pseudonyms – Vigilius represents a stance bordering the religious and Anti-Climacus represents the Christian stance to an extraordinary degree – they are in agreement on the distinctions and relations between psychological and anthropological reflection on the one hand, and explicitly theological reflection on the other.[19]

---

[17] *CA* 25–26 (*SV* IV 297–98).
[18] It also touches on what we will turn to later in this study, viz., the relation between ethics, religion, and Christianity.
[19] Although *The Concept of Anxiety* (1844) comes from the earlier pseudonymous literature and *The*

Both books emphasize the independence of psychology, and claim to give a universal account of psychology, i.e., a psychology that applies to all human beings as such. Vigilius uses techniques of descriptive observation and imaginative portrayal of the states of anxiety. So too, Anti-Climacus gives a phenomenology of despair as well as a wealth of vignettes describing despairing people that taken together provide a kind of "anatomy" of the concept that carries descriptive force. Vigilius' introduction to *The Concept of Anxiety* is especially clear in reflecting an Aristotelian concern with delineating the bounds of the science of psychology in relation to dogmatics. In language anticipating the *Postscript*'s critique of the confusion of logic and existence in Hegelian philosophy, Vigilius complains that the problem with the "System" is that it merges the various sciences and disciplines, thus ignoring the particular *mood* appropriate to each.[20] This matter of mood (Danish *Stemning*, compare German *Stimmung*) is especially important to Kierkegaard, for he conceives that what distinguishes different fields of inquiry ("sciences") is not only their subject matter, but the mood or modulation in which they are approached. For example, one must distinguish between the interest of the psychologist and of the dogmatician in "anxiety." The psychologist will possess an observational interest in anxiety: "the mood becomes that of persistent observation, like the fearlessness of a secret agent, but not that of the victorious flight of earnestness out of sin."[21] Vigilius is clear that there is a distinction between the psychological account that he gives and the concerns of Christian dogmatics. Indeed, he says that, having completed his analysis of the phenomenon of anxiety, it can be "delivered to dogmatics," which has very different interests in the psychological phenomena.[22]

Important to note is how psychology has its own domain independent of Christian concepts, yet, on the other hand, despite this independence, the overriding interest is specifically Christian. It is not that dogmatic concepts govern the psychological analyses themselves; rather, the psychological investigation is made in the interest of a

Sickness Unto Death (1849) from the later "second literature," I find them in essential agreement on these issues. For a treatment of *The Concept of Anxiety* that sees it as primarily belonging to the religious stage of existence, see Stephen Dunning, "Kierkegaard's Systematic Analysis of Anxiety," in Perkins, ed., *International Kierkegaard Commentary:* The Concept of Anxiety, especially 109.

20 *CA* 9 (*SV* IV 281), 14n. (*SV* IV 286–87). On the confusion between logic and existence in Hegel's philosophy, see *CUP* 109–25 (*SV* VII 88–103).

21 *CA* 15 (*SV* IV 287). Compare Barrett, "Kierkegaard's 'Anxiety,'" 40–42.

22 *CA* 162 (*SV* IV 428).

religiously oriented reflection: hence the subtitle of *The Concept of Anxiety*: "A Simple Psychologically Orienting Deliberation on the Dogmatic Issue of Hereditary Sin." Just as much with Vigilius as with Anti-Climacus the psychological phenomena of anxiety that are revealed by observation will be seen in a different light once they are placed within the different linguistic context of Christian dogmatic concepts like sin. In his "Introduction," Vigilius states that "the present work has set as its task the psychological treatment of the concept of 'anxiety,' but in such a way that it constantly keeps *in mente* [in mind] and before its eye the dogma of hereditary sin. Accordingly, it must also, although tacitly so, deal with the concept of sin. Sin, however, is no subject for psychological concern."[23]

Two points about this passage show the careful interplay Vigilius sets up between psychology and dogmatics. First is the theme of the independence of disciplines; psychology has its proper mood, domain and procedures, and that of dogmatics is different. In contrast to the mood of observation that characterizes psychology, the concept of "sin" immediately takes the subject of anxiety out of the realm of psychology: for "sin" is a stance before God, and to call "anxiety" by the name of "sin" requires one to shift the mood to one of "earnestness."[24] "Sin" is not a topic that can be dealt with in a disinterested fashion, or even in the mood of psychology's "antipathetic curiosity."[25] Rather, the proper mood for "sin" is not any science at all, but the sermon, "in which the single individual speaks as the single individual to the single individual."[26]

Second, in terms of the interest of the pseudonyms' investigations, psychology plays a subordinate role in relation to Christian concepts (dogmatics). Psychology "keeps *in mente* [in mind] and before its eye the dogma of hereditary sin. Accordingly, it must also, although tacitly so, deal with the concept of sin."[27] The metaphor of "delivering anxiety" to dogmatics that Vigilius uses at the end of *The Concept of Anxiety* continues this theme: although psychology is distinct from dogmatics, it is also in some sense a "serviceable spirit" to the religious and dogmatic enterprise and is even subordinate to it, in "a feminine way."[28]

This subordination theme, particularly using the gender-metaphor

[23]   *CA* 14 (*SV* IV 286).
[24]   *CA* 15 (*SV* IV 287).
[25]   *Ibid.*
[26]   *CA* 16 (*SV* IV 288).
[27]   *CA* 14 (*SV* IV 286).
[28]   *CA* 162 (*SV* IV 428), 15 (*SV* IV 287).

describing psychology as "feminine," sounds unfortunate to modern ears. Yet that should not obscure a point of considerable interest in describing the relations of psychology and dogmatics. Vigilius says that as psychology observes the phenomena of anxiety, psychology itself becomes filled with anxiety at what it discovers about human nature. In its "antipathetic curiosity," however, it becomes fascinated with anxiety as a state of the human spirit instead of seeing anxiety for what it is (viewed theologically): sin that must be resisted with courage.[29] I take this to mean that psychology quite properly limits itself to the role of observer, but that the object of its observation, human anxiety, is so distressing that *as an existing human being* one cannot simply retain the role of observer. Psychology must raise fundamental questions concerning this anxiety, but discovers that it cannot by itself answer those fundamental questions. In other words, psychology drives beyond itself, pushes issues it cannot answer, seeks its own downfall.[30]

Why does Kierkegaard relate psychology and dogmatics in this way? The answer is that Kierkegaard believes that only when one sees anxiety *theologically* does one find an adequate mood and science with which to deal with psychology and anthropological contemplation. This is because basic to Kierkegaard's understanding of the human self are explicitly dogmatic Christian concepts, such as the creation, fall, and sin. Kierkegaard's psychology plays upon two principles: that "the truth is the measure of itself and of the false," i.e., that the Christian understanding of anxiety and sin is true;[31] and, second, Christian concepts are *diagnostic* concepts. Thus, without violating the independence of psychology, dogmatics nonetheless has a determinative role as the goal of psychological investigation.

In the "Preface" to *The Sickness Unto Death*, the Christian pseudonym Anti-Climacus begins by saying that the role of Christian reflection on human beings is analogous to that of the doctor by the sickbed: "Everything essentially Christian must have in its presentation a resemblance to the way a physician speaks at the sickbed; even if only medical experts understand it, it must never be forgotten that the situation is the bedside of a sick person."[32] For Anti-Climacus, the dogmatic concepts of the Christian faith – particularly that of despair

---

[29]　*CA* 15 (*SV* IV 287).
[30]　Compare this to the way in which thought (illustrated by Socrates' quest for self-knowledge) seeks its own downfall, in *Philosophical Fragments*, especially chapter 3; see *PF* 37 (*SV* IV 204).
[31]　On truth as "the criterion of itself and of the false" (*index sui et falsi*), freely rendered from Spinoza, see *SUD* 42 (*SV* XI 155) and n44; compare *PF* 50 (*SV* IV 217).
[32]　*SUD* 5 (*SV* XI 117).

as the opposite of faith – direct his psychological interests. In this sense, Anti-Climacus' psychology and anthropological reflection are un-apologetically Christian. Unlike Vigilius, who keeps the doctrine of hereditary sin *in mente* and only hands over his analyses to dogmatic reflection at the end of the book, Anti-Climacus *begins* with Christian dogmatic presuppositions that are logically essential for his psychological analysis of despair. In either case, Kierkegaard's analysis of the relations between psychology and religious conceptions is already theologically oriented.

Dogmatics and apologetics

This analysis of Kierkegaard's reflections on the relations between psychology and dogmatics allows us now to gain some insight into another theological issue central to understanding his religious thought. Should Kierkegaard as a religious thinker – particularly as one concerned with communicating the "how" rather than the "what" of Christian faith – be seen primarily as a systematic apologist, sharing in the broad tradition of Schleiermacher's concern to relate Christian concepts to general claims about human experience? Or should he be seen rather as a religious thinker within the traditions of Christian dogmatics, perhaps even, despite important differences, closer to a modern theologian such as Karl Barth?

This theological issue reflects also current debates concerning the relations between psychological and theological discourse. Contemporary theologians more oriented to the "public" character of theology can (if they so choose) claim Kierkegaard as an important antecedent of apologetic theology, the need to begin theological discourse by grounding it (in some sense) in universally understandable claims concerning human experience. A dogmatic theologian on the other hand might well charge that if Kierkegaard's anthropological reflection is such an apologetic theology, it is a primary example of what is wrong with apologetics. To put the issue more sharply, a dogmatic theologian can charge that Kierkegaard's religious thought in its orientation to psychology is essentially *independent* of Christian purposes, and even that his understanding of Christianity is severely *distorted* by being forced to address questions that are arrived at independently of Christian presuppositions.[33]

---

[33] For a helpful discussion of these debates in contemporary theology, in terms of "revisionist" and "postliberal" options (roughly correlating to my use of "apologetic" and "dogmatic"),

We cannot answer all of these questions directly, especially not whether Kierkegaard's anthropological starting-point distorts Christian dogmatic interests; that must wait until further chapters concerning the shape of his understanding of Christ and salvation. What we can indicate at this point is how Kierkegaard can be "placed" on a modern map of theological approaches.

At first glance Kierkegaard's anthropological reflection appears to be essentially an "apologetics," for several reasons: his interest in communicating Christian concepts, his concern with the "how" of Christian abilities, his placing of Christian concepts within a wider area of "religion," and his use of psychology to diagnose a universal human malady to which Christianity is a proposed solution. Such an interpretation can point, for example, to Kierkegaard's study of Schleiermacher and his early remark in the journal that *"every dogma is nothing but a more concrete extension of* the universal human consciousness."[34] On this understanding, Kierkegaard's literature provides a faith-neutral or foundational or at least independent account of the human self, for example, an ontology of the self, that serves as the governing conceptual entry-point for religious and specifically Christian interests.[35]

In the previous section, however, we have seen that psychology does not have such determinative control over dogmatic concepts and language. Kierkegaard's stress on an Aristotelian separation of different disciplines means that psychology is not a foundation for dogmatic language. More than that, despite its independence from dogmatics, psychology for Kierkegaard is not even faith-neutral, but is put to the service of a religious and specifically Christian interest.

Instead of an apologetic approach to theology that enters into dialogue with a cultural situation in terms of its own conceptual frameworks, I would argue rather, especially in light of the passages from *The Concept of Anxiety* and *The Sickness Unto Death* that we examined

---

see William C. Placher, *Unapologetic Theology: A Christian Voice in a Pluralistic Conversation* (Louisville, KY: Westminster/John Knox Press, 1989), especially ch. 10.

[34] *JP* III 3273 (*Pap.* II A 440, May 22, 1839). In *The Concept of Anxiety*, Vigilius Haufniensis speaks of "Schleiermacher's immortal service to" dogmatics, and he adds that "Schleiermacher was a thinker in the beautiful Greek sense, a thinker who [unlike Hegel] spoke only of what he knew" (*CA* 20 [*SV* IV 292]). Kierkegaard appreciated in particular Schleiermacher's reflections on "original sin," that in relation to original sin all human beings are in the same position as Adam. See *JP* IV, p. 626.

[35] Approaches to Kierkegaard that stress an ontology of selfhood are Hermann Diem, *Kierkegaard's Dialectic of Existence*, trans. Harold Knight (London: Oliver & Boyd, 1959) and John Elrod, *Being and Existence in Kierkegaard's Pseudonymous Works* (Princeton University Press, 1975).

in the previous section, that Kierkegaard keeps apologetics within the purview and domain of dogmatics. Instead of attempting to adapt Christian belief to the canons of secularism, science, and rationality, Kierkegaard instead sees Christian faith as critically and polemically placed against these assumptions of modernity. His anthropological reflection is rather expressedly "confessional" in its stance, and indeed assertively so. Whereas the "apologetic" account of Kierkegaard tends to see his anthropological reflection as controlling his religious thought, the opposite is actually the case: Kierkegaard is a thinker for whom the religious and Christian concepts provide the governing concepts for his psychological reflection. He is a specifically *Christian* psychologist for whom the practice of psychology and of anthropological reflection is logically grounded in his belief in the truth of Christianity.[36]

This is why, in *The Sickness Unto Death*, Anti-Climacus speaks so harshly about any apologetic enterprise that wishes to provide a reasonable defense of Christianity, saying "it is certain and true that the first one to come up with the idea of defending Christianity in Christendom is *de facto* a Judas No. 2."[37] Christianity for Anti-Climacus is not defense, but offense, and any purported defense is treason.

Nonetheless, despite the weight given to the side of the dogmatic in his anthropological contemplation, and the veto against an independent foundational apologetics that is determinative for dogmatics, Kierkegaard has room for a "religiously determined" and "dogmatically determined" apologetics, just as he has room for an independent psychology.

We should note four aspects to this apologetic. First, Kierkegaard is "apologetic" in that he wishes to "take as good money" the self-understanding of his audience ("all in Christendom are Christian"), but apologetics for Kierkegaard is a *tactical* move within an essentially polemical *strategy* aimed at subverting illusions.

Second, in such an apologetic literature, the aim is to introduce religious and Christian concepts to the reader as capabilities. What one learns from psychology, not only gives one a context for

---

[36] Evans, *Søren Kierkegaard's Christian Psychology*, 39.
[37] *SUD* 87 (*SV* xi 198). Compare Kierkegaard's remarks in *The Point of View for My Work as an Author*, 38: "All the old military science, all the apologetic and whatever goes with it, serves rather – candidly speaking – to betray the cause of Christianity. At every instant and at every point the tactics must be adapted to a fight which is waged against a conceit, an illusion." Kierkegaard increasingly turns to this theme in the later writings; see *CD*, the epigraph to part 3, "Thoughts Which Wound from Behind – For Edification," 168; compare *JP* vi 6708 (*Pap.* x³ A 663, n.d., 1850), *JP* iv 3862 (*Pap.* x⁴ A 280, n.d. 1851).

approaching Christian dogmatic concepts, but helps a non-religious or non-Christian reader obtain a discursive or descriptive understanding of religious and dogmatic concepts. Here the independent "science" of psychology is indeed theologically relevant even if not determinative.

Third, a tempered apologetics is possible, not as an independent conceptuality that governs dogmatic language, but one that, for Kierkegaard, is based on a Christian dogmatic postulate, viz., the doctrine of creation. Hence, the self is created by God and in need of God. Anti-Climacus' definition of the self at the beginning of *The Sickness Unto Death* reflects clearly this explicitly dogmatic orientation to the doctrine of creation as the basis of his anthropological reflection: the very definition of the self is that it is a "relation that relates itself to itself," but moreover is ultimately dependent as "a derived, established relation, a relation that ... in relating itself to itself relates itself to another," that is, upon God as the "power" upon which, when despair is completely rooted out, this self rests "transparently."[38] Given that dogmatic postulate of creation, it is no surprise that human beings will display in their lives signs of that origin, need, and goal. Because of this orientation of the self to God, it is possible for a Christian diagnostician to locate elements of human experience that indicate that basic relationship to God. Further, a Christian teacher can nurture people along the path to the knowledge of God. The task of self-reflection addresses people with considerations touching on such matters as "purity of heart," of ethical responsibility, and the need for a lasting happiness, matters not in themselves specifically Christian. In this mood, Kierkegaard can even speak of a "natural knowledge" of God arising for a person as one seeks self-knowledge.[39] It is important to notice however that this tempered apologetics proceeds from a dogmatic postulate, the doctrine of creation, i.e., what we can term "the logic of belief" rather than "the logic of coming to belief."

---

[38] *SUD* 13–14 (*SV* xi 128).

[39] Here the difference between Kierkegaard and a theologian like the later Barth is most pronounced. Both disavow natural theology, and both see Christ as (in some sense) the governing formal and material principle of dogmatics that prevents an independent apologetics. Yet, within that position, Kierkegaard allows more scope to the doctrine of creation in dogmatics (and hence allows a *tempered* apologetics and natural knowledge of God) in a way that Barth will not countenance. For an account of a natural knowledge of God given in ethical existence, see *EO* ii 177 (*SV* ii 160), where Judge William speaks of the appearance of the "eternal Power" to an ethically formed person. See Robert C. Roberts, "The Socratic Knowledge of God," in Perkins, ed., *International Kierkegaard Commentary: Volume 8:* The Concept of Anxiety, 133–52. We will turn to this "natural knowledge of God" in chapter 3.

Fourth – and to anticipate matters we will discuss in chapters 3 and 4 – dialectical as Kierkegaard is, this apologetic task of preparing persons for the understanding of God, this development of a generalized religious spirituality, even though it is grounded in the dogmatic postulate of the doctrine of creation, faces another and ultimate limit. The religious quest for, as Kierkegaard puts it, "repetition," that is, the search for spiritual depth and integration, finally reaches the paradoxical conclusion that this repetition and self-integration are impossible. Ironically, the apologetic tactic of nurturing persons in their understanding of God leads them to frustration, whether it is the frustration facing God's command to Abraham to sacrifice Isaac, or – much more common – the breach with one's self-understanding in admitting that one is a sinner (*Philosophical Fragments, Postscript*). In addition, and most important, Christ is the limit and "reversal" of that attempt at self-understanding. Therefore, Christian dogmatics finally is not something deduced from "consciousness" or "experience," not even Christian consciousness or experience, but depends upon the *external* act of God in Christ, the miracle of revelation that negates the self-understanding one arrives at in one's attempts to make sense of existence.[40] This means that an apologetics that is dogmatically determined must constantly be aware of its own limitations, especially the requirement that it dialectically hand over its own efforts to the more complex dialectic of Christian faith. In chapter 4, we will return to this understanding of Christ as an "offense" against the understanding; the point to be made now is that this *material* point, that Christ is an offense against the understanding, undergirds a *formal* decision on the relations of dogmatic Christian affirmations to general anthropology. Because of the breach that Christ causes with the understanding, an independent or foundationalist apologetics is not possible, and is indeed contrary to the mood and substance of Christian faith. Apologetics in other words has *instrumental* value within a dogmatic *purpose*; it prepares people for encountering the paradox of Christian faith.[41] It is in *this* sense, I

---

[40] *JP* II 1100 (*Pap.* III A 39, n.d., 1840): "in faith we assume something which is not given and can never be deduced from the preceding consciousness ... the consciousness of the forgiveness of sins is linked to an external event, the appearance of Christ in his fullness"; see also Malantschuk, *Kierkegaard's Thought*, 20. Thus, despite Vigilius' praise of Schleiermacher in *The Concept of Anxiety*, Kierkegaard increasingly criticizes the "feeling of absolute dependence" for reducing faith to the "sphere of being," ignoring the sphere of "becoming," the ethical striving and obedience that attend faith. *JP* IV 3853 (*Pap.* x² A 417, n.d., 1850). We will return to this issue in chapter 4.

[41] Thus, despite their differences on the role of creation and of apologetics, I see Kierkegaard as religious and theological thinker much closer to Barth than to theologians like Schleiermacher

believe, that Kierkegaard contemplated (but for other reasons discarded) this subtitle for *Philosophical Fragments*: "The Apologetical Presuppositions of Dogmatics or Thought-Approximations to Faith."[42]

To summarize our conclusions from this and the previous section: Kierkegaard relates the psychological and dogmatic, and the apologetic and dogmatic, in complex ways:

First, psychology and dogmatics are independent of one another. They should not be subsumed into one another, much less (*contra* Hegel) into some meta-system, speculative or otherwise. Psychology and dogmatics have their own methods and language, and the concepts basic to each should not be confused with one another.

Second, psychology and dogmatics also "impinge upon" one another, but in some ways and not in others:

(a) Psychology for Kierkegaard provides neither a foundational/evidential conceptual framework for Christian language, nor a faith-neutral account of human experience to which dogmatics must correlate systematically. In this sense Kierkegaard's psychological, anthropological reflection is not apologetic. This is why, as I argued in the Introduction, Kierkegaard is quite distinct from the apologetic strategies of a Tillich (correlation) or a Bultmann (translation). Yet he also differs from an enterprise such as Schleiermacher's attempt to ground the vocabulary for dogmatic language systematically in experiential language. In terms of the language of revelation, the transcendent source of Christian faith – beyond all human capacity and hope – means that dogmatic language is independent of psychological concepts and experience.

(b) Yet psychology and anthropological contemplation are for Kierkegaard apologetic in some more restrained senses, all of them dialectically governed by dogmatics: first, he wishes to assume the standpoint of his audience in order to subvert it; second, he wishes to provide a context for approaching religion and Christian faith – to use Hans Frei's term cited in the Introduction, this theological strategy focuses on "the logic of coming to belief"; and third, the dogmatic belief that the person is created by God supports the apologetic tactic of identifying elements of human experience that reflect that basic

and Tillich. On Christ as the material and formal center of dogmatics, see, for example, *CA*, p. 187 (*Pap.* v в 53:17, n.d., 1844) on how dogmatics *begins* with the atonement "and by explaining the Atonement it indirectly explains sinfulness." We will return to this in chapter 4.

[42]   *Pap.* v в 7–8, n.d., 1844, cited in *PF*, p. 217 and the Hongs' "Historical Introduction," p. xvii.

relationship to God (here Kierkegaard shifts from "the logic of coming to belief" to "the logic of belief").

Hence, Kierkegaard's anthropological contemplation and psychology, far from being "descriptively foundational" or "primarily apologetic" are "contextual" and "primarily dogmatic." By "contextual" I mean that, for Kierkegaard, reflection on the human self (psychology) does not take place in a vacuum, divorced from religious and, in this case, even Christian presuppositions. On the contrary, his authorship works *from* the dogmatic presuppositions *to* their implications for an understanding of human existence. Despite the independence of psychological, anthropological contemplation, and the apologetic elements in his thought, his psychology and anthropological contemplation have primarily in view a dogmatically Christian presupposition and goal, viz., the doctrines of creation, sin, and salvation. Hence, the very task of reflecting on the self is one that is already dogmatically oriented according to "the logic of belief."[43]

Returning for a moment to Kierkegaard's psychology, the question arises whether his dogmatic orientation will distort one's observation and imaginative construction as a psychologist. And that is a question that, as far as I can see, Kierkegaard does not answer. Rather, he confidently goes forward with his psychological and anthropological reflections, without worrying about such a question. There are, I think, two reasons for this. First, his concern as a psychologist is conceptual rather than empirical. As C. Stephen Evans has put it, his interest is

---

[43] Claiming that Kierkegaard is concerned with "the logic of belief" as well as "the logic of coming to belief," I have in mind a helpful typology devised by Hans Frei in his posthumously published *Types of Christian Theology*. I see Kierkegaard in some ways closer to Frei's Type 4 theology, which emphasizes theology as "the logic of belief": "the practical discipline of Christian self-description governs and limits the applicability of general criteria of meaning in theology, rather than vice versa" (4) (examples are Barth, Newman, and Edwards). I would also argue that Kierkegaard is closer to Type 4 in seeing doctrines as having "a status similar to that of grammatical rules implicit in discourse" (4) than to Frei's Type 2, attempts "to correlate specifically Christian with general cultural meaning structures such as natural science or the 'spirit' of a cultural era" (3) (such as Bultmann's theological existentialism) or Type 3, in which Christian theology must develop an independent, faith-neutral philosophical account of the self that then provides the vocabulary for theological language or correlation (Schleiermacher and Tillich). In other ways, Kierkegaard shares characteristics of Frei's Type 5 (what he calls "Wittgensteinian fideism," attributed to D. Z. Phillips) combining Christian self-description with appeals to prereligious and nonreligious life attitudes: this fits Kierkegaard's tempered apologetics. Yet, in contrast to Type 5, I am claiming that Kierkegaard gives greater room to "the logic of belief" ("dogmatics") and does *not* "relegate doctrinal theology to a subordinate position" beneath "the logic of coming to belief" (4). I do not claim that Professor Frei would have agreed with my placing of Kierkegaard in his typology.

not in psychology as an empirical science, but as an interpretive and value-critical "science" of meanings.[44] He is not concerned with quantitative research (which could be distorted in view of a "Christian" result, whatever that might be); rather, he sees in Christian faith an inexhaustible conceptual resource for illuminating human behavior. Second, the adequacy of the Christian conceptual scheme cannot be demonstrated, but only *tested* in the process of employing it. It is not validated, but rather becomes persuasive (or not) only as one practices the anthropological contemplation he recommends.

Does this mean that Kierkegaard is finally uncritically Christian in his psychology? If we allow the issue to remain one of "relating psychology and dogmatics," it does perhaps appear uncritical, for certainly one can give other accounts of such psychological dilemmas as anxiety and despair, and other solutions to those dilemmas. But two comments are in order, based on Kierkegaard's remark that the "human" (for example, anthropological reflection, psychology) and the "Christian" (dogmatics) "are equally necessary ... Christianity is something which did not arise in any man's thought and yet since it is given to man is natural to him because here also God is creating."[45] The first comment is that, as Alastair Hannay suggests, the alternative to seeing Kierkegaard (in the negative sense of the term) dogmatically or uncritically *presupposing* Christian belief is to see him proposing Christianity as a solution to the universal spiritual malady of anxiety and despair.[46] This is correct as far as it goes, and reflects Kierkegaard's insistence on the human analysis; on the other hand, it is Kierkegaard's frankly dogmatic standpoint that confessionally posits this fittingness between malady and cure, despair and the faith that there can be help from God beyond all expectation. Finally, however, from the standpoint of Kierkegaard's anthropological reflection, the issue is not the possibly abstract one of how one relates disciplines such as psychology and dogmatics; the issue is, as Hannay rightly indicates, the question of "refuge," that as Wittgenstein put it – in words echoing Anti-Climacus' metaphor of the sickbed – Christian faith is a person's refuge in an ultimate torment.[47]

---

[44] Evans, *Søren Kierkegaard's Christian Psychology*, 31–33.
[45] *JP* II 2277 (*Pap.* III A 211, n.d., 1840). See also Malantschuk, *Kierkegaard's Thought*, 20.
[46] Alastair Hannay, "Refuge and Religion," in George L. Stengren, ed., *Faith, Knowledge, and Action: Essays to Niels Thulstrup* (Copenhagen: Reitzels Forlag, 1984); compare Hannay, *Kierkegaard*, 331.
[47] Hannay, *Kierkegaard*, 331, citing Wittgenstein's comment in *Culture and Value*, trans. Peter Winch, ed., G. H. von Wright (Oxford: Basil Blackwell, 1980), 46e.

KIERKEGAARD'S RELIGIOUS UNDERSTANDING OF THE SELF

I have argued that Kierkegaard's anthropological reflection is at once oriented to psychological analysis and is also strongly theological, Christian, and dogmatic in character. He gives room for a relatively independent psychology, and a tempered apologetics, but within the context of specifically religious and Christian concepts. Kierkegaard attempts, therefore, to combine analysis of the human with straight-forwardly Christian reflection. Thus, he stands fundamentally at odds with some later appropriators of his work, such as Martin Heidegger and Jean-Paul Sartre, who employ Kierkegaard's categories, but omit or radically alter his religious orientation of the self. And he also stands at odds with Christian dogmatists who do not see how psychology can illuminate (rather than govern) Christian concepts.

We can now turn to some central elements in Kierkegaard's religious conception of the self, focusing on three related issues. First, we can look at the fundamental orientation of the self to God in creation, and how this relates psychologically to emotions and moods, which in turn are theologically interpreted in relation to "sin." Second, this will lead us to consider the purpose of Kierkegaard's "stages on life's way," proceeding from the aesthetic to the ethical to the religious and finally to the Christian, which will lead us, third, to Kierkegaard's essentially narrative understanding of the self.

The orientation of the self to God: creation, emotions, moods, and sin

Central to Kierkegaard's conception of the self is, as we have seen, the conviction that persons are created by God. As is clear from the definition of the self as grounded in God as "the power that established it" in *The Sickness Unto Death*,[48] this means that, speaking diagnostically, all human beings, whether they are conscious of it or not, exist in, and are intended for, relation to God.

One of Kierkegaard's most profound insights is that he sees this self, related to God in creation, in strongly dynamic terms, and here his psychological analysis contributes immensely to the dogmatic under-standing. As created by God, a human being is a relationship of

---

[48] *SUD* 14 (*SV* xi 128). On the original gift of creation, see, for example, Nordentoft, *Kierkegaard's Psychology*, 76; Niels Thulstrup, *Commentary on Kierkegaard's* Concluding Unscientific Postscript, 103–04, has a useful citation of extensive literature on this aspect of Kierkegaard's anthropology.

factors, a component of various forces that one must relate together, and in turn relate to God. In place of the traditional concept of the substantive self as a "something" naturally enduring through time, Kierkegaard emphasizes the self as a temporal and dynamic process of relating. This is why one "is" not a self, but "becomes" a self, why the self is "open-ended," and ever-changing. Kierkegaard describes the self as a synthesis of *relations* of body and psyche, finite and infinite, necessity and possibility, the temporal and eternal, consciousness and unconsciousness.[49] But this synthesis is not a simple synthesis: if this were the case, then there would be no distinction between, say, the psychic and bodily relation that one finds in animals. What distinguishes the human self is, as we noted in chapter 1, the role of *consciousness* or what Kierkegaard calls *spirit* in relating these factors to one another. Consciousness is the "third term" necessary to becoming a self, for it is in bringing these factors consciously into relation to one another that a self emerges. When consciousness is lacking, we have a "human being," but not, strictly speaking, a "self." The "self" for Kierkegaard emerges only when one consciously relates these factors. For example, in relating "possibility" and "necessity," it is only when one reflects upon the given factors of one's life, then imaginatively "reflects" a possibility for oneself, and then finally acts to bring that about concretely within one's existence that a "self" emerges.[50]

This understanding of the self as composed of dynamic factors requiring relationship, one ultimately grounded in God as Creator but calling for a human task, provides Kierkegaard with a powerful vocabulary for discussing human emotions. A fundamental contribution of Kierkegaard's thought is that he widens the conception of the "human" to include a consideration of the emotions as central to human life. Behind this consideration of the emotions is, for Kierkegaard, a conviction that a central problem with the Western theological and philosophical tradition has been its consistent, even systematic, underrating – even suppression – of the emotions in understanding what it is to be a human being. The rationalist tradition, from Descartes to Leibniz and Baumgarten, locates the essence of thought in

---

49 Kierkegaard's terminology varies in describing these factors. In *The Concept of Anxiety* (85 [*SV* IV 355]), the categories are "psyche and body" and "temporal and eternal." In *The Sickness Unto Death* (29 [*SV* XI 142]), the categories are "finitude/infinitude, possibility/necessity, and consciousness/unconsciousness."

50 See especially Judge William's account of selfhood in *Either/Or* II. The Judge's description is consistent with the overall picture given elsewhere in the pseudonymous and non-pseudonymous literature.

"clear and distinct ideas," and the philosophical *desideratum* is then to attain clarity; the by-product of this rationalism is that emotions are thereby dismissed as impediments to that clarity. The culmination of this tradition, Kierkegaard thought, was the Hegelian elevation of reason over against the Romantic celebration of the "untamed" emotions.[51] But, for Kierkegaard, the Romantic error was just as great, and resulted in an anti-intellectualism that was just as personally destructive as Hegelianism's etiolated rationalism.[52]

Over against both of these distortions, Kierkegaard attempts to reinstate the emotions to their proper place in philosophical and Christian theological reflection. Avoiding both a dismissal of the emotions and an undue elevation of them, Kierkegaard provides a map of the human heart, a logic of the emotions, articulating patterns of action, motivation, belief, and emotion, plotting their mutual interrelationships. Significantly, at the beginning of his first pseudonymous work, *Either/Or* I, he places as an epigraph these lines from Edward Young: "Are passions, then, the pagans of the soul? Reason alone baptized?"[53]

Thus, we find in Kierkegaard's writings, pseudonymous and non-pseudonymous, a focused analysis of the wide range of human emotions. These analyses can take the form of fictional epigrammatic self-revelations (the aesthete – or aesthetes – of *Either/Or* I), epistolary arguments and exhortations (Judge William in *Either/Or* II), studies of the literary depiction of emotion (for example, "The Tragic in Ancient Drama Reflected in the Tragic in Modern Drama" and "Silhouettes" in *Either/Or* I, the Young Man in *Repetition*, Quidam in *Stages on Life's Way*, and the analyses in *Fear and Trembling* of Abraham's faith in contrast with the dilemmas of tragic heroes), upbuilding discourses on the passions of faith, hope, and love, and, finally, the "algebraic" treatises on the forms and structures of emotions (*The Concept of Anxiety*, *The Sickness Unto Death*). All of them taken together provide a striking passional literature that not only describes but depicts the emotional lives of human beings.

[51] See the young Kierkegaard's treatment of the Hegelian suspicion of Romantic irony in his dissertation, *The Concept of Irony*. Kierkegaard shared Hegel's critique of Romantic irony, yet he distributes his suspicion against the Hegelians' dislike of irony too: irony for Kierkegaard becomes a "controlled element," but controlled in a way that gives greater and continuing importance to Socratic irony. See *CI*, especially 324–29 (*SV* XIII 388–93).

[52] For Kierkegaard's critique of rationalism and romanticism, see my *Kierkegaard's Dialectic of the Imagination*, chs. 1–3.

[53] *EO*I 1 and 603n.

We can now say something more about how Kierkegaard's under-standing of emotion differs from other accounts. Emotions are not, as in the Rousseauian tradition, simply evidence of sentiment or a tender heart, neither are they, as in the related Romantic tradition, simply direct expressions of untamed spontaneity and vitality. In particular, Kierkegaard's analysis differs from the attempt, attributed by some to Friedrich Schleiermacher and the tradition that follows him, to distinguish emotion as precognitive, as a feeling distinguish-able from thought and action, independent of concepts, grammatical rules, practices, and beliefs.[54] One of Kierkegaard's criticisms of Schleiermacher is that he "treats religion in the sphere of being," "esthetically-metaphysically merely as a condition," with little regard for "striving."[55] While Kierkegaard grants an important role for precognitive "immediacy," he does not find emotions to be im-mediate. Neither are emotions "nominative," names of physiological sensations.[56] Nor are they names for episodic "feelings" or "sensa-tions," inchoate and inexpressible. And, despite all of his talk of "inwardness," Kierkegaard does not give evidence of a view that we *identify* our emotions by a process of introspection.[57] Introspection is used not to identify an inner something, but to reflect upon one's life.

Emotions, Robert C. Roberts suggests, are "concern-based con-struals" that depend upon how one sees one's circumstances.[58] Emo-tions are not the same as beliefs or judgments, but are occurrences in consciousness. Yet there is a cognitive dimension to emotions, related to how one "construes" or imagines circumstances. As in Jastrow's "duck–rabbit," used to effect by Wittgenstein, one can "construe" a

54   Wayne Proudfoot, *Religious Experience* (Berkeley: University of California Press, 1985), 77, 228. For another reading of Schleiermacher, see Nicholas Lash, *Easter in Ordinary: Reflections on Human Experience and the Knowledge of God* (Charlottesville: University Press of Virginia, 1986), see 7n6, 127ff.; Lash, with Richard Crouter, sees Schleiermacher's identification of "God" as the "whence" of "the feeling of absolute dependence" "within an interpretative or 'hermeneutical' tradition of theological discourse," (129) closer to Wittgensteinian gramma-tical remarks (127) addressed to the Christian community. In any event, Kierkegaard is critical of Schleiermacher on immediacy.

55   *JP* IV 3852, 3853 (*Pap.* X² A 416, 417, n.d., 1850).

56   Proudfoot, *Religious Experience*, 91, asks rhetorically, "Are we ready to posit physiological differences, or even different states or events, to correspond to the subtle differentiation between the various forms of despair described by Kierkegaard in *The Sickness Unto Death*?" Compare 219–20.

57   Proudfoot, *Religious Experience*, 92.

58   Robert C. Roberts, "What an Emotion Is: A Sketch," *The Philosophical Review* 97 (April 1988): 195–201. See also his *Spirituality and Human Emotion* (Grand Rapids, MI: William B. Eerdmans, 1982).

figure differently, can "see it as" a duck or rabbit. So too, emotions are construals. Emotions are moreover "concern-based," reflecting cares and interests. "Emotions *are* our concern" about other things.[59]

The emotions that a person experiences are not accidental or unrelated to a person's beliefs about herself or the situation in which she finds herself. For example, the despairing sorrow experienced by each of the women described in *Either/Or* 1's "Shadowgraphs" – Marie Beaumarchais, Margarete in Goethe's *Faust*, and Donna Elvira in Mozart's *Don Giovanni* – is nuanced in a particular way that depends upon the beliefs that each holds on her own situation. For example, Margarete's despair is inseparable from her beliefs about her abandonment by Faust and her shame at her seduction. Her shame contrasts strongly with the anger of Donna Elvira's despair against Don Giovanni. By placing these figures in relation to one another, an anatomy of the concept of "despairing sorrow" comes into view. Thus, one can learn from studying Kierkegaard as psychologist of the emotions the subtle nuances of the topography of the human heart.

Finally, religious emotions, too, are shaped by beliefs. In his book on Magister Adler, Kierkegaard notes that the problem with Adler is that he is an "enthusiast" who is not tempered by concepts. In contrast, Kierkegaard writes:

Emotion which is Christian is checked by the definition of concepts, and when emotion is transposed or expressed in words in order to be communicated, this transposition must occur constantly within the definition of the concepts ... In order to express oneself Christianly there is required, besides the more universal language of the heart, also skill and schooling in the definition of Christian concepts, while at the same time it is of course assumed that the emotion is of a specific, qualitative sort, the Christian emotion.[60]

Kierkegaard speaks here of specifically Christian concepts and emotions, but the conceptual shaping of emotions applies also to what he calls "the language of the heart."

Much of Kierkegaard's concern in these analyses is to outline a distinction between emotions and moods. Both emotions and moods may be concern-based construals, but what distinguishes moods is that they are unanchored, episodic, and troubling. As Vincent A. McCarthy indicates, Kierkegaard traces out a "phenomenology of moods" of

---

[59] C. S. Lewis, "The Language of Religion," in Walter Hooper, ed., *Christian Reflections* (Grand Rapids, MI: William B. Eerdmans, 1967), 139.

[60] *OAR* 163–64 (*Pap.* VII² B 235, pp. 200–01). See also Don E. Saliers, "Religious Affections and the Grammar of Prayer," in Bell, ed., *The Grammar of the Heart*, 188–205.

anxiety, irony, melancholy, and despair. These moods, Kierkegaard believes, are universally applicable experiences that can be diagnostically described and applied from both a psychological and a specifically Christian theological standpoint.[61] Moods indicate, for Kierkegaard, the dynamic and tension-ridden features of human life, as persons live within time, oriented from a past through a present to an undetermined future. In moods too, concerns are at work, and one construes or sees one's life in a certain way. Because human beings live toward the future, one can be anxious. And, as one lives oriented to that future of possibilities, one can also suffer through other moods, such as irony (the detachment from one's environment necessary to any truly human life), melancholy (the unutterable sadness that arises as a person becomes aware of his or her need for the "eternal"), and finally – whether unconscious or conscious – despair (arising from the failure in this striving to relate the complex elements of the self, with all of its necessities and possibilities, into a coherent whole, related to God).

One mark of moods is their fragmented and episodic nature. This tempest of moods is most brilliantly displayed in the first part of *Either/Or*, the letters of the aesthete (or aesthetes?) A. Using the literary device of the "discovered papers," and employing indirection superbly, the book does not instruct, but depicts the life of one who, pursuing a life of pleasure without commitment, is victimized by conflicting episodic and turbulent moods. Most importantly, Kierkegaard does not lecture, does not preach, but allows the aesthetes to speak on their own behalf; and, to his credit, the life of the aesthete is portrayed in all of its strengths and not only its vulnerabilities. The aesthete, significantly nameless, is cultured, witty, passionate, now manic in his enthusiasms and loves (such as the essay on Mozart), now cast into the depths of despair and hopelessness; now sentimental, now ironic; now devoted to sensual pleasure, now satisfied only with the most refined intellectual amusements. Yet for all of his brilliance and attractiveness (and his friend Judge William, who admonishes him in part II of the book, shows great affection for A) his life is despair, without purpose or direction, and dissolves into a paradox of sheer fantasy and dreamlike unreality. In the final scenes of "The Seducer's Diary" – which may merely be A's literary creation – Johannes the Seducer, in the culmination of his erotic quest, disappears into unreality; on his way to reap the fruits of his seduction, and already looking forward to

[61]   Vincent A. McCarthy, *The Phenomenology of Moods in Kierkegaard* (The Hague; Boston: Martinus Nijhoff, 1978).

abandoning the young woman, he says, "I myself am a myth about myself, for is it not as a myth that I hasten to this tryst?"[62] In the end, the Seducer is insubstantial, ghostlike, a mere bundle of contradictory moods.[63]

But, as we have seen, Kierkegaard as religious thinker is not content with the psychological analysis or even with the literary presentation of human moods. In *The Concept of Anxiety* and *The Sickness Unto Death*, the treatises on the moods of anxiety and despair, he relates moods immediately to a theological understanding of the self as sinner. Psychology serves to illuminate these theological concepts in new ways; theology, on the other hand, gives further explanation of psychological phenomena "before God." Hence, for Kierkegaard, the universality of anxiety reflects not simply personal idiosyncrasy, or adolescent development, or cultural malaise, but a basic disorientation of the self away from God. So, too, despair is seen not simply in terms of abnormal psychology, but, as the Christian pseudonym Anti-Climacus puts it, as a universal illness that indicates at once the saddest defect and the most glorious excellence of being a person.[64]

Kierkegaard's psychological account of moods sheds light on the traditional Christian understanding of sin. Psychology shows that the basic problem of becoming a self is that one *cannot* relate these factors to one another in a harmonious way. One runs the risk, perhaps, of forgetting possibility by anxiously remaining in a "vegetative" or bourgeois-Philistine state, or one loses oneself in dreams of possibility without actualizing one's visions in concrete existence. In either event, the Christian diagnosis places these psychological phenomena in religious categories: anxiety is the mood that explains sin retrogressively in terms of its origin;[65] despair, when it becomes fully conscious is the potentiation of this spiritual malaise: "Sin is: before God, or with the conception of God, in despair not to will to be oneself, or in despair to will to be oneself".[66] Anxiety and despair are indicators of the "eternal" in the human being; they point beyond themselves to a person's need to be grounded in God.

---

[62] *EO*I 444 (*SV*I 411).
[63] *Either/Or*, I also presents a whole range of other aesthetic possibilities "below" the etherealized reflective Seducer; contrast especially the "immediate" or unreflective forms of aestheticism portrayed in the essay on Mozart, "The Immediate Erotic Stages or The Musical Erotic," *EO*I 45–135 (*SV*I 31–113).
[64] *SUD* 22–28 (*SV*XI 136–41), 14–15 (*SV*XI 129).
[65] *CA* 46 (*SV*IV 317).
[66] *SUD* 77 (*SV*XI 189).

Kierkegaard relates his psychological observation and dogmatic analysis with great care, not only in theory, but also in practice. As a psychologist, his task is to give an accurate and persuasive account of these moods. Theologically, his problem is to give a psychological account of the self that illuminates (in contrast to much traditional dogma) the role of the individual in talk of "creation" and "sin," yet without "psychologizing" the doctrine in unacceptable ways. The discussion of the doctrine of original sin in *The Concept of Anxiety* shows the delicacy of Kierkegaard's task. Four aspects of this careful relating of psychology and dogma deserve mention.

First, Kierkegaard's psychological account of anxiety enables him to criticize traditional dogmatic accounts of "original sin" that place "Adam" outside the human family, accounts that need criticism because they explain nothing about sin as it is experienced by human beings. Whether in Roman Catholic theology (grace as a superadded gift) or in Protestant federal theology (for example, Coccejus, where Adam is the "head" of the race), traditional dogmatics tends to place "Adam" outside the human race, and so explains nothing either about Adam's sin or the dynamics of subsequent sin ("our sin"). In contrast to these traditional discussions, Vigilius offers a psychological account of original sin, rather than an historical account, that reorients the dogmatic discussion toward explaining sin in terms of each individual's transition from anxiety to sin.[67]

Second, he also wishes to avoid Hegelian accounts of the Genesis myth that "demythologize" the account of the Fall by translating the fall from "innocence" into such foreign philosophical concepts as "immediacy," removing entirely the ethical component, and confusing the categories of logic and ethics.[68]

Third, he must give an account that avoids the traditional problem of making sin part of created human nature; such an ontological account would make "hereditary sin" mere fate, robbing the person of responsibility for his or her own sin. It would also call into question the goodness of creation. He must therefore give a central place to "freedom" and "guilt" in the origin of sin.

At the same time, however, and fourthly, Kierkegaard is quite aware that any psychological account of "sin" or "original sin" that stresses freedom runs the risk of Pelagian errors that ignore what Augustine recognized so clearly: that sin is a condition that persons *find* themselves

---

[67]   See the helpful notes in *The Concept of Anxiety*, in particular, 230n1.
[68]   *CA* 35–37 (*SV* IV 306–09).

in, prior to their particular sinful actions, and that this bondage of the will characterizes the entire human race.[69] So, too, Kierkegaard does not wish to isolate the individual, in Pelagian fashion, from solidarity with the human race by denying that sin is a "state."

The power of Kierkegaard's account is that he gives a psychological analysis relevant to the doctrines of sin and original sin without compromising what he sees to be the central theological interest of those doctrines: maintaining both the individuality of human guilt and freedom and also the solidarity and "givenness" of sin. In his treatments of anxiety and despair, as well as the additional moods of irony and melancholy, Kierkegaard unites successfully a psychology of moods with a dogmatic Christian understanding of the self as fundamentally oriented to God.

But to speak diagnostically of the spiritual illness of anxiety and despair as "moods" and "sin" is already to point to the cure; the metaphor of the physician at the bedside in *The Sickness Unto Death* gives the proper viewpoint for speaking of religion and of Christianity. Addressed to the despairing, those who are buffeted in a complex chaos of moods, apparently with no hope, the offer is that through despair and sin there may be not a suppression of one's affective life, but self-integration, hope, and even blessedness in nurturing longterm emotions.

The stages on life's way

How one can make a transition from moods to emotions, from chaos to continuity, from sin to blessedness, Kierkegaard sums up in his well-known categories of the "stages" or "spheres" (*Stadier*) of existence: the aesthetic, ethical, religious, and within the religious sphere a "natural" religiosity (Religiousness A) and Christianity (Religiousness B). These categories are often taken as basic to Kierkegaard's thought, and, indeed, they are central especially to the earlier pseudonymous authorship beginning with *Either/Or*, describing the contrast and possible transition between the aesthetic and the ethical stages of life. So, too, *Repetition, Fear and Trembling, Stages on Life's Way, Philosophical Fragments* (less directly) and *Concluding Unscientific Postscript* all develop the concept of the religious stage of existence as another way of life beyond (yet continuing) the ethical.

---

[69] On Vigilius' awareness of the dangers of Pelagianism, see, for example, *CA* 28 (*SV* IV 300), 34 (*SV* IV 306), 37–38 (*SV* IV 309).

The concept of the stages is best seen within the context of Kierkegaard's larger purpose of providing an account of human moods and emotions and the quest for continuity and unity in one's existence – what Kierkegaard calls "the eternal," and which for him is grounded finally in the relationship to God as the source and goal of one's existence. For Kierkegaard, the task of human existence, and of Christian therapeutic, is in large part that of sorting out the complex chaos of one's emotional life – the problematic of moods – into a life that is characterized rather by the consistency and stability of emotions. In this transition from moods to emotions a dominant theme is that of attaining a unity in one's life.[70] But, for Kierkegaard, this goal of continuity, integration, and stability is also theologically oriented; Kierkegaard's famous doctrine of the "stages on life's way" embodies this religious teleology.

As accounts of human emotional life with a religious teleology, the stages also envision a particular goal for human existence, what Kierkegaard terms *Salighed,* a supple term that for him embraces "happiness," "eternal happiness," "blessedness." It is crucial to see that this goal is anything but hedonistic; rather, it carries strong overtones of "task" and "striving." Concerned not only with "feelings," it aims at the transformation of a person (including emotional transformation) as one who is earnestly oriented toward the task and gift of relating to God.[71]

Thus, another way to approach the stages is to see them as strategies for happiness. An "aesthetic" way of life, one fundamentally oriented to pleasure and away from pain, sees pleasure as a supreme good, whether in "lower" forms of unreflective immediacy (here the model is Don Juan) or "higher," more cerebral forms of reflectiveness (like the cold, ethereal "Seducer" of *Either/Or* or the "Professor" satirized in *Postscript*). But, as we have already seen in discussing A, the striking feature of human beings is that, as they pursue aesthetic existence, they find themselves to be not happy, but unhealthy, personally fragmented, and living in self-contradiction. Created by God to be a self, enduring through time, related to a lasting good – "the eternal " – the episodic nature of aesthetic living reveals its inadequacy. As a quest for happiness, it is self-defeating.

Ethical and religious (including Christian) existence can then be seen

[70] See George Connell, *To Be One Thing.*
[71] Abrahim H. Khan, Salighed *as Happiness? Kierkegaard on the Concept* Salighed (Waterloo, ON: Wilfrid Laurier University Press, 1985), see especially 84–91.

as strategies for resolving the dilemmas brought about by the failure of the previous stage to obtain that happiness. The condition of the aesthete is that he or she is dis-integrated, lacking a self, and this may reveal itself to the aesthete in the emotional disharmony of moods. What recommends ethical existence (*Either/Or* II's Judge William claims in his letters to the aesthete) is that it allows one to move from the misery of moods, through despair, to the consistency of emotions as longterm belief-oriented construals of one's life. Relating to "the eternal" – for example, an ethical ideal such as marriage – allows one to relate the day-to-day episodes of life into a continuous whole.

As we will see in chapters 3 and 4, religious and Christian existence can also be seen as a strategy for redefining happiness as one reaches problems in the ethical (or religious) quest to relate to "the eternal." This is why Johannes Climacus puts the problem of "becoming a Christian" in this way:

I, Johannes Climacus, born and bred in this city and now thirty years old, an ordinary human being like most folk, assume that a highest good, called an eternal happiness, awaits me just as it awaits a housemaid and a professor. I have heard that Christianity is one's prerequisite for this good. I now ask how I may enter into relation to this doctrine.[72]

As Climacus develops in *Concluding Unscientific Postscript*, there are various reasons for moving from an ethical existence to an explicitly religious existence, and from a religious existence to Christian existence, but the point to see now is that these transitions too arise out of the concern to find a blessedness – an "eternal blessedness" – that might resolve the dilemmas of anxiety and despair.

Having briefly described the structure and religious teleology of the stages, three comments are in order on how the "stages" function in support of Kierkegaard's map of human emotions: first, how the concept of "stage" contributes to the "logic" of moods and emotions by showing how certain moods and emotions attend each stage; second, whether the stages should be seen as a temporal "progression," so that one must move from the aesthetic, then through the ethical, religious, and the Christian stages; and third, how the schema of the stages as an account of human moods and emotions throws light on the "context-dependence" of human existence.

(1) The notion of the stages on life's way enables one to gain a reflective grip on human subjectivity by providing a framework that

[72]   *CUP* 15–16 (*SV* VII 7).

describes how particular moods and emotions attend a particular way of life. The notion of the "stage" thus allows one to see that moods and emotions are not accidental, but that certain moods and emotions are typical of a particular stage; this contributes to the "logic" of moods and emotions.

To see a person's (including one's own) existence as "aesthetic" allows one, perhaps for the first time, to *identify* and *name* the moodiness and instability that may afflict one. The aesthete A's self-description in *Either/Or* reveals a heightened, almost manic, awareness of the turbulence of his moods, but at the same time shows his blindness to his condition. It is only in Judge William's analysis of the connection between the aesthete's moods and his way of life – how he flits from one interest to another, lacking decisiveness – that the aesthete can (perhaps) locate the source of his emotional malaise. In advocating to his young friend that he throw himself into his despair, and that despair may drive him to choose an ethical way of existence dedicated to an ideal, the Judge also holds out to the aesthete a richer *emotional* life as well.[73] The ethical way of life possesses "aesthetic validity," greater emotional range, indeed greater passion and enjoyment, than the aesthetic way of life offers. Far from portraying the ethical way of life as devoid of pleasure, divorced from considerations of pleasure, the Judge gives an account of the ethical way of life as a fulfillment of the restless quest of the aesthete for emotional depth and personal unity.[74]

So, too, in the transition from the ethical to the religious sphere of existence, Kierkegaard's account pays attention again to the passion involved in attempting to find the emotional range required for human existence. Abraham's dilemma in *Fear and Trembling*, for example, is not a dilemma forced upon him by an abstract consideration of a conflict between duties to Isaac and to God; it is also a conflict of loves: his love for Isaac and his love for God. "Love" here means not simply inclination, but a passion that is indeed reinforced by law, yet not to the exclusion of the passion.[75] To take another example, in *Philosophical Fragments*, Socrates attempts to attain self-understanding, but meets puzzlement about himself. This puzzlement is, however, a product not simply of an abstract consideration of his life, but of passion, what Climacus describes as the Greek pathos for self-understanding. In

[73]   *EO* II 218–22 (*SV* II 196–99).
[74]   *EO* II, especially "The Balance between the Esthetic and the Ethical in the Development of the Personality," 155–333 (*SV* II 141–299).
[75]   *FT* 31 (*SV* III 83).

short, the transition to the religious (and in the case of *Fragments*, the Christian) stage of existence is a product of passion; its concern is with the emotional life, considered not as peripheral to one's life, but as related to the deepest passions of the person.

The stages therefore provide an account of the emotions and passions that come to characterize each stage. Far from moods and emotions being fortuitous, there are reasons for them, and those reasons relate to how a person seeks happiness.

(2) The metaphor of the "stage" indicates that there is a *progression* from the aesthetic to the ethicoreligious (and also from the ethical to the religious). Kierkegaard's notion is that human beings, given their orientation toward pleasure and away from pain, and their anxiety about past and future, will naturally opt for the aesthetic way of life. As a result of the personal and emotional disharmony that results from the aesthetic stage, a person may move to the ethical and religious stages.

It is important to notice that this progression between stages is not a "natural" or necessary development. Becoming ethical or religious is not a result of attaining a certain chronological age; indeed, many, if not most, adults remain aesthetes their entire lives.[76] Becoming ethical or religious is rather for Kierkegaard a function of the formation of character and longterm interest. One *becomes* ethical by *choosing* to become ethical. So, too, one *continues* to be ethical by maintaining that original commitment. Becoming and staying ethical are not done thoughtlessly, or without effort. Thus, a mark of being truly ethical, as distinct from conventionally moral, is that one is dedicated to ethical ideals. This is why the conventionally moral are unlikely to suffer for justice, and will find reasons for compromising their standards. But, if one is ethical, one is willing – indeed expects – to suffer for justice. For Kierkegaard, such personality characteristics as will, continuity, dedication, and the willingness to suffer for an ideal are necessary marks of ethics and religion.

Nonetheless, it is important to see that the "progression" from the aesthetic to the ethical or religious does not necessarily mean that one must go through these stages in lockstep fashion. Kierkegaard

---

[76] Contrast Kierkegaard to someone such as James W. Fowler, who in *Stages of Faith: The Psychology of Human Development and the Quest for Meaning* (San Francisco: Harper & Row, 1981) attempts to map out a relation between chronological age and various religious capacities. Kierkegaard's conception is quite different. I am indebted on this point to an unpublished paper by Robert L. Perkins.

does outline a progression of stages from the aesthetic to the ethical to the religious and then finally to Christianity (Religiousness B).[77] And sometimes Kierkegaard speaks of the stages, taken together, as a life-development that is "the condition for properly embracing Christianity."[78] This schema of the stages is then taken to mean that any particular individual must progress through each of these stages in order. But in other writings Kierkegaard implies that one may make a transition, say, from the aesthetic *directly* to the boundary of the religious.[79] In favor of the first point of view, one can say that the issues of religion would not make sense to a person lacking ethical capacities. But in favor of the latter interpretation, one can argue that, given the diversity of human life and spiritual development, there is no a priori reason why someone cannot emerge from aestheticism directly into the religious or Christian spheres.

(3) The notion of "stages" as an account of human moods and emotions throws light on the "context-dependence" of human existence. One can philosophically plot emotions, in other words, in relation to the kinds of judgments, evaluations, attitudes, and beliefs that people hold. For example, to live aesthetically is not only to experience certain moods, it is also to adopt a certain range of beliefs: that pleasure is to be desired above all, that pain is to be avoided, that boredom is one of life's greatest evils, that existence is essentially episodic, that virtuosity is preferable to continuity in one's life, that fantasy is more important than reality, that the accidental features of one's life (such as beauty or intelligence or wealth) are crucial, etc. To the aesthete, this way of life is glorious. To the ethical person, however, the *judgments* an aesthete holds are in error and the moods accompanying aesthetic life are tragic. In their place the ethical person holds radically different beliefs and proposes different emotions.

Now what is interesting is that, while the stages provide an overall map of human subjectivity, that overall map respects the differences between the stages, and, indeed, highlights the limits of communication, understanding, and "reason-giving" that obtain between these different philosophies of life. The discussion between A and Judge William in *Either/Or* "has no conclusion," as its editor Victor Eremita

[77] See, for example, Johannes Climacus' discussion of the earlier pseudonymous literature from the standpoint of the stages, in *CUP* 251–300 (*SV* VII 212–57).
[78] Or at least Johannes Climacus sees it this way; see for example *CUP* 292 (*SV* VII 250).
[79] See Lee Barrett, "Kierkegaard's *Two Ages*: An Immediate Stage on the Way to the Religious Life," in Robert L. Perkins, ed., *International Kierkegaard Commentary, Volume 14: Two Ages* (Macon, GA: Mercer University Press, 1984), 53–71.

points out.[80] The book does not result in a conclusive argument that defeats one of their positions. It shows rather that – to take the Judge as example – the *reasons* that an ethical person provides for living ethically (even arguing that ethical existence is more aesthetically pleasing) are themselves dependent upon the ethical way of life (i.e., context-dependent); there is no way of rationally *demonstrating* the superiority of the ethical way of life to the aesthete or proving the truth of such an ethical way of life from an external point of view. It is only by losing the desires of the aesthete and adopting the desires of the ethical person that one will come to see the ethical way of life as superior and "true." (So, too, by losing the desires appropriate to the ethical person one can go back to aestheticism.) In this sense, the transitions between the stages on life's way depend not upon "reasons" alone, but upon "motives." Yet "motives" must not be seen as logically excluding "reasons." Rather, they constitute a type of "reason-giving." Kierkegaard's understanding of the transitions between the stages of life should not then be seen as "irrational." His claim is rather that there is no possible *overall* account of "reasons," outside of the *particular* sphere of existence within which those reasons and motives obtain, that is compelling.[81]

The Christian narrative understanding of the self

This dynamic image of the self's journey to God raises, finally, a fundamental point concerning Kierkegaard's understanding of the self that is often misunderstood. The point can be put metaphorically: Kierkegaard's conception of the self and his language of moods and emotions are frequently misunderstood in existential phenomenology when they are interpreted as employing primarily the metaphor of "depth structures." On this view, moods and emotions are prelinguistic and precognitive expressions of psychological structures. Furthermore, the aim of philosophical and psychological analysis is the explication and "uncovering" of these moods and emotions. The "explanation" of a mood or emotion is that it is to be explained in terms of these dynamics. As in Freudian and also Heideggerian terminology, moods and emotions are best seen in terms of the basic ontological structures of the self.[82]

---

[80] *EO* I 14 (*SV* I xv).
[81] Compare Mehl, "Kierkegaard and the Relativist Challenge to Practical Philosophy," 265.
[82] Martin Heidegger, *Being and Time*, trans. John Macquarrie and Edward Robinson (New York and Evanston: Harper & Row, 1962).

Now Kierkegaard does indeed employ the "depth structure" meta-phor to speak of the self and its moods. And, as we have seen, he also employs an ontological vocabulary stressing the dynamics of the factors of finitude and infinitude, etc. But Kierkegaard's anthropological reflection differs from Heideggerian and Freudian "depth structure" language in that it employs more fundamentally a quite different metaphor, that of "patterns of life."[83] As Vincent McCarthy has put it, the phenomenology of moods in Kierkegaard sees emotions more in terms of their relationship to beliefs, attitudes, actions, and feelings, that is, in terms of broad patterns of a person's life that are observable and describable, rather than to a Heideggerian ontology of moods.[84] Jeremy Walker also rightly points out that Kierkegaard is concerned as a psychologist with the phenomena of the psychological life; rather than being concerned with psychoanalytical theories of hidden mech-anisms, his interest as psychologist is closer to the tradition of Christian writings about temptation, sin, prayer, and purification.[85]

This is an important point, since it is tempting to link Kierkegaard with a "depth structure" language used in Idealism and existentialism in which emotions are seen as prelinguistic and precognitive structures, immediately "present" to the self, despite the reality of self-deception promoted by the dynamic factors of the self. Such a theory of emotions is increasingly seen, however, as a problematic way of speaking of psychological terms and categories. Not only does it play upon a notion of immediate self-presence, and so the notion of a sovereign self divorced from its environment, it also affirms a prelinguisticality to experience that ignores the extent to which experience is shaped by cultural and linguistic concepts.

Kierkegaard's psychological terminology, however, is, I want to argue, much more closely allied with another tradition that predates the Idealist–existentialist tradition of immediate self-presence, and that is an Augustinian narrative understanding of the self. For the August-inian tradition, the self is to be seen in terms of a temporal narrative of one's journey from and to God. The project of self-understanding is to gain clarity about oneself by rehearsing the narrative of one's own life, not in isolation, but in terms of two additional factors: the "ordinary experience" of daily life and also the relation of the self to God as the

---

[83] This will be especially important when we turn in chapters 4–7 to Christ as "Pattern" (*Forbilledet*) for Christian existence. See Dewey, *The New Obedience*, 222n42.

[84] McCarthy, *The Phenomenology of Moods in Kierkegaard*, 124.

[85] Walker, *Kierkegaard: The Descent into God*, 218.

source and goal of one's happiness: in Augustine's famous words in his *Confessions*, "you made us for yourself and our hearts find no peace until they rest in you."[86] The project of "understanding oneself" is therefore a matter of forming such a narrative and also placing this narrative in its theological context. With regard to moods and emotions, these are seen (usually) less as functions of hidden psychological mechanisms than as functions of the actions, attitudes, judgments, and decisions that a person makes. To understand a mood or an emotion is to understand the surface of life, its narrative flow, rather than the hidden dynamics of the psyche.[87] And the goal of life is to find one's home in God as the result of a journey of self-clarification and purification.[88] Michael Plekon lists some of the "kinetic metaphors" that erupt in Kierkegaard's language for the self:

The self is variously described as a "wanderer" (*Vandrer*), a "wayfarer" or "pilgrim" [*sic*] (*Vandringsmand*), a "traveller" (*Reisende*), and as a "seeker" (*Søger*). Kierkegaard visualizes human existence as a "journey" (*Reise*) or "way" (*Vej*) ... Similarly, such theologically derived metaphors are applied to the path of the religious individual, in particular the Christian, who is called to "imitate," literally to a "following after" Christ (*Kristi Efterfølgelsen*). Other images include characterizations of the self as a "stranger" (*Fremmed*), an "alien" or "foreigner" (*Udlænding*) in the world, and "emigrant" (*Udvandrer*) consigned to "restlessness" (*Uro*) in existence.[89]

In the end, Kierkegaard's anthropological contemplation results in a dynamic vision of the self on pilgrimage ("stages on life's way") that stands in marked contrast to traditional metaphysical "substantive" visions of the self. The self is not a static "something," possessed or lost like "an arm, a leg, five dollars, a wife, etc."[90] To be a self is to be

---

[86] Augustine, *Confessions*, trans. with an Introduction by R. S. Pine-Coffin (Harmondsworth: Penguin Books, 1961), Book I, I, 21.

[87] An immediate objection to this might be that this narrative account of Kierkegaard's psychology ignores the central place given to "hidden inwardness." We will return to this later; for the moment, it need only be noted that "hidden inwardness" indicates not the *source* of moods and emotions or the essential *privacy* of the self, but rather the difficulties of *communication* between persons who do not share the same conceptuality – which is quite another matter altogether.

[88] Mark C. Taylor uses the image of the journey to God in his study of the conflicting "journeys to selfhood" of Kierkegaard and Hegel. But Taylor's insightful study nonetheless continues stereotypes of the Kierkegaardian "solitary individual" that require qualification; see Mark C. Taylor, *Journeys to Selfhood: Hegel and Kierkegaard*, 272. We will return to this in chapter 7.

[89] Michael Plekon, "'Anthropological Contemplation': Kierkegaard and Modern Social Theory," *Thought* 55 (1980): 349.

[90] *SUD* 33 (*SV* XI 146).

engaged in a dynamic process, one involving a journey or progress of self-purification of one's moods and emotions on the way to self-clarification, what Kierkegaard calls "becoming a self before God." It is to the shape of that spiritual "progress" that we will turn in the remainder of this study.

CHAPTER 3

Becoming religious: upbuilding before God

Kierkegaard sees "becoming religious" in terms of "upbuilding" and "forming" the individual. In this chapter we need to examine more closely Kierkegaard's vision of becoming religious as the shaping of the heart, the development of longterm personal emotions and particularly virtues that characterize both ethical and religious existence. And we will see how he also alters that virtue tradition in considering the dynamics of religious existence before God. Finally, at the end of this chapter, we will briefly situate his understanding of religion in relation to others current in his time.

Ethics and religion are related closely for Kierkegaard. Of course, the ethical and religious are distinct stages in much of Kierkegaard's published and unpublished writings, especially in such works as *Stages on Life's Way*, *Fear and Trembling*, and *Postscript*. He makes clear that ethics, while inherently religious, is not the whole story of religion, and, conversely, religion is never simply the ethical; there are crucial differences between ethics, religion, and Christianity. Nonetheless, ethics and religion can also be seen *together*, over against, in contrast to, the disorder of aesthetic life. As Alastair McKinnon has written, the great divide, the decisive fork in the road, the great either/or for Kierkegaard is between the aesthetic and the Christian, with the ethical and religious subsumed under the Christian.[1] This is especially so in light of his strategic purpose to lead persons from an aesthetic approach to life (including aesthetic intellectualism) to decisive Christian categories. Ethics is the entry-point for religious and for Christian concern, and each of the religious spheres *builds upon* the ethical. Ethics and religion therefore share longterm passionate concerns as a person seeks refuge and recovery from the disorder of the aesthetic. Thus, we can

---

[1]   Alastair McKinnon, "Søren Kierkegaard," in Ninian Smart, John Clayton, Steven Katz, and Patrick Sherry, eds., *Nineteenth Century Religious Thought in the West*, 3 vols. (Cambridge University Press, 1985), I, 189.

speak of "ethicoreligious" capabilities that are by and large shared by
ethics and the religious spheres, and we will rely on the upbuilding
literature as well as the pseudonymous works to describe these virtues.[2]

G. E. Arbaugh notes that, while Kierkegaard accepts the importance of virtue, its philosophical conception does not weigh heavily
with him.[3] This is true on the face of it, for reasons we will explore in
this chapter, yet a careful appreciation of his thought on ethicoreligious existence will confirm the essential significance of virtue in his
thought. In contrast to what I have called the existentialist depiction
of the person as being simply a sovereign, self-created, and isolated
will, Kierkegaard's own ethicoreligious thought focuses on images of
"continuity," of "character," "soul-making."[4] Important as "will" and
"decision" are for him, Kierkegaard stands rather in the broad
tradition – extending from Plato and Aristotle through Plutarch,
orthodox Christianity and addressed anew in Pietism and in moral
philosophers such as Kant – of ethics as virtue, the development of
ongoing intentions, dispositions, judgments, and motivations that
characterize a person over time.[5] Virtues are not limited to the "will"
or "behavior" or "motivation," but are, as one student of the virtues
argues, "*patterns* of action, emotion, and motivations typical of [that
virtue] and the circumstances in which actions and emotions exempli-
fying the virtue are appropriate."[6] This aptly fits Kierkegaard's

2   In terms of the stages, I approach these upbuilding discourses as reflecting an immanent
    religiosity. Johannes Climacus describes the discourses in terms of the "ethical categories of
    immanence, not the doubly reflected religious categories in the paradox" (*CUP* 256 [*SV* vii
    216]). Malantschuk, *Kierkegaard's Thought*, 311, sees them as addressing the aesthetic person with
    the eternal in terms of steadfastness, but not yet with the eternal as the ethical. This is
    unlikely, given the strong conceptual similarities to Religiousness A's concern with the
    ethicoreligious tasks required by patience, courage, and so forth, grounded in resignation and
    reliance upon God. Evans, by contrast, affirms the parallels with *Postscript*, and sees the
    Upbuilding Discourses as an excellent guide to the *Postscript* (*Kierkegaard's* Fragments *and*
    Postscript, 50).
3   G. E. Arbaugh, "Christian Virtues," in Thulstrup and Thulstrup, eds., *The Sources and Depths
    of Faith in Kierkegaard, Bibliotheca Kierkegaardiana*, ii, 100.
4   As Evans puts it, Kierkegaard's ethics is concerned with "soul making"; see Evans,
    Kierkegaard's Fragments *and* Postscript, 75–78, 86–92.
5   In contrast to the usual criticism of Kant's ethics as empty and formalistic – concerned simply
    with the categorical imperative as the definition of the good will – Ronald M. Green argues,
    in my view correctly, that Kant was deeply concerned with questions of personal virtue,
    questions of intention and willing as well as good deeds, and with the link (evident in the
    second *Critique*) between virtue and happiness. Green argues that in all of these concerns Kant
    influenced Kierkegaard, although Kierkegaard sought to hide the extent of that debt. Ronald
    M. Green, *Kierkegaard and Kant: The Hidden Debt* (Albany: State University of New York Press,
    1992); on happiness and virtue, see especially 47–55.
6   Roberts, "Therapies and the Grammar of a Virtue," in Bell, *The Grammar of the Heart*, 150
    (italics added).

understanding. "Morality is character; character is something en-graved ... but the sea has no character, nor does sand, nor abstract common sense, either, for character is inwardness."[7] In this he resembles many contemporary ethicists and theologians who wish to turn attention away from sole consideration of moral dilemmas (although Kierkegaard is, of course, concerned with moral dilemmas as well) to a consideration of "character" or "virtue."

Our approach will be to see Kierkegaard's ethicoreligious focus in terms of "upbuilding" into the religious, a shaping of character and virtue (including the Christian virtues of faith, hope, and love) – hence the title of this chapter, "*Becoming* Religious," and the later chapters, "*Becoming* Christian."[8] Throughout his authorship, his ideal is one shared by the virtue tradition, the ideal of personal "unity."

BECOMING A SELF: FORMING PERSONAL UNITY

Becoming ethical or religious is gaining a unified self. This involves not only the continuity of the emotions in contrast to moods, but also other dispositions. While emotions are dispositions, not all dispositions are emotions; dispositions include also other longterm "non-emotional" capacities that Kierkegaard finds at the heart of the ethicoreligious life, including virtues such as patience, humility, perseverance, and courage that he treats extensively in his upbuilding literature. These too form the continuity of a person over time. Whether a person *feels* hopeful or not, one may still be hopeful despite the discouragements of particular events. A patient person is one who is disposed to be patient even if she does not feel patient. It is the "building up" of such dispositional virtues that Kierkegaard envisions in his literature.

In one sense, however, "disposition" is inadequate to speak of patience, humility, and so forth. As is often noted, a "disposition" may be seen simply as a tendency to *act* in certain ways in certain circumstances. This is inadequate to describe ethical and religious existence, however; a patient person may sometimes exhibit impa-tience, and a patient act may be done by someone who is generally impatient.[9] Neither do "skill" and "technique" suffice. Kierkegaard is

---

[7]   *TA* 77–78 (*SV* viii 73).

[8]   Kierkegaard sometimes equates the terms "upbuilding" and "religious," as in a journal entry that speaks of the course of his authorship from the aesthetic to the religious. See *JP* vi 6238 (*Pap.* ix a 227, n.d., 1848).

[9]   See for example Gilbert C. Meilaender, *The Theory and Practice of Virtue* (University of Notre Dame Press, 1984), 7–8.

most interested therefore in a more "hidden" element in such characteristics as patience, humility, and courage, matters of what he often
calls "the heart."

Such capabilities are "earnestness" and "inwardness and passion."
In terms of his understanding of the self, these capacities point, not
only to dispositional behavior, but to the "depth" factors of the self. In
The Concept of Anxiety, Vigilius Haufniensis gives an account of "earnestness" as "the acquired originality of disposition" [*Gemyt*].[10] The
adjective "acquired" is crucial, for "no one is born with earnestness."
The point is to distinguish ethicoreligious continuity from "habit."
Vigilius' answer is that a person must depend, not upon feeling, for
"the inwardness of feeling is uncertain in its mood," nor upon habitual
action alone, but upon "earnestness" as the originality which directs
the person to his or her freely chosen task.

"Earnestness" requires also "inwardness and passion." Kierkegaard's
term "inwardness" or "hidden inwardness" points to the hiatus
between the "inner" and the "outer," the distinction between action
and motivation, the difficulties of communication between persons, the
"hiddenness" of one's relationship with God, indeed, the incognito of
the "God-man." As we will see, Kierkegaard later criticized his earlier
emphasis on "hidden inwardness." But, calling up as it does images of
"the turn inward" or "private meaning," one might think that
Kierkegaard is speaking of an *essentially* private interiority, Gilbert
Ryle's "ghost in the machine," divorced from external actions, and
since dismantled or deconstructed by recent analytic philosophy.[11]
Now one can grant that the inner–outer distinction and the themes of
privacy and incommunicability are certainly important for Kierkegaard, but it is a serious distortion of "inwardness" to see it apart from
the ethicoreligious formation of the person. "Inwardness," rather, "is
earnestness."[12] "Inwardness" finds its natural home in relation first of
all to such matters as ethical thoughtfulness and self-reflection.

The truly ethical person is not simply the one who performs certain

---

[10] *CA* 149 (*SV*IV 414).
[11] Gilbert Ryle, *The Concept of Mind* (London: Hutchinson, 1949). See Iris Murdoch's protest
"Against Dryness: A Polemical Sketch," in Stanley Hauerwas and Alasdair MacIntyre, eds.,
Revisions: Changing Perspectives in Moral Philosophy (Notre Dame and London: University of Notre
Dame Press, 1983), 43–50. Kierkegaard's concepts of "inwardness" and "passion" provide an
antidote to such "dryness" and quasi-behaviorism, without committing him to an essentially
private self.
[12] *CA* 146 (*SV*IV 412); compare *JP*II 2112 (*Pap.* v в 65, n.d., 1844).

actions (which may be done from base motives), but one who possesses a concern, which involves introspection and self-examination.[13] The relation between inwardness and concern is clearly stated in an 1843 upbuilding discourse on "Strengthening in the Inner Being," where Kierkegaard writes of the person in whom there awakens not just a concern for things in the world, but "a concern about what meaning the world has for him and he for the world ... only then does the inner being announce its presence in this *concern*."[14] The juxtaposing of "inner being" and "concern" is central: to speak of having "the inner being" means not locating an inner something, but exercising a concern. He points out next that this concern is not temporary, something decided "once and for all" after which one is "finished with it," but that one has it as a continuing concern.[15]

Inwardness as a longterm and intensive concern constitutes a *passion*. In *Postscript*, Climacus writes that "at its highest, inwardness in an existing subject is passion."[16] By passion (Danish *Lidenskab*; compare the German *Leidenschaft*) he means an extensive interest that shapes a person's life in great breadth. To say that a person has a passion for justice tells one about a wide range of that person's preferences, desires, intentions, emotions, and actions. We come to characterize a person's entire life as "seeking justice."

VIRTUE, VISION, AND WILL

Kierkegaard's virtue ethic, with its stress on passion and interest, emphasizes vision and not simply the will. We can see this in looking briefly at two ways that passion is related to the imagination.

As noted earlier, the self is a synthesis of the temporal and eternal, the finite and infinite. Terms like the "eternal" and "infinite" point to the expansive capacities of the self, linked with imagined possibilities. M. Jamie Ferreira suggests another role for the imagination in relation to passion, and that is to hold the infinite and finite, the eternal and the temporal, in dynamic tension.[17] This is reflected in Judge William's comment, "Whoever has not understood the eternal correctly, understood it altogether concretely, lacks inwardness and

---

13 On introspection, see *JP*ɪɪ 2124 (*Pap.* x³ ᴀ 251, n.d., 1850).
14 *EUD* 86 (*SV*ɪɪɪ 302) (original italics).
15 *EUD* 87 (*SV*ɪɪɪ 303).
16 *CUP* 199 (*SV*ᴠɪɪ 166).
17 Ferreira, *Transforming Vision*, 32.

earnestness."[18] In choosing to be a concrete self, I choose "myself in my eternal validity," and this too is a function of the imagination in ethicoreligious existence.[19] Hence, ethical existence is eternal in two ways, relating one to imagined possibilities, and in calling one back to commitment and duty.

Ferreira suggests that passion plays another imaginative and crucial role, one that we will see both in this chapter and throughout our examination of Kierkegaard's religious thought: passion is both active and passive. The passionate, concerned life is actively self-directed, involving free acts of will in envisioning possibilities and making them concrete. Yet a passionate person is not self-creating; one cannot simply generate a passion by arbitrary choice. Rather, one is engaged. The accidents of aesthetic immediacy – one's talents, skills, abilities, and moods too – become the raw material for passion. For example, as Judge William notes, one passively, as it were, inherits certain talents, but "the talent is not beautiful until it is transfigured into a calling."[20] Only when the material of received talents is formed into callings can one relate what one passively is to what one can actively become. The ethical person, the Judge says, sees life as passive and active, as gift and task (Danish *Gave/Opgave*). In relating the passive and active in this dynamic way, we will see a continuing element in Kierkegaard's religious and Christian thought, gathering up receptivity and activity, suffering and active virtue.

Imaginative vision is central in Judge William's letters to A, which are not solely philosophical arguments, but also rhetorical appeals aimed at altering how A *sees* himself and others. He urges A to examine his own life, to see it in a certain way so that it is no longer material for ironic amusement, but for self-despair. He invites A to see other people not as source of amusement, but as an "other," over against himself. He portrays the ethical life in such a way that A might be led to see marriage as "beautiful" (hence "aesthetically valid"). The judge's aesthetic defense of the ethical way of life, of marriage and duty, is not therefore merely a shrewd appeal to an aesthete who regards the ethical as tedious and is only interested in pleasure. The judge's arguments for the *aesthetic* validity of marriage are also totally consistent with the ethical way of life, because ethics for the Judge (and for Kierkegaard) is never a matter simply of sheer obligation, duty, or

18   *CA* 151 (*SV* iv 417).
19   *EO* ii 214 (*SV* ii 192).
20   *EO* ii 293 (*SV* ii 263).

moralism, but of envisioning new desires and needs, indeed, a new vision of happiness.

In speaking of "desire," "needs," and "happiness" as well as "virtue," it is not that Kierkegaard is eudaemonistic, justifying ethical existence on the basis of a *prudential* desire for happiness. Like Kant, he rejects the notion that ethical life is grounded on prudential concerns; happiness (conceived as a reward for virtue) is distinct from virtue, and the ethical person acts out of moral obligation rather than a desire for some external reward.[21] But Kierkegaard is able to include not simply duty, but also desire in his ethicoreligious vision, since the object of desire, "an eternal happiness" [*en evig Salighed*], is redefined; it is not a finite good, but is itself the absolute *telos* of duty, and, as we will see, "the God-relationship." Thus, eternal happiness is the "internal reward" of one who does his or her duty.[22] But this rethinking of "happiness" in terms of virtue allows Kierkegaard to give the desire for happiness wide scope. For Kierkegaard, as one writer puts it, "happiness is the intrinsically satisfied state of the person who fulfills his moral duty."[23]

Conceiving a desire for happiness takes irony, which is another exercise of imagination. Unlike purely aesthetic irony, which can itself be a destructive mood, ethical concern employs irony to enable one to stand back from the givens of one's life and to question them.[24] Irony's ethicoreligious roles in *mirroring* the self are explored in many places in Kierkegaard's writings.[25] For example, in an upbuilding discourse from 1844, "To Need God Is a Human Being's Highest Perfection,"

---

[21] Ronald M. Green, *Kant and Kierkegaard*, 100.

[22] See Khan, *Salighed as Happiness?*; compare Evans, *Kierkegaard's* Fragments *and* Postscript, 141–47, who in turn is indebted to Jeremy Walker, "The Idea of Reward in Morality," *Kierkegaardiana* 8: 30–52.

[23] Evans, *Kierkegaard's* Fragments *and* Postscript, 147.

[24] *CI* 324 (*SV* xiii 388). In *Either/Or*, ii Judge William is unaware of the seriousness of the questions raised against his position in the final sermon he himself appends to his letters to A (*EO* ii 338 [*SV* ii 304]; compare *SLW* 184 [*SV* vi 174]). On the irony directed against both the young man and the ironist Constantin in *Repetition*, see my "Understanding, Imagination, and Irony in Kierkegaard's *Repetition*," in Robert L. Perkins, ed., *International Kierkegaard Commentary: Fear and Trembling and* Repetition (Macon, GA: Mercer University Press, 1993), 283–308. Socrates' ironic conclusion that his attempts at self-knowledge fail is found in *PF* 37 (*SV* iv 204). The ironic religious and Christian failure is the focus of such concepts as striving, repentance, guilt, and sin.

[25] Kierkegaard notably applies the image of "mirror" not only to self-reflection, but to Scripture in "What Is Required in Order to Look at Oneself with True Blessing in the Mirror of the Word?" in *FSE* 9–51 (*SV* xii 301–37). It implies other images, such as the depth of the sea reflecting the height of the skies, applied both to Christ's divinity and humanity (*JP* i 284 [*Pap.* ii A 595, n.d., 1837]).

Kierkegaard suggests that when a person "turns and faces himself in order to understand himself," he is no longer identified with "the first self," the external self that has particular desires and cravings and is invested in "gaining the whole world," but "the deeper self" (more conscious or reflective self) "lets the surrounding world remain what it is – remain dubious."[26] The immediacy of one's life is surveyed and choices are made as to what projects one will pursue or not pursue. This "deeper self" points not to an ontological substratum in the self, but to the cultivation of ironic-edifying capacities for self-questioning and self-examination, a spiritual and moral discipline, as one is trained toward imagining and enacting the good. The mirror-image implies attaining not only "reflection" and "depth," but also a "transparency" in place of the opaque character of the aesthetic.

This brings us to the will. Vision and desire are, of course, not enough in describing ethical and religious existence. Vision and desire by themselves may, of course, remain abstract, examples of imagination leaping into possibility, unresolved into a concrete, visible life: the good one desires or envisions may always remain unactualized. As we have seen, passion is active and not simply contemplative, actual and not just *possible*, concerned to form a concrete life. The will also is needed; ethicoreligious existence is shaped by commitment and choice. What is required in addition are the "motive forces" of "choice," "will," and "passion." Judge William thus counsels his young friend that he must despair of himself and choose the ethical, which first and foremost is "to choose to choose," to be committed, whatever it is one chooses: "the point is not the reality of that which is chosen but the reality of choosing."[27] Herein lies, for Kierkegaard, the heart of human freedom, the *kinesis* or movement by which one moves from the entertainment of possibilities to the actualizing of possibilities in one's own life. Johannes Climacus agrees, speaking in *Postscript* of the superiority of ethical to poetic ideality: in ethical ideality, possibility becomes actuality, not in the sense of the mere "outer," but as actuality that is "interiority infinitely interested in existing," that is, translated into the actual and concrete individual.[28]

We saw earlier that ethical dispositions are not only skills, since that ignores the dimension of inwardness. But for Kierkegaard it is important to speak of active virtues that are like skills, involving will-power and

---

[26]   *EUD* 314 (*SV* v 95).
[27]   *EO* ii 176 (*SV* ii 160).
[28]   *CUP* 324–25 (*SV* vii 279–80).

self-control.[29] Indeed, Kierkegaard's suspicion of Aristotle's under-standing of virtue is that "the so-called moral virtues" in Aristotle are simply matters of moderation dealing only with habit, not with free acts.[30] (This is part of his concern too that patience, courage, and temperance can be simply instrumental requirements for a successful temporal and aesthetic life, quite apart from seeing oneself before the requirements of the good or God.) But in the margin of this same journal entry on Aristotle, he adds with appreciation:

that he [Aristotle] does not believe virtue to be the postulated midpoint at all times can be seen in his distinction between virtue and voluntary acts. The voluntary is the discreet [sic]; virtue is the continuous. He therefore says most profoundly that free action lies totally in a man's power; virtue does not, except with respect to the beginning, because it is a competence (continuity).[31]

Kierkegaard is not saying that the virtuous life is devoid of continuity, but is distinguishing here again between the bare continuity of habit and a truly ethical disposition that includes freedom and will. Part of this stress on the active virtues is the Kantian background, locating the good in the good will. With Kant's *The Doctrine of Virtue* and against Aristotle, Kierkegaard locates virtue not in habit, but in active resolu-tion.[32] This focus on active virtue has another important source in Kierkegaard's understanding of the *healing* required of the disorder of the aesthetic sphere. The will is active and must struggle through despair to reach ethical existence, to weave a life of continuity and inwardness out of the chaos of the aesthetic. Many of the virtues do include skill-like struggle. When the judge says to A that he must "choose to choose," which is the heart of freedom, he indicates formally the role of the will in ethicoreligious life.[33]

Yet Kierkegaard's language of "will" points not simply to a discrete act of willing (the "leap"), but to "activating resolution" and self-control. In his upbuilding discourses, Kierkegaard stresses the active cultivation of "strengthening in the inner being."[34] In "Against

[29] See Robert C. Roberts, "Will Power and the Virtues," *The Philosophical Review* 93 (April 1984): 227–47.

[30] *JP* I 892 (*Pap.* IV c 16, n.d., 1842–43).

[31] *JP* I 893 (*Pap.* IV c 17, n.d., 1842–43). This passage helps explain one reason that the term "virtue" appears so seldom in Kierkegaard's writings. It is not that the concept is lacking, but that the word "virtue" is associated with habit.

[32] George B. Connell, "Judge William's Theonomous Ethics," in George B. Connell and C. Stephen Evans, *Foundations of Kierkegaard's Vision of Community: Religion, Ethics, and Politics in Kierkegaard* (Atlantic Highlands, NJ; London: Humanities Press, 1992), 58.

[33] *EO* II 176 (*SV* II 160).

[34] *EUD* 79–101 (*SV* III 296–315).

Cowardliness," Kierkegaard describes courage and perseverance as *active* resolution. But in what sense is perseverance "active"? Here Kierkegaard is quite clear that resolution is not *momentary* decisiveness. Indeed, it is not a "leap," since a leap may simply be impetuosity: "it is a question not of boldly leaping out but of saving" oneself.[35] Resolution is described (with echoes of Kant) dispositionally, not as a leap but as coming "into stride."[36] Resolution relates to endurance, to a continuous struggle to renew one's resolution.[37] The will is spoken of as developing a disposition of resolution. This includes acts of will, but is not restricted to such acts.

The will, even conceived of as "the discrete," does not "create" the self in a moment of existential decision, but rather is embedded in a fabric of developing emotional continuities, new desires, and active virtuous dispositions. Vision and desire, as well as choice and acts of will, are at the heart of the formation of ethical and religious existence for Kierkegaard. I have been arguing throughout that Kierkegaard does not see the self as a "thin sliver of will." The will is central to his thinking on human existence, especially in contrast to hyperintellectualism and aestheticism, but he discusses the will within a broader context. "Purity of heart" is to will one thing, but this means shaping a heart within the continuities of emotions and dispositions.

THE GRAMMAR OF "SEEING AND KNOWING GOD"

"Blessed are the pure in heart, for they shall see God" (Matthew 5:8). In becoming aware in ethical obligation of the "eternal within," one also becomes aware of the "Eternal," of God. It is, I believe, important to see how the ethical sphere, for Kierkegaard, is itself religious, a point which a number of commentators miss.[38] As George B. Connell argues, Judge William's ethics, in contrast to Kant, is theonomous;

---

[35]　*EUD* 349 (*SV* v 126).
[36]　*EUD* 351 (*SV* v 128).
[37]　*EUD* 352 (*SV* v 128).
[38]　Anthony Rudd, *Kierkegaard and the Limits of the Ethical* (Oxford: Clarendon Press, 1993), correctly criticizes Jeremy Walker and Alastair Hannay on this point (135–37). In contrast to Walker, Rudd is correct to see both Judge William and *Purity of Heart* as broadly theonomous rather than autonomous. "Kierkegaard's whole concern is with self-realization, the individual's quest for fulfillment," rather than universalizability of action, as (he alleges) in Kant. Yet Rudd's contrast of eudaemonism and duty runs the risk of downplaying the Kantian element in Kierkegaard's understanding of ethics; Walker correctly stresses that Kierkegaard's "happiness" is internally related not to reward, but to "duty."

God's authority is the ground of moral obligation, yet this does not result in heteronomy, for the relationship to God is freeing rather than confining.[39] In "choosing to choose," one relates to God.

This affects how Kierkegaard as well as Judge William understand "knowledge of God." We will turn to this again in the next chapter on Christian faith and knowledge, where we will see that the claim to "know God" is called into question. For now I simply wish to indicate that Kierkegaard's descriptions of "immanent" religion, apart from a special revelation, allow room for speaking of "knowledge of God." His attacks on a propositional understanding of knowledge, his criticisms of empirical or rational proofs for God's existence and the entire project of "natural theology," do not rule out speaking of a "natural knowledge" of God available in ethicoreligious existence. His interest is not to deny such knowledge, but to describe the subjective qualifications necessary to speak of "knowing God."

The central point is that such knowledge is not gained dispassionately, but is a matter of passionate personal commitment. Knowledge of God is discovered as one gains knowledge of oneself. "Self-knowledge is a difficult matter; although it is easy to understand the rest of the world, the understanding suddenly changes very substantially when it pertains to oneself."[40] Knowledge of God is intimately tied to self-knowledge. As a person is formed in ethical concerns and duty, concerned to maintain the continuity of life brought by ethics, such a person will look to God for sustenance, or, as Judge William says, "refers" everything to God within the context of obligation to God.[41] The context of "referring" is not an objective inventory of the world that then adds, "God exists too." "Referring" is rather seen in the judge looking to God as Providence and supreme Judge, turning to God in hope of being given the strength to fulfill his ethical obligations.

For Judge William, ethical existence is therefore inseparable from a God-relationship. Johannes Climacus agrees, saying that "only in the inwardness of self-activity ... does [one] become aware and capable of seeing God."[42] It is in ethical existence, specifically the attempt to relate to an absolute duty and good, that a person learns to see God. In the discourse I have just cited, Kierkegaard says that

---

[39] Connell, "Judge William's Theonomous Ethics," in Evans and Connell, *Foundations of Kierkegaard's Vision of Community*, 63.

[40] *EUD* 275 (*SV*IV 157–58).

[41] *EO*II 58 (*SV*II 53).

[42] *CUP* 243 (*SV*VII 204–05).

even though in every other sense it is just a figurative expression to say that we see the finger of God in life, a person who is concerned about himself understands it quite literally, because all deeper and more inward self-knowledge is under divine guidance and continually sees the finger of God that points to him.[43]

As Kierkegaard puts it in a journal entry, "the medium, the only medium, through which God communicates with 'man,' the only thing he will talk about with man is: the ethical."[44]

This calls to mind Wittgenstein's remark that when someone speaks of the "eye of God," one will not draw conclusions about, or speak of, the eyebrows of God.[45] In Wittgenstein's terms, this reference to the "finger of God" is a remark on the "grammar" of the word "God." In saying that one sees the "finger of God" or hears God in ethical concern, Kierkegaard indicates the proper context for "using a picture," a context of concern for one's ethical duty and ethical formation. That is, Kierkegaard indicates what one may or may not say about God, in Wittgenstein's terms the "depth grammar" of the concept "God." The "depth grammar" of speaking of God points not only to the rules of correct usage, but also to the personal capacities, the passion, that the use of the concept "God" requires.

Climacus indicates this when he says that "God is indeed a postulate, but not in the loose sense in which it is ordinarily taken."[46] This "postulation" is rather a matter of passion. The passion of a person who seeks to relate to God despairs over reaching an objective proof that God exists, and so in faith grasps God "by virtue of the infinite passion of inwardness." This "postulate," Climacus says, "far from being the arbitrary, is in fact *necessary* defense [*Nødværge*], self-defense; in this way God is not a postulate, but the existing person's postulating of God is – a necessity."[47] The surprising use of "defense" and "self-defense" puts the passional stamp on the matter. What is ruled out here is treating the knowledge of God as a detached question of epistemology or an inference; Climacus rather points to the passional reasons that lead one to speak of God. It is not that one first establishes, hypothesizes, or even presupposes a prior belief in God's necessary existence to talk about God's love and judgment. Rather, it is in the

---

43   *EUD* 276 (*SV* iv 158).
44   *JP* iii 2823 (*Pap.* x⁵ A 73, n.d. 1853).
45   Ludwig Wittgenstein, *Lectures and Conversations on Aesthetics, Psychology and Religious Belief*, ed. Cyril Barrett (Berkeley and Los Angeles: University of California Press, 1972), 71.
46   *CUP* 200n (*SV* vii 167n).
47   *Ibid.*

context of developing those prior passions and using the concept "God" that give force and even necessity to postulating God.[48] Such a postulation is hardly "arbitrary," Climacus suggests, for it is a matter of deepgoing personal concern. In contrast to both objective demonstration and arbitrary assertion, belief in God arises in the passion of inwardness.

We have already seen Kierkegaard's logical explorations of object- ivity and subjectivity, why he emphasizes "subjectivity" in order to specify the quality of "interestedness" and commitment required in ethicoreligious truth. But, if belief in God is "using a picture" or a "postulate" required by ethical existence, can we speak of ethics and religious belief as "objectively true"?

The literature on these issues is immense.[49] Some argue that Kierkegaard is "subjectivist" in the sense that "believing something makes it true." On this understanding "passion" is simply "willing makes it so." A more plausible case can be made, however, that Kierkegaard's concern for truth as subjectivity is not a denial of an objective pole of truth, but is concerned with *how* one relates "in truth" in ethical and religious passion. Jeremy Walker distinguishes between the epistemological and metaphysical issues in "objectivity and sub- jectivity." He writes that, when Kierkegaard *appears* to imply that words such as "good" and "God" do not name external objective realities, the force of such arguments is epistemological rather than metaphysical.[50] If by "epistemological" we mean a search for transcen- dental guarantees, an attempt to prove God outside the commitment and decisiveness of ethicoreligious existence, this is certainly true to Kierkegaard's thought. Important textual support for the importance of "metaphysical" objectivity in ethicoreligious existence is found in the following passage from *Postscript*:

Just as important as the truth, and of the two the even more important one, is the mode in which the truth is accepted, and it is of slight help if one gets millions to accept the truth if by the very mode of their acceptance they are transposed into untruth.[51]

Climacus' concern, then, is not to attack the notion of an objective truth, but rather to clarify that in ethics and religious belief the only

---

[48] D. Z. Phillips, *Wittgenstein and Religion* (New York: St. Martin's Press, 1993), 17.
[49] See David R. Law, *Kierkegaard as Negative Theologian* (Oxford: Clarendon Press, 1993), chs. 3 and 4, for a good survey of the discussions on both epistemology and truth.
[50] Walker, *Kierkegaard: Descent into God*, 39.
[51] *CUP* 247 (*SV* vii 208) (italics added).

possible means by which one comes to the truth is by way of developing one's "inwardness" and "subjectivity." In contrast to science, history, and other "objective" pursuits, in ethics and religion the many attempts to demonstrate the objective truth of morality or God's existence will fail.

The metaphor of *vision*, of "seeing the good and God," enables Kierkegaard to steer between ethical and religious subjectivism and objectivism, for it is a metaphor with both subjective and objective dimensions. On the one hand, for Kierkegaard (as for Aristotle), willing the good (required in virtue) is *envisioning* and *desiring* the good as an object toward which one strives. This envisioning and desiring the good does not "create values," but is a *conforming* and *transforming* of the person who "sees" a value or a good or God outside the self. Virtue is learning to see things and persons as they are, to give them attention.[52] The person who learns to see a situation as unjust does not think that this is a mental construction, that one can simply choose not to see an injustice; she will say, "Don't you see this injustice?" As Edward F. Mooney puts it, the realm of moral and religious value has an objectivity; otherwise, we could not make sense of error in evaluative judgments; neither can we simply dictate at will the meaning of those concepts of value that provide sense for our lives.[53] The denial of this kind of realism or objectivity often depends upon an implicit empiricism, a distinction between "fact" and "values" embedded in certain non-cognitivist theories of moral and religious language.[54]

Yet, on the other hand, Kierkegaard's focus on the subjective qualifications for knowing the good and God is a careful attempt to pry us from the idea that "knowing" the good and God are like a neutral, uninvolved "representing" of reality. He highlights the subjective capacities in ethics and religion in that he holds that seeing and doing the good require personal capacities, including "purity of heart." Again, it is the urge to think that there is a way to know the good or God apart from such formation that is so tempting. But Kierkegaard suggests that one cannot relate to the good or God without caring for it or perceiving it or desiring it. This is where the subjective qualifications of passionately learning to see and desire the good become crucial.

[52]   In addition to Iris Murdoch and Simone Weil (among others), see Stanley Hauerwas, "The Significance of Vision: Toward an Aesthetic Ethic," in *Vision and Virtue: Essays in Christian Ethical Reflection* (Notre Dame, IN: Fides Publishers, 1974), 30–47.
[53]   Mooney, *Knights of Faith and Resignation*, 93.
[54]   Sabina Lovibond, *Realism and Imagination in Ethics* (Minneapolis: University of Minnesota Press, 1983) and also Charles Taylor, *Sources of the Self*.

Here again is where the emotions come into play in one's values, since values are not simply objects to be known, but enter our lives through the emotions.[55] It is by relating to the good ("purity of heart is to *will* one thing"), that is, by one's emotions and passions and will directed toward the good, that one knows the good.

Judge William refers his life to God. Wittgenstein's thought can illuminate how this "referring" finds a path between objectivism and subjectivism. As Hilary Putnam has recently argued (following Rush Rhees), for Wittgenstein, "referring" does not have an essence.[56] "Referring" is not limited to examples of pointing; as Putnam writes, religious thinkers are the first to confess that "referring to God" is quite unlike the use of "referring to one's brother in America."[57] Neither, he continues, is it helpful to distinguish some realms of discourse as "cognitive" in contrast to other "non-cognitive" discourses. For Putnam, both "relativism *and* the desire for a metaphysical foundation are manifestations of the same disease."[58] Kierkegaard's thought on these matters, I suggest, is no more "subjectivist" or "relativist" than is Wittgenstein's in Putnam's reading.[59] In the end, Kierkegaard too seeks to avoid the subjectivism that sees us creating a private world in morality or religious faith; he avoids at the same time an empiricist realism that assumes that we relate to God as one relates to "objects in the world," in an "obsession with representation, and of the accompanying picture of the self as observer of the passing scene."[60]

The metaphor of vision helps too in thinking about transitions to ethics and to religious belief. In rejecting a single universal rational standard for ethics and religion, the alternative is not that transitions are "irrational" or arbitrary. In chapter 2, discussing the "stages on life's way," I suggested that, while there is no overall account of "reasons" outside a particular sphere of existence, these transitions are not simply "motives" opposed to "reasons." In describing ethical

55 Evans, *Kierkegaard's Fragments and Postscript*, 69.
56 Hilary Putnam, *Renewing Philosophy* (Cambridge, MA; London: Harvard University Press, 1992), 167–78.
57 Putnam, *Renewing Philosophy*, 168. The reference to "his brother in America" is to Wittgenstein, *Lectures and Conversations*, 66–68.
58 Putnam, *Renewing Philosophy*, 177.
59 Compare also Cyril Barrett, *Wittgenstein on Ethics and Religious Belief* (Oxford and Cambridge, MA: Blackwell, 1991), chs. 7 and 13, who concludes (with criticism of Rhees as well as D. Z. Phillips) that Wittgenstein's relativism was not "hardline" but "moderate." While not seeing Kierkegaard as a relativist, Barrett nonetheless still seems to see him advocating an "irrational" leap (156).
60 Fergus Kerr, *Theology After Wittgenstein*, 134.

existence, including referring all things to God, Judge William does not prove, but attempts to persuade, by giving an account of a moral vision of a way of life that appeals to the aesthete's vision of his life as it is and may be. It is not an exhortation to *blind* choice, but to imaginative revisioning.

VIRTUE, ETHICS, AND RELIGION

From ethics to religion

Judge William says of the ethical individual that "He is going to develop in his life the personal, the civic, the religious virtues, and his life advances through his continually translating himself from one stage to another."[61] But does Kierkegaard really fit into the tradition of an ethic of virtue that, in Gilbert C. Meilaender's words, "seeks to focus not only on ... moments of great anxiety and uncertainty in life but also on the *continuities*, the habits of behavior which make us the persons we are"?[62] Is not Kierkegaard the thinker of discontinuities and breaches, of spiritual trial and anxiety? Kierkegaard *distinguishes* the "religious" sphere of existence from the "ethical," and he is concerned to show the limits of the ethical.[63] He exhibits to his readers a further "language of the heart" that arises from the crises or breaches a person encounters that throw into question one's attempt to form an ethical character before God.

Kierkegaard is certainly concerned with the anxieties and uncertainties, the breaches and discontinuities in ethicoreligious life (witness *Fear and Trembling*). He also distrusts a simply civic concept of virtue (especially if it overstresses the golden mean), as a Christian sees forgiveness as "far beyond sin – and virtue."[64] And, as a Lutheran, he rejects "works-righteousness." Yet his concern with such breaches *presupposes* the continuities that shape ethicoreligious existence, the continuities of the virtues, and he also *retains* the concepts of the virtues within these higher conflicts. This is why his language of "upbuilding" and "practice" or "training" [*Indøvelse*] applies appropriately to religion, including Christianity, as well as to ethics.

Part of our task in this chapter and the next is, therefore, to see how Kierkegaard rethinks the virtue tradition in light of the tensions and

---

61 *EO*II 262 (*SV*II 235).
62 Meilaender, *Theory and Practice of Virtue*, 5 (italics added).
63 Rudd, *Kierkegaard and the Limits of the Ethical*.
64 *JP*II 1218 (*Pap.* IX A 482, n.d., 1848).

discontinuities of religious and Christian faith. In the remainder of this chapter we will see how ethical virtue as the *realization* of the good is for Kierkegaard an impossibility, while retaining the concerns of a virtue ethic for personal formation.

The virtue ethic carries with it the seeds of its own *possible* surpassing (*possible*, because these are transitions in existence, not in "a logical system"), yet the language of virtue is refined, not eliminated, in religion. Let us return to Judge William, the representative of the "ethical stage" of existence. Judge William's ethical formation still assumes an essential *self*-reliance. Despite the loftiness of the ethical ideal, and his reflections on the need of "repenting oneself" into the ethical, he still believes that a person has the power to repent and so relate oneself to the ideal and to God. Guilt is an occasion for further struggle and hoped-for victory, but not for ultimate despair over one's ethical task or powers.

Beyond the ethical sphere of life, in the religious stage, however, a person may confront an inability to fulfill the dictates of ethical striving. Ironically, it is Judge William himself who includes in his letters to A the "Ultimatum," a sermon written by the Judge's friend the Jylland pastor, who writes of "the upbuilding that lies in the thought that in relation to God we are always in the wrong."[65] But the Judge himself ironically misses the point that if one is always in the wrong before God then one *cannot* fulfill the ethical law. The ethical person, typified by Judge William, is still self-reliant, and one might even say that the thought that one is always in the wrong before God does not fully penetrate his self-understanding. But the religious person relates to God "not in self-confident action but in repentance."[66] One turns to God not to confirm and encourage the integrity of one's own action, but to be transformed by God.

The "religious stage" for Kierkegaard looms up as a vast, varied, and troubled terrain. Passion burgeons forth in the upbuilding discourses and in a number of his pseudonymous books, ranging from the "Ultimatum" at the end of *Either/Or* II, to *Fear and Trembling* (Abraham as a righteous person who nonetheless relates to God above all, evident especially in the fearful teleological suspension of the ethical) and

---

[65] *EO* II 339–54 (*SV* II 306–18).

[66] Evans, *Kierkegaard's* Fragments *and* Postscript, 140. Johannes Climacus writes in *CUP* that the upbuilding thought that in relation to God we are always in the wrong "is no qualification of sin as fundamental," but is the cry of the finite spirit to God: " 'I cannot understand you, but I will love you.' " (*CUP* 268 [*SV* VII 228]).

Repetition (the possibility of hope and the reintegration of life in the face
of personal disintegration), *Stages on Life's Way* (on resignation, suffering,
and guilt), *The Concept of Anxiety* (which as we have seen outlines the
specifically Christian understanding of anxiety in light of the doctrine
of original sin), and *Concluding Unscientific Postscript*, which delves deeply
into both "immanent" religion (Religiousness A) and the "transcendent" religion (Religiousness B) that is Christian faith. The variety of
these works explores in breadth and depth the multifaceted issues
surrounding the distinctiveness of the religious sphere. Many of those
issues are beyond the scope of this study, but we may turn to the
culmination of the series in *Postscript*, where Johannes Climacus
develops at great length the characteristics of immanent religion, and
especially the religious person's reliance upon God. And this will help
us rethink "virtue."

Religiousness A

This reliance on God is what Climacus terms "Religiousness A" or
"immanent religion."[67] By "immanent," Climacus means that it is not
dependent upon any "transcendent," historical revelation, but is
generated from a universally available experience, the religious person's attempt to stake her eternal happiness on God.[68] It is thus a
"pagan" religiosity, in the best sense, the highest religious expression
available to humanity apart from a transcendent revelation, and "in
Christianity it can be the religiousness of everyone who is not decisively
Christian, whether baptized or not."[69] It is exemplified by someone
like Socrates, who strenuously seeks to live the ideal, yet increasingly
questions himself. While Religiousness A is not specifically Christian, it
continues into the Christian faith; "Religiousness A," Climacus writes,
"must first be present in the individual before there can be any
consideration of becoming aware of the dialectic B [Christianity]."[70]

Religiousness A is a new "pathos" or passion that brings one
beyond ethical self-reliance. It is progressively and dialectically
shaped, Climacus argues in *Postscript*, by three factors: resignation,
suffering, and guilt.[71]

---

67 *CUP* 559 (*SV* vII 488): "Religiousness A ... has only universal human nature as its
    presupposition."
68 Evans, *Kierkegaard's* Fragments *and* Postscript, 45.
69 *CUP* 557 (*SV* vII 486).
70 *CUP* 556 (*SV* vII 486).
71 *CUP* 387–555 (*SV* vII 335–484).

In the "initial expression" of pathos in Religiousness A, a person relates absolutely to the absolute *telos* (an eternal happiness as a relationship with God) and relatively to the relative. The goal here is "the transformation by which the existing person changes everything in his existence in relation to that highest good."[72] This also entails resignation.[73] By "resignation" Climacus means the willingness to sacrifice the relative for the sake of one's relation to the absolute. Climacus sees this resignation as required by the idea that one relates absolutely to the absolute, for if one desires an eternal happiness as one good among others ("a good job, a beautiful wife, health, the rank of a councilor of justice – and in addition an eternal happiness"), one is not thinking of it as either the absolute or as something to which one relates absolutely.[74] It is not to be confused with apathy, neither is it that one gives up all relation to relative goods, but that, while living in the world and firmly enjoying relative goods, one is *willing* to give these up for the sake of the absolute relation to the absolute.[75] This is, obviously, a philosophical rendition of Christ's understanding of the First Commandment, although it is certainly not limited to the Christian faith: "You shall love the Lord your God with all your heart, and with all your soul, and with all your mind." To love God as one good among others is not to love God as *God*. The task then is one of pathos: "the pathos lies not in testifying to an eternal happiness but in transforming one's own existence into a testimony to it."[76]

The second, "essential" expression of immanent religion follows from this: a specifically religious type of *suffering*, which results as one realizes the difficulty in this task of relating absolutely to the absolute *telos* and relatively to relative ends. One realizes the extent to which one has not "died away from immediacy" but is absolutely related to the relative.[77] A person may think that she loves God above all, but then realizes that what is of utter importance is some finite or relative good. The great actor Seydelmann, on the night he was crowned with a wreath, went home and fervently thanked God; Climacus observes:

With the same passion with which he gave thanks, he would have revolted against God if he had been booed. If he had given thanks religiously and

72 *CUP* 389 (*SV* VII 337–38).
73 *CUP* 387–431 (*SV* VII 335–74).
74 *CUP* 391 (*SV* VII 339).
75 *CUP* 393 (*SV* VII 341). On resignation not being apathy or "minimal concern," see *JP* III, p. 916.
76 *CUP* 394 (*SV* VII 342).
77 *CUP* 431ff. (*SV* VII 374ff.).

therefore thanked God, then the Berlin public and the laurel wreath and the applause lasting several minutes would have become equivocal in the dialectical uncertainty of the religious.[78]

This produces an inner and continuing suffering; whether one is fortunate or unfortunate, one realizes how difficult it is to shift absolute allegiance from the host of relative goods to the absolute good that is God.

Here we come to a central element in Kierkegaard's pseudonymous and upbuilding literature, that of "dying away from immediacy" and realizing that before God one is "nothing." This is important not only in *Postscript*, but also in the upbuilding writings, including Kierkegaard's discourses on the earnestness one may gain from contemplating death.[79] These concepts – a commonplace in the Christian ascetic and mystical traditions as well as in other religious traditions – may appear to subvert the active resolution virtues require. It is important to pause a moment over these ideas that loom so large in Kierkegaard's religious thought, and see how they alter yet preserve the virtue-ethic.

The first point to be made is that Climacus develops the notion that in learning to "die away from immediacy," one learns to rely, not on oneself, but on God; hence, one learns also that apart from God one is "nothing."[80] Becoming "nothing" before God, "dying away from immediacy," "self-denial," and "self-annihilation," dramatic as these terms are, as reminiscent as they may be of Schopenhauer's extinction of the will, are not world-denial, since the task is to relate simultaneously to the absolute and to the relative.[81] Rather, in learning how deeply one relates absolutely to the relative, one sees also how radically *dependent* one is as a creature upon God the Creator, that one therefore has no *independent* source of life and power. This is not the same as Friedrich Schleiermacher's "feeling of absolute dependence," since this is not a precognitive intuition, but an adoption of a point of view, a learned dependence arising specifically from striving. The sense of "annihilation" comes from the difficulty of the attempt to relate absolutely to the absolute: "he wants to hold on to the conception absolutely, and this is what annihilates him; he wills to do everything, and while he is willing it, the powerlessness begins."[82]

[78]   *CUP* 446 (*SV* vii 388).
[79]   *TDIO*, "At a Graveside," 69–102 (*SV* v 225–53).
[80]   Evans, *Kierkegaard's* Fragments *and* Postscript, 170.
[81]   *CUP* 422 (*SV* vii 366).
[82]   *CUP* 484 (*SV* vii 421).

This "annihilation" is a realization of one's createdness. A person does not *disappear* into annihilation, for the movement is dialectical, from one's "self-annihilation" to God's "creation"; apart from God one is nothing, with God one becomes something, for God is the Creator who brings forth life out of nothingness. Kierkegaard describes this in an upbuilding discourse from 1844, "To Need God Is a Human Being's Highest Perfection," where he develops further the thought of how a religious person comes to "know God":

Just as knowing oneself in one's own nothingness is the condition for knowing God, so knowing God is the condition for the sanctification of a human being by God's assistance and according to his intention. Wherever God is in truth, there he is always creating. He does not want him to be spiritually soft and to bathe in the contemplation of his glory, but in becoming known by a person he wants to create in him a new human being.[83]

One's nothingness in the God-relationship is not absorption into God, but a recognition of one's radical dependence at every moment upon God; one sees one's "nothingness" before the utter reality of a transcendent, omnipotent, and providentially creating and sustaining God, the God who "*is* [*er til*]."[84] Apart from God, one is nothing; with God, one is indeed something, in radical dependence.

Climacus dwells extensively upon all of these themes in the famous Deer Park passage from *Postscript*. As a humorist, he begins with his witty examination of people who listen on Sunday to the pastor's words: "You must not put your trust in the world, and not in people, and not in yourself, but only in God, because a human being is himself capable of nothing."[85] But the question is what happens on Monday. The religious person who takes an outing to the Deer Park not only cancels the notion that he can do anything by himself; he then must do something else that is equally difficult: "with God to be capable of it."[86] Where God is, "there he is always creating" a "new human being," just as Moses, cited earlier in the above-mentioned discourse, "was capable of nothing at all and the work was the Lord's."[87] The finite creature, incapable of independent action, arrives not at mystical contemplation of God, or mystical dissolution into God, but sees her or his "highest perfection" in being recreated and sanctified by God. Just

---

[83] *EUD* 325 (*SV* v 105).
[84] *EUD* 321 (*SV* v 102).
[85] *CUP* 467 (*SV* vii 406).
[86] *CUP* 486 (*SV* vii 423).
[87] *EUD* 311 (*SV* v 93).

as God enables one to go to the Deer Park or empowers Moses, this "nothing" with God is a "something." In a discourse "Against Cowardliness," Kierkegaard writes that "no one should fear to entrust himself to God with the idea that this relationship would deprive him of his power and make him cowardly. It is just the reverse."[88] One can do nothing without God, but God gives the creature power of action and the task. As Climacus says, "This does not mean that such a religious person becomes inactive ... [but] deepens his outward activity by acknowledging that he is capable of nothing ... even though he still works to the utmost of his ability."[89] As we will see, this is a theme that Kierkegaard pursues throughout his religious authorship; in *Judge for Yourself!*, it culminates in the famous image portraying God as a coachman who drives the (human) horses. The point of all of this is not idle speculation on God and creation, but to make clear the relation of God to the human being, and what the human being is called to be: "In self-knowledge and before God, to come to oneself *as nothing* ... To become nothing before God, *and nevertheless infinitely, unconditionally engaged.*"[90]

This theme of human nothingness before God combined with engagement points also to the dialectic of the active and the passive, the active and receptive virtues, between life as task and as gift. As we have seen, Judge William too describes the ethical stage as gift and task, receiving what one is, and then making that into one's task. Yet he stresses more the active virtues. But in *Postscript*'s depiction of specifically religious activity and receptivity, one turns more from the activity of ethical self-reliance to a religious suffering that is passive. Nonetheless, this too is dialectical; Climacus says that

to act might seem the very opposite of to suffer, and thus it might seem strange to say that the essential expression of existential pathos (which is acting) is suffering. But this is only apparently the case, and again the sign of the religious sphere is manifest here – that the positive is distinguished by the negative ... that to act religiously is marked by suffering.[91]

As Louis Mackey has put it (speaking of Kierkegaard's upbuilding discourses), because God is all in all, acquiring one's life as a task is the same as receiving one's life as gift; herein lies the divine circularity.[92]

---

[88]   *EUD* 352 (*SV*v 129).
[89]   *CUP* 506 (*SV*vii 440).
[90]   *JFY* 106 (*SV*xii 388).
[91]   *CUP* 432 (*SV*vii 376).
[92]   Mackey, *Kierkegaard: A Kind of Poet*, 106.

This receptivity before God is important to Kierkegaard's religious thought, not least because it sets in a new framework the ethical project of virtue-formation that we have been tracing out. More and more there is in the religious sphere the notion that finally, standing before God, a person is like the Young Man in *Repetition*, who at the end of his story confesses to his confidant that his healing is not self-created, but that he has received himself back again.[93]

Receptivity is gratitude. One of his discourses on "Every Good and Perfect Gift Is from Above," on James 1:17–22 (Kierkegaard wrote three discourses on this passage in *Eighteen Upbuilding Discourses*) reflects on the receptive humility and receptivity that allow gratitude and thanksgiving in all circumstances. God's good gifts are not only the good things for which we wish, for

when your wish was denied, did you thank God? And when you yourself had to deny your wish, did you thank God? And when people wronged you and insulted you, did you thank God? We are not saying that their wrong thereby ceased to be wrong ... It is up to you to decide whether it was wrong; but have you taken the wrong and insult to God and by your thanksgiving *received* it from his hand as a good and a perfect gift?[94]

"Every good and every perfect gift is from above if it is received with thankfulness."[95] It is in inwardness and the "heart to be humble," "trustful," and "receptive" that experience is *transformed* by trust in God's sovereign providence. This receptivity is akin to the path of "humble diversion" taken by the visitor to Deer Park. Rather than go to the monastery (which is "too exclusive"), one lives in the finite, truly enjoys an excursion to Deer Park, "because the humblest expression for the relationship with God is to acknowledge one's humanness, and it is human to enjoy oneself."[96]

This discourse shows another crucial element at the heart of the religious stage, that it is finally not anthropocentric, but theocentric. Kierkegaard's language of receptivity and suffering indicates this crucial new element. As Merold Westphal has noted, a problem with using Aristotelian ethics as a paradigm of religious existence is that it so singularly seeks an answer to the question of how one can be happy.[97] We have seen how Kierkegaard rethinks eudaemonistic ethics, recasting

---

93   *R* 220 (*SV*III 253).
94   *EUD* 43 (*SV*III 47) (italics added).
95   *EUD* 48 (*SV*III 51).
96   *CUP* 493 (*SV*VII 428).
97   Westphal, *God, Guilt, and Death*, 133.

it in terms of an equivalency between happiness, duty, and a relationship with God. And this same question of happiness will continue in Climacus' consideration of the specifically Christian sphere, for, as we have noted, Climacus too asks how one can relate to Christianity's promise of an eternal happiness. But the stress on receptivity and the religious pathos of suffering shows that already in the immanent religious sphere there is no simple eudaemonism. An *aesthetic* understanding of happiness is purged away. This is why Johannes Climacus speaks of the religious sphere as showing how "the positive is marked by the negative": like the aesthetic person, a religious person experiences joys and sadness, but she rejoices over her sufferings and sorrows over her guilt. Most centrally, God is not merely an instrumental means for acquiring independent goods, not even solutions to psychological dilemmas or the judge's cultivation of character. For all of Kierkegaard's anthropocentrism, focused on "the solitary individual," "eternal happiness," or "immortality," his thought is finally oriented to God, not to oneself. C. S. Lewis has written,

> I cannot help thinking that any religion which begins with a thirst for immortality is damned, as a religion, from the outset ... For the essence of religion, in my view, is the thirst for an end higher than natural ends; the finite self's desire for, and acquiescence in, and self-rejection in favour of, an object wholly good and wholly good for it.[98]

Kierkegaard's reflections on religious suffering and receptivity seek, like Lewis, to avoid the dangers of narcissistic self-absorption, including the dangers of self-absorption that lurk in the project of cultivating the virtues. Of Christian writers, Kierkegaard is one of the most "theocentric" and even "God-intoxicated."

This does not cancel the project of character formation, nor does it, as one might think, replace "virtue" with "repetition." Kierkegaard's thought on virtue and repetition is too dialectical for that kind of "either/or." "Virtues" as the formation of dispositions like patience, courage, and expectation are hardly eradicated, but are positively required in religious and Christian existence. Virtue is dethroned (not eliminated) as one discovers that finally the project of forming one's character is fraught with difficulties; "the *examined* life is not worth living for man."[99]

Gilbert C. Meilaender describes two ways of speaking of virtue in

[98]   C. S. Lewis, "Religion Without Dogma?," in *God in the Dock: Essays on Theology and Ethics*, ed. Walter Hooper (Grand Rapids, MI: William B. Eerdmans, 1970), 131.

[99]   Meilaender, *Theory and Practice of Virtue*, ch. 5.

the Protestant tradition, especially in Lutheranism, that we can use to illuminate Kierkegaard's thought, showing how virtue is dethroned and yet retained. The first is to speak of virtues *substantively*, as traits of character developed over time; here, life is a journey and progression over time. This fits Judge William's ethical project nicely, but so does the active ethical formation of specifically religious existence. But virtues are also spoken of *relationally*: the virtuous person is the one who is *accepted* by God. We are not simply bundles of deeds and virtues, Meilaender argues, but are made for fellowship with one another and with God. We need to be loved and accepted, not just have our deeds or virtues commended. This is why we need to be *receptive* before God.[100] In Kierkegaard, we come close, then, not to the *cancellation* of the passions of virtue and character, but to the question that Luther put: how is one to stand before God?[101]

Kierkegaard's descriptions of immanent religion actually employ at one and the same time the language of "substantive" and "relational" virtues. The *Eighteen Upbuilding Discourses* parallels Climacus' discussion of immanent religion in *Postscript*. The discourses can be seen as essays in "substantive" ethicoreligious virtues: expectation and faith (in a general, not specifically Christian sense), patience, courage, and perseverance are recurrent themes. In his discourses on patience, he emphasizes how patience is "gained" and also "preserved."[102] He speaks of inwardness in dispositional language, as a "strengthening in the inner being."[103] He dwells upon courage and perseverance as "resolution" in "Against Cowardliness."[104] But the discourses also dwell upon how one's *need* for God constitutes one's highest perfection,[105] how "One Who Prays Aright Struggles in Prayer and Is Victorious – In That God Is Victorious."[106] Kierkegaard *combines* both ways of speaking of virtue, as substantive and relational, in these discourses. Here the dialectic of active and receptive, of substantive and relational virtues is carefully developed. Although describing immanent religion, the language of the discourses is infused with Christian terminology and concerns; they are not *limited* to immanent religion. And, as we will see, in describing the specifically Christian

[100] Meilaender, *Theory and Practice of Virtue*, 119–21.
[101] See Mooney, *Knights of Faith and Resignation*, on receptivity and action, stasis and movement.
[102] *EUD* 159–75 and 181–203 (*SV*IV 54–68 and 75–94).
[103] *EUD* 79–101 (*SV*III 296–315).
[104] *EUD* 347–75 (*SV*v 124–48).
[105] *EUD* 297–326 (*SV*v 81–105).
[106] *EUD* 377–401 (*SV*v 149–68).

passions of faith, hope, and love, Kierkegaard continues this language of substantive and religious virtues.

To recapitulate: we have seen how the immanent religious sphere is marked by two characteristics: resignation and suffering before God. Now we move on to *Postscript*'s third and "decisive" expression of immanent religion, guilt, and repentance, the increased awareness that one is *unable* to relate absolutely to God, that one is therefore *guilty* before God.[107] Already in the second expression, suffering, Climacus writes of spiritual trial (*Anfægtelse*; cf. German *Anfechtung*) as a specifically religious trial; it is not temptation (attraction to what is lower than God), but a person's fright at what is higher, the desire to flee from God's presence.[108] In the third and "decisive" expression of immanent religion, one confronts one's true stance: at once desiring God and fleeing from God. Here a person not only recognizes how far she is from realizing the goal of an eternal happiness or relationship with God (the moment of suffering), but also sees herself as "going backward," as guilty. Guilt, Climacus emphasizes, is a qualitative, not quantitative, concept: a person is not more or less guilty than her neighbor; Climacus says that the religious discourse should not browbeat persons into thinking themselves "more loathsome *than* others," for "a totality-qualification is never produced numerically."[109] The question is not how much or how little one has done in pursuing character, but how one stands before God. We are measured by the standard to which we aspire; the dignity of a person is therefore measured by the standard of relating to God; thus, however painful and a cause for sorrow, guilt is at once a direct index of failure and, ironically, an inverse indication of the glory of human beings as they stand before God. Yet the sorrow and repentance dominate, with a hope of possible help.

But how does Abraham stand in relation to this threefold portrayal of Religiousness A, especially guilt? Representing faith, he stands somewhat beyond Religiousness A. In addition, the source of his dilemma is not Religiousness A's guilt, but the spiritual trial of obedience. In moving beyond ethics, Abraham describes a trajectory to

---

[107] *CUP* 525–55 (*SV* VII 458–84). "Guilt" is not the same as "sin," which is a specifically Christian category, as Climacus makes clear (*CUP* 532 [*SV* VII 464]; *CUP* 583 [*SV* VII 508]). We will return to this in the next chapter.
[108] *CUP* 459 (*SV* VII 399).
[109] *CUP* 530n and 529 (*SV* VII 463n and 462).

faith and trust in God "by virtue of the absurd." Even more than in Religiousness A, the focus is on God; Johannes de Silentio writes, "he who loves God without faith reflects upon himself; he who loves God in faith reflects upon God."[110]

In Abraham the dialectic of active and passive continues, with even greater emphasis on receptivity. In his ordeal Abraham strives in obedience, yet he is receptive, not only in "fear and trembling," but also in receiving his son a second time.[111] Abraham is "great by that power whose strength is powerlessness."[112] In this depiction of faith, eternal happiness as the God-relationship is even more radically redefined as one's helplessness before God.[113]

The crucial category of "repetition" captures too Abraham's dialectic of striving and receiving. As Constantin Constantius says in *Repetition*, repetition (*Gjentagelse*) is literally a "taking again," the movement forward from past, through present, toward the future.[114] Repetition is "something inward," "freedom's own task," in which "Behold all things have become new."[115] But in Abraham repetition is a "transcendent" category; it is "received" as miracle and gift. In Abraham, the receptivity is even starker; the miracle is that he can receive Isaac back.

Abraham's dilemma is obedience, not guilt. But the final pages of *Fear and Trembling* point beyond Abraham to the dilemma not only of guilt, but also of sin.[116] So too, in *Three Discourses on Imagined Occasions*, Kierkegaard returns to the theme that only the pure in heart see and know God, and, as in *Purity of Heart*, he links it to confession, and to the manner of seeing and knowing God. "What it means to seek God" is defined in this way: "without purity no human being can see God and without becoming a sinner no human being can come to know

---

110   *FT* 37 (*SV*III 88).
111   *FT* 9 (*SV*III 61). Compare Mooney, *Knights of Faith and Resignation*, ch. 6, on "getting Isaac back."
112   *FT* 16 (*SV*III 69).
113   Khan, *Salighed as Happiness?*, 85, notes the etymological root of the Danish "*Salighed*" as "*salig*," which means "weak or helpless." See also the connection between *Salighed* and "fear and trembling" as an expression of human impotence in matters of faith.
114   *R* 149 (*SV* III 189). See Nelly Viallaneix, "The Law of 'Gjentagelse,'" in Bertung, ed., *Kierkegaard – Poet of Existence*, 120–31.
115   *CA* 17n-18n (*SV* IV 289n-90n). Thus, Vigilius quotes Constantin Constantius in *Repetition*, "repetition is the interest [*Interesse*] of metaphysics, and also the interest upon which metaphysics comes to grief; repetition is the watchword [*Løsnet*] in every ethical view; repetition is the *conditio sine qua non* [the indispensable condition] for every issue of dogmatics" (*CA* 18n [*SV*IV 290n], quoting *R* 149 [*SV*III 189]).
116   Ronald M. Green, *Kierkegaard and Kant*, ch. 5, sees this as part of the "hidden message" of *Fear and Trembling*, and relates it to Kant's concern with radical evil.

him.">[117] How Kierkegaard will further that discussion, moving from
"guilt" to "sin," from virtue as a human project to virtue as a God-
given gift in faith on the other side of confession and sin, we will
examine in the next chapter.

KIERKEGAARD ON RELIGION: POLEMICAL POINTS

We can now contrast Kierkegaard's understanding of religion to other
alternative proposals current in his day and ours. For Kierkegaard, (1)
"religion" is not primarily a matter of propositional metaphysical belief
(an assumption widely shared in eighteenth-century natural theology
and orthodoxy, as well as by Enlightenment critics of natural theology,
like David Hume); (2) while religious concern arises from ethical
concern, religion is not *dependent* upon morality (as when belief in God
is a postulate of ethical concern "within the limits of reason alone," as
in Kant or classical liberal Protestant theology), but is a separate sphere
of existence, characterized by a particular set of passions before God;
(3) religion is not immediacy or a prelinguistic and precognitive
intuition (as in some readings of Schleiermacher), but is conceptually
defined; (4) nor is the transition to religious belief, in "seeing" and
"referring" to God, arbitrary and irrational.

By contrast, Kierkegaard's understanding of religion as a stage of
existence, focusing on "passion," far from suggesting a foundationalist
(or reductionist) account of religion, indicates rather the complexity of
the religious sphere, a complexity that discourages foundationalist or
reductionist explanations. Entailing beliefs, religion is not simply
assent. Based upon ethical formation, religious existence is not simply
ethics. Aimed at healing the waywardness of moods, religion is not
simply precognitive self-expression or intuition. Using representational
and metaphorical language, religious belief is not for that reason
inferior to abstract thought.

Kierkegaard's extensive descriptions of religious existence argue
against all of these foundationalist or reductionistic accounts. The
result is an analysis, akin to that of Wittgenstein, in which the passions
and beliefs of the religious life are seen not as requiring a foundation,
but as *sui generis* to that form of life. Religious existence is a pilgrimage, a *way of life* for *homo viator*, characterized by particular passions
and cares, that does not stand in need of foundational theoretical

---

[117]   *TDIO* 15 (*SV* v 182).

justification. To understand religious existence, one must attend carefully to the *particular* characteristics of that way of life, the learned disciplines of self-examination, repentance, and confession. The justification of religious existence rests not upon some other activity or interest, but upon itself.

A final word about narrative and its role in religion is called for at this point. A substantive view of virtue often sees life as a journey and progression over time, while a relational view of virtue tends to speak of the self more "vertically" in relation to God. But Kierkegaard's relational view of virtue also has a narrative shape: the narrative may be less "horizontal" and more "vertical," but it is the narratives of God – such as God's dealings with Abraham and Job – that give the framework for religious self-reflection.[118] So, too, Kierkegaard gives a narrative form to describing the crises on the borders of religion, whether in the letters of the young man to Constantin Constantius in *Repetition* or the diary of the nameless Quidam of the "Story of Suffering" in *Stages on Life's Way*. Even if the "growth" metaphor of virtue is altered, the narrative shape is not given up. It is the tales of standing before God – Abraham's obedient answer to the divine call; Job's suffering and complaint in the face of catastrophe – that now define the divine context: that it is joyful but also fearful to stand before the living God. In these religious stories the narrative pattern is the same: the past is called up in recollection and sifted and redefined; the suffering person looks for the stories and paradigms that will make sense of experience; and a future is looked for in which one can breathe. The narrative shaping of human life in religious existence is also the concern of the next chapter.

[118] Mark Lloyd Taylor, "Ordeal and Repetition in Kierkegaard's Treatment of Abraham and Job," in Connell and Evans, *Foundations of Kierkegaard's Vision of Community*, 33–53.

CHAPTER 4

Becoming Christian I: responding to Christ in faith

> Sins' forgiveness belongs to the pure God-relationship, far beyond sin – and virtue.   *JP* II 1218 (*Pap.* IX A 482, n.d., 1848).
>
> Faith . . . is a battle of character.
>   *JP* II 1129 (*Pap.* X¹ A 367, n.d., 1849).

Thus far we have examined Kierkegaard's psychological, moral, and religious analyses of human existence: his diagnostic critiques of misplaced objectivity, his anthropological reflection relating psychology and theology, and his carefully textured portrayals of how the emotions, passions, and virtues are shaped in ethicoreligious existence. And we have seen too his rethinking of the "virtue tradition" in the context of Religiousness A. All of this is prologue, however, to his central interest, depicting the logic and passions of Christian faith.

In chapters 4–6, we turn to "becoming and being a Christian." Wittgenstein suggested that in looking at religious images and stories we need to see how they are used. This study is an exercise in the use of the portrayal of Christ as Redeemer and Pattern, and Kierkegaard's concern to see Christian existence as centrally *response* to Christ. We will explore this in terms of his investigations of upbuilding in the Christian passions or virtues of faith, hope, and love.

Kierkegaard wrote that "*the category* for my undertaking: is *to make men aware* of the essentially Christian."[1] Possessing less a sense and taste for the infinite than a sense and taste for the particular, his interest is in the specific shape and dynamics of Christian faith.[2] Just as his analyses of religious existence are meant to prevent misunderstandings concerning religion, he strives in the words of one commentator to distinguish Christianity's categories from those of philosophy, mythology, poetry,

---

[1]   *JP* VI 6533 (*Pap.* X² A 196, n.d., 1849).
[2]   Hans W. Frei, *Theology and Narrative: Selected Essays*, ed. George Hunsinger and William C. Placher (New York: Oxford University Press, 1993), 27.

Christianity's categories from those of philosophy, mythology, poetry, history, and morals.[3] As Johannes Climacus puts it in *Concluding Unscientific Postscript*, Religiousness A, with its descriptions of resignation, suffering, and guilt, is assumed before the concerns of Religiousness B, specifically Christian faith, come alive for a person.[4] Yet Christian passion is "dialectically" defined further, both in terms of "the logic of belief" and "the logic of coming to belief."

The range of issues in connection with Kierkegaard's understanding of faith are extraordinarily broad and many are beyond the scope of this chapter. I will focus rather on the interrelation between the "what" and the "how" of Christian faith, first by looking at some of Kierkegaard's strategies for describing the relations between Christ and the believer, including Christ as Redeemer and Pattern, then turning to offense and faith as possible responses to Christ, and finally reflecting on Kierkegaard's understanding of Christ and salvation. Throughout I will draw upon a range of Kierkegaard's literature, from the Climacean and also later writings.

THE "WHAT" AND THE "HOW"

I want to begin by examining how Johannes Climacus pursues three strategies to elucidate Christian faith, all of which speak of Christian faith as a "how" of subjectivity and also as a relation to "what," the "teacher." In the first two we will examine, the starting-point is the passional qualifications of the subject; in the third, however, the focus is more on the passion of "the god." Taken together, all three seek to elucidate the notion that "Christianity is not a doctrine" and that in Christian faith "the how and the what are a mutual fit."

First, at the end of *Postscript* Climacus says that he has attempted to describe Christian faith not from the standpoint of "what" it is, which he grants, but from the standpoint of subjectivity alone, its particular "how" or passion. It is not precise enough to say even that faith is "appropriating" the doctrine, that one will "live and die for it." The Christian pathos "cannot be confused with any other pathos," but is distinct.[5] The result is his well-known definition of Christian faith as "an objective uncertainty with the repulsion of the absurd, held fast in the passion of inwardness, which is the relation of inwardness

---

3   Nielsen, *Where the Passion Is*, 203.
4   *CUP* 555–86 (*SV* vii 484–511).
5   *CUP* 608–09 (*SV* vii 530–31).

intensified to its highest. This formula fits only the one who has faith, no one else, not even a lover, or an enthusiast, or a thinker."[6]

Nonetheless, Climacus' very definition points to a relation and an object of faith; this definition fits "solely and only the one who has faith, *who relates himself to the absolute paradox.*"[7] Climacus' attempt to describe the particular "how" requires him to speak of the content or object of that unique relation: the absolute paradox. The particular distinctiveness of Christian faith is therefore twofold: it has a distinctive "how" (faith) *and* a distinctive "what" (Christ) as the object of faith.

Second, in *Fragments,* Climacus approaches this task of contrasting immanent religion and Christianity humorously and indirectly by postulating Socrates and a nameless "teacher," and posing a seemingly non-threatening question, "Can the truth be learned?" or "Can virtue can be taught." Here too the relation of the "how" to the "what" is central. Socrates' passion is recollection and eliciting the truth within the learner. The other unnamed teacher, however, does not see the learner as "in the truth," but as being in untruth. Climacus marshals the contrasts between the situation established in Socratic faith and by this unnamed teacher. (1) For Socratic faith, the *preceding state* was *ignorance* that one possessed the truth within; for this other faith ("if the moment is to have decisive significance"), the preceding state is that one is "outside the truth (not coming toward it like a proselyte, but going away from it) or as untruth."[8] And, since the responsibility for being in untruth lies with oneself, this "untruth" is redescribed as "sin," in which one chose to become "unfree" and "bound."[9] Sin is not simply "ignorance" or even "guilt," but is rebellion, slavery, and death. (2) For Socratic faith, the *teacher* is only an occasion, since one already possesses the "condition" for knowing the truth within. Like the slaveboy in Plato's *Meno,* the task is simply to elicit what is already known. For this other faith ("if the moment is to have decisive significance") the teacher must give the learner the condition for understanding the truth, must transform the learner, and be the one on whom the pupil continually depends – such a teacher we might call "savior," "deliverer," and "reconciler."[10] (3) For Socratic faith, the follower moves from ignorance to self-knowledge, but there is essential

6   *CUP* 611 (*SV* VII 532).
7   *CUP* 611 (*SV* VII 532) (italics added).
8   *PF* 13 (*SV* IV 183–84).
9   *PF* 15 (*SV* IV 185).
10 *PF* 17 (*SV* IV 187).

continuity within the self in the sense that one develops one's own inner subjectivity in "recollection." For this other faith, the condition is not found "within," but must be given, and only thus does one become a "new person," undergoing a change Climacus suggests we call "conversion," repenting her or his former state, moving to "rebirth."[11]

Third, in chapter 2 of *Fragments*, Climacus shifts to another strategy of exploration, from a "thought-project" about two teachers to a "poetical venture," focusing even more on the "what." Yet this "what" is described lyrically, in "the god's poem," and within this poem is the analogy of the king and the maiden, intended to suggest the pathos of divine love found in this "teacher and savior."[12] The king's dilemma is that of unhappy love: how can he win the maiden without either deceiving her by elevating her to his station (she is not royal) or overwhelming her by his splendor (in which he is glorified, but she not)? Appearance in an incognito resolves his dilemma. Without deceiving or falsely elevating the maiden, the king finds a way for his love to be returned – as an equal.

The analogy is meant to suggest the pathos of "the god." But the analogy fails at one important point, Climacus adds; not, as one might suspect, because the analogy stretches the metaphor of the incognito too far, but because the analogy cannot present the reality of the god's incognito strongly enough. In the story, the king only *appears* to be a servant; the incognito is not his real being. By contrast, the incognito of the god is no mere appearance: "this form of a servant is not something put on like the king's plebeian cloak, which just by flapping open would betray the king ... but it is his [the god's] true form."[13] So strong is the stress on the *divine* passion in Climacus' parable that he emphasizes how "the form of the servant was not something put on," and so "the god must suffer all things, endure all things, be tried in all things ... absolutely the equal of the lowliest of human beings." "His whole life is a story of suffering, and it is love that suffers."[14] The analogy fails, and yet its lyricism points the way to an "apprehension of the truth," which is to be found not in poetic contemplation, but in a new self-evaluation and loving response to this suffering divine love that seeks communion without compulsion.

---

[11]   *PF* 18–19 (*SV* IV 188–89).
[12]   *PF* 26–32 (*SV* IV 195–200). Paul Müller, "The God's Poem – The God's History," in Bertung, ed., *Kierkegaard – Poet of Existence*, 83–88.
[13]   *PF* 31–32 (*SV* IV 199–200).
[14]   *PF* 32–33 (*SV* IV 200–01)

Anti-Climacus writes, "The qualitative distinction between paganism and Christianity is not, as a superficial consideration assumes, the
doctrine of the Atonement. No, the beginning must start far deeper,
with sin, with the doctrine of sin – as Christianity in fact does."[15]
Actually, the logic of both Climacus' and Anti-Climacus' position is
that "the god" in time establishes at once a dual situation: one is utterly
unlike God, lacking the truth within, a sinner, and also (as is clear in the
king and maiden analogy) the God passionately desires to *abolish* that
difference, not in divinizing the sinner, but in love and salvation. The
ground of *both* sin and the offer of atonement is the Incarnation as the
expression of God's love. In terms of God's intent, the desire for
atonement takes priority; realizing that one is a sinner then becomes a
possibility on the way to accepting that offered atonement. The teacher
who comes in love with the intent of atonement is the occasion,
showing both sin and the way of salvation.

In these three approaches, we can already say something about the
"what" of Christian faith. The "how" of subjectivity does not create its
object, for faith is a *response* to that object. This means at least three
things: first, while Christianity *is* not a doctrine, Christianity *has*
doctrines.[16] There is a "what," a conceptual content, that distinguishes
Christian faith: it "makes conditions in such a way that the conditions
are not the dialectical concentrations of inward deepening but a
definite something that qualifies the eternal happiness more specifically..."[17] Yet, second, the "what" is a human being, "the actuality of
another person," not a teaching.[18] Unlike Religiousness A, which sees
the reality of another person as irrelevant to anyone's project of inward
deepening aimed at an eternal happiness, in this faith one is called to
stake eternal happiness on another human being who lived at a
particular time. But, third, this object is not simply another person, but
God incarnate, the "wonder" and the "absolute paradox." The
"what" is not only "what Christianity's doctrine is," neither is it Christ
as simply a human being, but the "absolute paradox" of Christ as the
revelation and incarnation of God in time and history who seeks
sinners.[19] Revelation points to the transcendent source of this
"wonder," that the "poem of the god" did not arise from the human

---

[15]   *SUD* 89 (*SV* xi 201).
[16]   *CUP* 379 (*SV* vii 328).
[17]   *CUP* 556 (*SV* vii 485).
[18]   *CUP* 580 (*SV* vii 506).
[19]   *CUP* 611 (*SV* vii 532).

heart or earthly poets; "perhaps it is not a poem at all," for to whom would it occur "that the god poetized himself in the likeness of a human being, for if the god gave no indication, how could it occur to a man that the blessed god could need him?"[20] Revelation shows the god's poeticizing, which is not in contemplation alone, but in history. It at once transcends human poeticizing, calling into question one's natural "knowledge of God," and yet expands the boundaries of the imaginable as it breaks into the world of actuality. "When an oak nut is planted in a clay pot, the pot breaks; when new wine is poured into old leather bottles, they burst."[21] What happens then to the learner? Ironically, as the *god's* poeticizing, when the poetic is broken, new imaginative engagement is required, for the invitation is to see the god and the teacher in a new way, not in "direct recognizability," for the god is truly incognito, but seen *in* and *as* the suffering teacher who also calls to one in a new way.

CHRIST AS REDEEMER AND PATTERN

The god's poem seeks equality with the hearer; so too the story of the god's passion does not compel response, but invites it. The story is not ended for the reader until response is made. Before treating the possible responses to this "what," the responses of offense and faith, it is important to mention another aspect of Kierkegaard's thought on Christ, that he is both "Redeemer" and "Pattern." Climacus is essentially concerned with Christ as Redeemer or atoner. But in *Practice in Christianity* Anti-Climacus extends the image to Christ as Pattern (*Forbilledet*). Both titles are necessary in order to understand clearly the two possible responses of "offense" or "faith" to which we will turn in the next sections, and throughout the next chapters. We will postpone looking at Christ as Redeemer in detail until later in this chapter, and make a few preliminary comments focusing on Christ as Pattern.

Kierkegaard's thought on Christ as Pattern or prototype as well as Redeemer is developed most fully in his later works, such as *Practice in Christianity, For Self-Examination*, in the posthumously published *Judge for Yourself!*, as well as in his journals. The relation of Christ as Redeemer and Pattern is a dialectical one; both elements are necessary. Without atonement, the Pattern is simply an external demand or "law," leading either to "works righteousness" or despair. Without the Pattern or

---

20 *PF* 35–36 (*SV* IV 203).
21 *PF* 34 (*SV* IV 202).

prototype, Christian existence is "free from works," or else is indistinguishable from worldly life.[22]

The function of the prototype is therefore twofold for a person who believes or is offended (one can be offended at various stages). First, the prototype convicts one of sin. If one is not offended, and seeks to imitate the prototype, one strives to be what he or she admires.[23] But one soon discovers that she or he is not like him at all, "not even in what you call your best moment; for in such a moment you are not in the corresponding tension of actuality but are spectating."[24] Second, therefore, after the prototype has "crushed" one, then one will "effectively learn to flee to faith in grace."[25] In relying upon Christ as atoner, one is *not* engaged in imitation: "For Christ's death is not a task for imitation [*Efterfølgelse*] but is the atonement." Christ is not only "a historical, actual person" whom one imitates, but "Christ is also the dogmatical. Here is the distinction. His death is indeed the atonement." "It is not simply a matter of Christ's being the prototype and that I simply ought to will to resemble him. In the first place I need His help in order to be able to resemble Him, and, secondly, insofar as he is the Savior and Reconciler of the race, I cannot in fact resemble him."[26]

Third, Christ as prototype re-enters as a model for discipleship. In contrast to Luther, who stressed Christ as the atoner against "a too zealous and too enthusiastic desire to make Christ only the prototype," Kierkegaard's emphasis on the prototype is meant to redress the balance. Christ helps the believer, but to an end: the end of imitation. The atonement is not an end in itself, but is meant to issue in a life. In this sense, the "subjective" moment takes precedence as the goal of the objective atonement. But it would be a mistake to see this as a completed dialectic; Christian existence is a continuing three-stage cycle of "imitation – reliance on Christ as atoner – imitation." As one is convicted of sin, one continually has recourse again to the atonement, which leads to renewed attempts at imitation within "actuality."

OFFENSE AND THE PARADOX

Despite the lyricism of the king–maiden story in *Philosophical Fragments*, not all will find such a picture attractive, anymore than all will find the

22 FSE 16–17 (SVxii 307–08).
23 PC 241 (SVxii 220).
24 JP1 692 (Pap. ix A 153, n.d., 1848).
25 Ibid.
26 JP1 693 (Pap. x¹ A 132, n.d., 1849).

story of "teacher B" attractive. The analogy may fail not only because it is imperfect, but because what may be attractive meets with *resistance*. By "offense," Climacus means something quite specific: that a person's "understanding" will have an unhappy encounter with the paradox and the person.[27] In *Practice in Christianity*, Anti-Climacus alludes to Bertel Thorvaldsen's statue of Christ in Copenhagen's cathedral, which stands as an image of inviting: "Come here, all you who labor and are burdened, and I will give you rest" (Matthew 11:28). But the irony is that it is as if this statue, or the gospel, were saying "*Procul o procul este profani* ["Away, away, O unhallowed ones"].[28] And the response is prompted by Christ as "Pattern" in the situation of modern Copenhagen.

That the "offense" at the "sign of contradiction" of the Incarnation is not the reasonable person's puzzlement about a *formal contradiction* in uniting the divine and the human, or eternity and time, is crucial to understanding Kierkegaard's overall understanding of offense. Much ink has been spilled on this matter. A number of commentators have argued that Climacus is an irrationalist because the absolute paradox presented to the understanding is the logical offense of a formal contradiction involved in saying that a person is at once "God" and "a human being."[29] Most recently, C. Stephen Evans has argued extensively, and in my view persuasively, that the Incarnation is not a formal contradiction of the union of the eternal and the temporal, an unchanging eternal God opposed to a human being, but is rather an apparent contradiction.[30] He supports this with arguments both from Climacus' overall strategy and with particular textual support. I will not rehearse those arguments, which focus on the Climacus writings, but rather cite a passage from Anti-Climacus. It quite clearly distinguishes between Christ as the "sign of contradiction" and "nonsense." He says that

A sign of contradiction ... is a sign that contains a contradiction in its composition. To justify the name of "sign," there must be something by which it draws attention to itself or to the contradiction. *But the contradictory parts must not annul each other in such a way that the sign comes to mean nothing or in such a way that it becomes the opposite of a sign, an unconditional concealment.*[31]

27　*PF* 49 (*SV* iv 215).

28　*PC* 5 (*SV* xii xiii). This is the Sybil's cry when Aeneas entered the underworld in Virgil's *Aeneid*, vi, 258. See *PC*, notes, 381.

29　So argue Alastair Hannay, *Kierkegaard*; Louis Pojman, *The Logic of Subjectivity: Kierkegaard's Philosophy of Religion* (University of Alabama Press, 1984).

30　Evans, *Passionate Reason*, 96ff.

31　*PC* 125 (*SV* xii 117) (italics added).

The sign of contradiction does not dissolve into nonsense: "the contradiction is between being God and being an individual human being."[32]
Note that Anti-Climacus is not saying that placing the *concepts* of God
and humanity together is a contradiction, for "what contradiction, if
any, could there be at all in the speculative unity of God and man?"[33]

The Hegelian background is helpful to understanding Anti-
Climacus' point: speculative thought finds no offense in the Incarnation
because it interprets the Incarnation as a "speculative unity of God and
man." The actual historical "scandal of particularity" is thereby lost;
the scandal is that any *particular* individual is God incarnate, to say
nothing of the scandal of the "how" of *this* life. But note that the
"contradictory parts must not annul each other in such a way that the
sign comes to mean nothing." In a formal contradiction, such annulment occurs, but Anti-Climacus denies that such an annulment occurs
in seeing a human being as God. The contradiction is not a formal
contradiction. Neither is the contradiction "an unconditional concealment," for, as we have seen, while Christ's divinity is in no way directly
recognizable, Christ puts the issue of his identity in the form of a
question. In this he is "the sign of contradiction."

The contradiction is then, I agree with Evans, apparent not formal.
The sign "signifies" rather than canceling itself, and yet the situation
the sign creates is a contradiction not between the elements of the
portrayal (God and human), but between the reader of the gospel (or
the viewer of Thorvaldsen's statue) and the figure presented. More
specifically, "the sign of contradiction" calls one, but the call is
spurned. The invitation is genuine and not a rejection, but rejection
occurs. Why is this? The contradiction is *passional*; it is an affront to
common conceptions of God, and also an affront against the assumption that one has the truth "within." This is particularly clear in *Practice
in Christianity*, where "the sign of contradiction" is that God is this
individual human being. First, it is deeply offensive if someone "loftily"
"speaks or acts as if he were God."[34] The offense is at the claim (verbal
or acted out) that one has the authority of God.[35] There may also be

---

32   *PC* 125 (*SV* XII 118).
33   *PC* 125 (*SV* XII 117–18).
34   *PC* 94 (*SV* XII 90).
35   I say "verbal or acted out" because Anti-Climacus and Kierkegaard both stress Christ's self-
      consciousness of divinity; Anti-Climacus also says Christ "speaks or acts as if he were God"
      (*PC* 94 [*SV* XII 90]). Kierkegaard is committed to the importance of Christ's self-consciousness
      of divinity. This functions not, however, as in Schleiermacher, as a "God-consciousness"
      communicable to believers, but in more traditional orthodox terms as Christ's self-awareness

offense at the "lowliness" of this person who speaks or acts as if he were God.[36] The person who is "lowly, poor, suffering, and finally power-less" offends human ideas of divine glory and grandeur.[37]

Second, the offense arises not only at the character of the God-man, but at the re-evaluation of oneself that this calls forth. The "absurd" suggestion is that one must see oneself not only as guilty (as in Religiousness A), but also as a sinner, living in "untruth," in need of a savior.[38]

In *The Sickness Unto Death*, Anti-Climacus employs psychology to amplify the dogmatic concept of sin in this way: sin – despair – offense. "Sin is: before God in despair not to will to be oneself, or before God in despair to will to be oneself."[39] Anti-Climacus adds that sin and despair are linked with offense, and that for a very interesting reason. The heart of "offense" is not that Christianity is gloomy and rigorous, but rather because it is so high; it envisions a goal that a person finds too lofty, too good to be true. Employing a poetic analogy similar to the king and the maiden used by Climacus, it is as if an emperor desired a day laborer for a son-in-law, and the day laborer said, "Such a thing is too high for me, I cannot grasp it; to be perfectly blunt, to me it is a piece of folly."[40] Christianity is offensive because it teaches that "every single individual human being ... this individual human being exists *before God* ... this person is invited to live on the most intimate terms with God."[41] The language of envy and self-assertion leads Anti-Climacus to the Augustinian understanding of sin: that a person is not simply ignorant of the good (Socratically, sin is ignorance), but that one is unwilling to understand himself as a sinner: "sin has its roots in willing, not in knowing."[42]

The "absolute paradox" is not an *intellectual* contradiction concerning the Incarnation; it is a passional collision, wherein Christ is "the sign of the possibility of offense." To speak of "doubt" as if the problem were simply one of intellectual clarification does not explain the recoil and vigor of the flight and attack in reaction to the God-man. This is why

of his identity. Whether Kierkegaard's position *requires* a "messianic" or "divine *consciousness*" is another matter.
[36] *PC* 102 (*SV* xii 98).
[37] *Ibid.*
[38] Evans, *Passionate Reason*, 105–07. There is another offense that we will turn to later in this study: the offense caused by Christ's opposition to the established order.
[39] *SUD* 81 (*SV* xi 193).
[40] *SUD* 84–85 (*SV* xi 195–96).
[41] *SUD* 85 (*SV* xi 197).
[42] *SUD* 95 (*SV* xi 206).

Anti-Climacus says that in modern philosophy "there is a confused discussion of doubt where the discussion should have been about despair," that "'despair' ... promptly points in the right direction by placing the relation under the rubric of personality ... so also, the practice has been to use the category 'doubt' where the discussion ought to be about 'offense.'"[43]

In *Practice in Christianity* Anti-Climacus says that Christ as the sign of contradiction "discloses the thoughts of hearts" (1 Corinthians 4:5). Christ "is anything but an assistant professor who teaches directly to parroters or dictates paragraphs for shorthand writers – he does exactly the very opposite, he discloses the thoughts of hearts."[44] Again we find the image of the mirror, but now instead of looking at oneself, one looks at Christ in this mirror, and

one comes to see oneself, or he who is the sign of contradiction looks straight into one's heart while one is staring into the contradiction ... As he is forming a judgment, what dwells within him must be disclosed ... The contradiction confronts him with a choice, and as he is choosing, together with what he chooses, he himself is disclosed.[45]

The sign of contradiction is a mirror who "discloses the thoughts of the heart"; here too the images of mirroring and transparency join together. Christ pushes the question of whether one will or will not respond in faith, whether one will stake one's eternal happiness not on oneself, but on this person.

Climacus in *Philosophical Fragments* speaks similarly of "offense" as an "acoustical illusion"; the absolute paradox is not hurt by being called that, and offense is merely parroting or repeating what the absolute paradox says of itself.[46] The paradox itself (Christ) asserts the possibility of offense. Offense (or faith) are "passive," that is, are *responses* to the object that proclaims itself to be a paradox.

Yet the tone in Anti-Climacus is quite different, conflating doubt with offense, sin, and despair. Now this is certainly apologetically unhelpful when dealing with honestly held doubts about Christian faith or any faith.[47] The difference in tone in the two pseudonyms stems from the difference of stance. Anti-Climacus, we need to remember, speaks from a Christian perspective, unlike Climacus the humorist. Yet

43   *PC* 81n (*SV* XII 78).
44   *PC* 126 (*SV* XII 118).
45   *PC* 126–27 (*SV* XII 118–19).
46   *PF* 52 (*SV* IV 218).
47   Evans, *Passionate Reason*, 85.

Anti-Climacus and Climacus both highlight that offense *just as much as faith* proceeds from an interest, rather than from neutral objectivity.[48] The "reason" may pretend to be neutral, objective, detached, in contrast to faith's attraction to the teacher. But how people react to a religious faith or belief or practice is often passional rather than neutral; one responds from deep antipathy, even disgust, or from an immediate sympathy. The strength of Climacus' treatment is that he does not skirt these factors. Particularly when confronting deeply held beliefs concerning one's *identity*, to hear that one is in "untruth" may be profoundly offensive. "The sign of contradiction" serves as a mirror that "discloses the thoughts of hearts."[49]

FAITH AS A "HAPPY PASSION"

Another response besides offense is possible to the God–man and the redefining of oneself as a sinner. Although all who encounter this sign of contradiction must go through the *possibility* of offense, not all are offended, for some may come to *faith*. Anti-Climacus speaks of faith in *The Sickness Unto Death* as follows: "*The opposite of sin is faith*, as it says in Romans 14:23 ... And this is one of the most decisive definitions for all Christianity – that the opposite of sin is not virtue but faith."[50] "Faith is: that the self in being itself and in willing to be itself rests transparently in God."[51] Climacus captures this "being" and "willing" and "resting" and "transparency" in another definition of faith, that it is a "happy passion."[52]

The heart of faith as a "happy passion" is "contemporaneity." A believer, of whatever generation, is contemporary with Christ in the relation of faith. *Philosophical Fragments* stresses that this contemporaneity negates the difference between believers in the past and present; no one has an advantage by being closer historically to this teacher, since He cannot be "known" historically, although he was a particular person living at a particular time and place in history.

"Contemporaneity" takes on greater depth and force in Kierkegaard's later writings. In *Practice in Christianity* faith becomes equivalent with "contemporaneity," but also with "discipleship." In looking at faith as

---

[48] I am indebted here to Evans' approach in *Passionate Reason*, 117–18. He identifies well the "interestedness" of reason, in contrast to the myth of reason's "objective neutrality."

[49] *PC* 126–27 (*SV* XII 118–19).

[50] *SUD* 82 (*SV* XI 194).

[51] *Ibid.*

[52] *PF* 59 (*SV* IV 224).

contemporaneity, we will use both the Climacean and later writings. Faith is a response both to Christ as Redeemer (Climacus' emphasis) and to Christ as Pattern (the main concern of Anti-Climacus and other later non-pseudonymous works).

The centrality of "contemporaneity" to faith is especially clear in the "Invocation" that opens the first series of discourses in *Practice in Christianity*. Anti-Climacus says that Christ's

presence never becomes a thing of the past ... As long as there is a believer, this person, in order to have become that, must have been and as a believer must be just as contemporary with Christ's presence as his contemporaries were. *This contemporaneity is the condition of faith, and, more sharply defined, it is faith* ... Lord Jesus Christ, would that we, too, might become contemporary with you in this way, might see you in your true form and in the surroundings of actuality as you walked here on earth ... Would that we might see you as you are and were and will be until your second coming in glory, as the sign of offense and the object of faith, the lowly man, yet the Savior and Redeemer of the human race.[53]

This passage points to key elements of contemporaneity to Christ as the response in faith. Several comments on faith as contemporaneity are called for; taken together these provide a series of "dialectical" or "grammatical" remarks outlining the rules of usage for the language of Christian faith:

(1) Christ as God incarnate is *present* to the believer in faith. This presence or communion follows from the divinity, in contrast to the presence of a "merely historical person." "Believe that Christ is God – then call upon him, pray to him, and the rest comes by itself. When the fact that he is present [*er til*] is more intimately and inwardly certain than all historical information – then you will come out all right with the details of His historical existence ... [Christ is] an eternally present one [*en evig Nærværende*] for he is true God."[54] Yet there is always a reserve in this, with little evidence of Pietism's erotic-mystical "friendship" and "love" for the Savior. "To call Christ a friend in heaven" is "a sentimentality which has made a thorough mess of Christianity."[55]

(2) Especially in Kierkegaard's later writings, Christ is understood not in terms simply of a bare historical "that" of "the moment" of Incarnation, an icon of eternity invading time, but increasingly in a *narrative framework*. Climacus says that it would be "more than enough"

53   *PC* 9–10 (*SV* xii 1–2) (italics added).
54   *JP* i 318 (*Pap.* viii¹ a 565, n.d., 1848).
55   *JP* ii 1285 (*Pap.* x³ a 200, n.d., 1850). Compare Dewey, *The New Obedience*, 128.

to know that "the god appeared in the humble form of a servant, lived and taught among us, and then died," but Climacus, I think, is making a logical point about the lack of need for extensive historical information about the teacher, not dismissing the narrative of "the god."[56] And it should be noted that even Climacus' bare minimum is a condensed narrative, including incarnation, life, ministry, and crucifixion.[57] Anti-Climacus more explicitly gives narrative content to Christ's life. Although one cannot learn Christ's identity from "profane history," the meaning and identity of Christ's life are shown in his story as "sacred history," "which must not be confused with world history and the history of the race."[58] He discusses that sacred history in terms of various periods of Christ's life that show increasingly a history of love, mixed with continuing misunderstanding, suffering, and abasement.[59] Furthermore, with Christ's ascension to glory, as we see in the invocation above, the church waits for his second coming; the church's whole existence on earth is a "parenthesis or something parenthetical in Christ's life," a time not of glory (for the church does not directly behold his glory), but of discipleship and testing.[60]

Operating here is a Christological pattern of thought in which the narrative of Christ, his particular life, gives the context for encountering him. Although Religiousness A provides the prelude for encountering Christ, the context of the encounter is given by who he is and what he did and suffered. The meaning of his life – as God incarnate – provides rather the only adequate context for encounter and response. Faith is made possible by him, not he by faith.

(3) *Faith relies on the forgiveness of sins.* As we have seen, the force of the authorship points to the increasing sensitivity of the moral conscience, the increase in guilt, and the final realization of oneself as a sinner. In classic Lutheran fashion, the life of faith follows the sequence of "law and gospel." In faith, relating to Christ as atoner, one finds forgiveness of sins, a dialectical realization that one is "totally sinner and totally justified."

Here the "active virtues" are suspended in relation to the receptivity of faith. It is in this sense that the forgiveness of sins is not a "virtue."

---

[56] *PF* 104 (*SV* IV 266).

[57] Climacus does not discuss the resurrection, but this does not mean it is unimportant in Kierkegaard's thought. We will turn to this in chapter 5.

[58] *PC* 221 (*SV* XII 203).

[59] *PC* 40–56 (*SV* XII 38–53).

[60] *PC* 202 (*SV* XII 186).

"The Christian's piety is the forgiveness of sins, that sins' forgiveness belongs to the pure God-relationship, far beyond sin – and virtue."[61]

This consciousness of sin is often portrayed as sheer terror, guilt, and anxiety before God. As suggested above, however, the basis for the consciousness of sin is "the god's" love seeking equality with the believer. We can add now that, for Kierkegaard, the believer's consciousness of sin is logically connected to one's own love for God. In a journal entry from 1848, Kierkegaard writes of the close inter-connection between the consciousness of sin and the passion of love – both the divine love and the human love for God. He begins by saying that no one "can by himself come to the idea that God loves him, in like manner no human being can come to know how great a sinner he is." This must be revealed "as the Augsburg Confession teaches":

> when a person does not comprehend what a great sinner he is, he cannot love God; and when he does not love God (through the proclamation to him of how much God loves him), he cannot comprehend how great a sinner he is. The inwardness of the consciousness of sin is the very passion of love. Truly the law makes one a sinner – but love makes one a far greater sinner. It is true that the person who fears God and trembles feels himself to be a sinner, but the person who in truth loves feels himself to be an even greater sinner.[62]

In his later thought, the forgiveness of sins as God forgetting of sins looms large. In contrast to resignation, which can endure the punishment for sins still assured that God is love, belief in the forgiveness of sins "means to believe that in time God has forgotten the sin, that it is really true that God forgets."[63] God's "forgetting" is an "uncreating": "It is the Deity's joy to forgive sins; just as God is almighty in creating out of nothing, so he is almighty in – uncreating something, for to forget, almightily to forget, is indeed to uncreate something."[64] Kierkegaard speaks of the forgiveness of sins as "a paradox, the absurd."[65] It addresses what Luther called the "terrified conscience": "The eternal consolation in the doctrine of the forgiveness of sins is this: You shall believe it. For when the anxious conscience begins with heavy thoughts, and it is as if they could never in all eternity be forgotten, then comes this: You shall forget. You *shall* stop thinking of your sin."[66]

[61] *JP* II 1218 (*Pap.* IX A 482, n.d., 1848).
[62] *JP* II 1216 (*Pap.* VIII¹ A 675, n.d., 1848).
[63] *JP* II 1123 (*Pap.* VIII¹ A 649, n.d., May 11, 1848).
[64] *JP* II 1224 (*Pap.* XI² A 3, n.d., 1854).
[65] *JP* II 1215 (*Pap.* VIII¹ A 663, n.d., 1848).
[66] *JP* II 1217 (*Pap.* IX A 177, n.d., 1848).

(4) *"Faith is not an act of will."*[67] The "condition" for faith is given by "the god" in the moment, in contrast to Socratic recollection. Climacus therefore sees faith as based upon grace, not upon an independent will. Faith is never "merit" for Climacus or Kierkegaard.

There are several recent interpretations of Climacus on faith and will. David Wisdo argues that faith as a gift of grace is completely beyond philosophical description.[68] Others take a straightforward volitionalist position: faith is a willed decision.[69] Others, like C. Stephen Evans, find a way to discriminate between the act of faith and the condition. "Faith is not an act of will"; faith is "the condition" given by God, and can never be claimed as something that a person wills. But the will operates in the following ways: first, the one thing the god in time can teach me Socratically is that I am in untruth; second, when the god reveals my sinfulness "I have a choice as to whether to accept this insight," which is "decisive for whether I acquire faith or not, since it in turn is decisive for whether I can come to understand the limitations of my reason." "Faith is not an act of will; it is a gift of the god. However, an act of will is necessary if the gift is to be received."[70]

Yet others, such as M. Jamie Ferreira, reconceptualize the issue. Her proposal is that the will should not be seen solely in volitionalist terms as a discrete willed act of belief, a "leap," but as involving various kinds of imaginative shifts and transitions, combining metaphors of the active and receptive sides of Christian faith. Yet faith involves the will; it is not sheer receptivity (as in thinking of a person as a *passive* recipient of the "condition" of grace).[71]

Ferreira's approach is suggestive, for it includes seeing faith as a passion as well as a leap, more clearly combining elements of the "passive" as well as "active." The transition to faith involves imaginative revisioning, engagement, and surrender, as well as decision. And this can illuminate how we see Kierkegaard thinking of the relation between the divine and human. Evans stresses "the condition" is given, yet still speaks of faith as if it were an *independent* act of the agent that one engages in order to "acquire faith." Ferreira suggests that faith is something more than an "independent" act. One receives

---

[67] *PF* 62 (*SV* iv 227).
[68] David Wisdo, "Kierkegaard on Belief, Faith, and Explanation," *International Journal for Philosophy of Religion* 21 (1987): 95–114.
[69] Pojman, *The Logic of Subjectivity*.
[70] Evans, *Passionate Reason*, 140.
[71] Ferreira, *Transforming Vision*.

the condition for a new self-understanding of oneself as redeemed sinner, yet receiving the condition includes an *active* response of a quickened will. In describing these "transitions," Kierkegaard is neither Pelagian in attributing merit to faith, nor does he think of the converted person as simply a passive recipient of a grace.

This can be seen in the way that Kierkegaard consistently affirms the role of human freedom in conversion. Early in his journal, he shows no patience with a doctrine of predestination, which he calls an "abortion," a rejection of the freedom involved in the response of faith.[72] Indeed, Kierkegaard's thought on predestination, unlike Schleiermacher's, is curiously undialectical, since he sees it as a threat to freedom, on a "competitive-agency" model between divine and human will. But he later speaks of divine and human activity as not being in competition. Ferreira cites this passage from the journals on God's omnipotence as the ground of human freedom:

The greatest good ... which can be done for a being, greater than anything else that one can do for it, is to make it free. In order to do just that, omnipotence is required ... If man had the slightest independent existence over against God ... then God could not make him free. Creation out of nothing is once again the Almighty's expression for being able to make [a being] independent. He to whom I owe absolutely everything, although he still absolutely controls everything, has in fact made me independent.[73]

Human beings have no "independent existence over against God"; divine creation and omnipotence are the very ground of freedom. Yet human freedom is truly independent.

(5) *Faith as a relational virtue continues the earlier religious dialectic of the active and the receptive.* What is true for the Climacean writings on grace and freedom is part of the larger pattern of Kierkegaard's authorship, extending back to the upbuilding discourses and continuing in the later literature. Faith is to be seen as an example of his dialectic of religious existence and human agency as active and receptive. Ethical existence for Judge William is both task and gift. The relation to God in faith's "expectancy" in the early upbuilding discourses, as we saw, combines active and receptive elements. In *Repetition* and *Fear and Trembling* the stance of the person in the religious sphere is both an active self-examination and also the humility and receptivity to "get oneself back

---

[72] *JP*II 1230 (*Pap.*. I A 5, August 19, 1834); compare *JP*II 1231 (*Pap.*. I A 7, November 23, 1834).
[73] *JP*II 1251 (*Pap.*. VII¹ A 181, n.d., 1846). See also Ferreira, *Transforming Vision*, 54. As we will see in chapter 6, this has important implications for God as the ground of love and maieutic of love, both of which aim at the good and the independence of the other.

again," to "get Isaac back" beyond the powers of human ability. In *Postscript* the religious person's passive suffering and "self-annihilation" are not world-denial, but an active process that opens the way for God to work in a person. And, as we have seen, in *Judge for Yourself!* Kierkegaard in his own name, immediately before the image of the royal coachman, speaks of how "in self-knowledge *and before God*," one becomes "nothing before God, and nevertheless infinitely, unconditionally engaged."[74] As we will see, this theme will emerge again later in our study.

(6) *"Faith is immediacy or spontaneity after reflection."*[75] In contrast to the "first immediacy" of childhood or immaturity ("God will make everything all right"), and in contrast to the resignation in which a person adjusts to realities, faith is a "second immediacy." Faith opens one to possibility; "the condition for a person's salvation is the faith that everywhere and at every moment there is an absolute *beginning*."[76] In specifically Christian terms, faith's spontaneity arises from trust in the forgiveness of sins for Christ's sake, and the beginning of a new life of gratitude.[77]

This new spontaneity is summed up as joy and gratitude. As Paul Minear has written, for Kierkegaard, no activity of the self is more creative or self-revealing than gratitude.[78] Gratitude is an eternal happiness as a synthesis of time and eternity, a synthesis revealed in the act of thanksgiving to God. Contrary to common impressions, Kierkegaard's reflection on faith abounds in gratitude and joy. In 1848, as part of *Christian Discourses* he published "Joyful Notes in the Strife of Suffering," indicating how joy sustains Christian existence in the midst of suffering, affliction, poverty, weakness, loss, and misfortune.[79] In deliberate and ironic contrast to the "anxieties of the heathen" of part 1 of *Christian Discourses* (anxieties all-too-common in "Christendom"), Christian existence is opened to a second spontaneity that survives those anxieties, and, by the "inverse dialectic" of faith, even flourishes in the midst of the negative. The inverse dialectic is Kierkegaard's

---

[74] *JFY* 106 (*SV* 388).
[75] *JP* II 1123 (*Pap.* VIII^1 A 649, May 11, 1848).
[76] *JP* II 1136 (*Pap.* X^2 A 371, n.d., 1850).
[77] See *JP* II 1202 (*Pap.*. III C 16, n.d., 1840–41).
[78] Paul S. Minear, "Thanksgiving as a Synthesis of the Temporal and the Eternal," in Howard A. Johnson and Niels Thulstrup, eds., *A Kierkegaard Critique* (New York: Harper & Brothers, 1962), 297.
[79] *CD* 101–63 (*SV* x 101–60).

preservation of joy in the midst of suffering – a theme we will treat more fully in the next chapter.

(7) *"Faith" is obedience in a life of discipleship following Christ as Pattern.* In contemporaneity, we have to do not only with relying upon Christ as atoner, but as the object of imitation. To say that Christ is the "truth" means that his life is "the way, the truth, and the life": "truth in the sense in which Christ is the truth is not a sum of statements, not a definition etc., but a life."[80] Therefore, faith is not only holding beliefs concerning him (true as that is), nor is it a timeless communion between the believer and Christ, but is rather a matter of following or imitating Christ's life (*Kristi Efterfølgelsen*). Here the language of Christ as "Pattern" becomes especially important for Kierkegaard. Christology and soteriology remain abstract or, worse yet, result in a cheap grace if the dialectic of Christ as Redeemer and Pattern is forgotten. The "Pattern" does not legislate a particular set of acts that constitute following Christ; there is no "facsimile imitation," as one commentator has put it; rather, imitation calls for creative improvisation and innovation.[81] One is called to a "way," in which the important matter is "how" one goes on the road of discipleship.[82]

(8) *Faith as discipleship includes a striving.* While Luther is right that striving for one's salvation leads to presumption or despair, and that there is no question of "merit" in the Christian life, this does not rule out striving or "good works," for "the very fact that I am saved by faith and that nothing at all is demanded from me should in itself make it possible that I begin to strive."[83] Here the dialectic of gift and task continues; eternal happiness is first of all gift, but to believe in it is arduous.[84] "Faith" is a "striving" "both in its beginning and during its progress."[85] As one commentator has put it, for Kierkegaard, the question of a "sequence" of grace or works does not arise, since God's grace and commands interpermeate one another without displacing one another.[86] Nonetheless, Kierkegaard can also speak of "grace in the first place" and "grace in the second place," which reflects what we noted earlier about how Christ as Pattern is first the ideal who leads to

---

[80] *PC* 205 (*SV* xii 189).
[81] Dewey, *The New Obedience*, 107.
[82] See for example, "The Joy of It That It Is Not the Road That Is Hard but That Hardship Is the Road," in *The Gospel of Sufferings*, *UDVS* 289–305 (*SV* viii 370–384). "The road is: *how* it is walked" (291 [*SV* viii 372]).
[83] *JP* ii 1139 (*Pap.* x³ A 322, n.d., 1850).
[84] Khan, *Salighed as Happiness?*, 99.
[85] *JP* ii 1139 (*Pap.* x³ A 322, n.d., 1850).
[86] Dewey, *The New Obedience*, 159.

acknowledgement of sin and second prompts the strenuousness of discipleship.[87]

(9) *Faith is a dispositional virtue.* Kierkegaard contrasts the forgiveness of sin as a "totality-qualification" of the "God-relationship" to "virtue."[88] The basis of the believer's status before God is not her virtue, but her faith. "The opposite of sin is not virtue, but faith." Despite these strictures on virtue language, Anti-Climacus increasingly speaks of faith not only in terms of active striving, but also dispositionally. Faith therefore is never a "possession," but it is an upbuilding in longterm capacities that "characterize" a life. Given the narrative understanding of Christ's life, and given also the Christian's striving, he now speaks of Christian existence, not as timeless communion with Christ, but in terms of "appropriation" that likewise is over a period of time. "Is *truth* such that in relation to it one may suppose that a person can appropriate it summarily with the help of another? Summarily, that is, without willing oneself to be developed in like manner, to be tried, to battle, to suffer as did the one who acquired the truth for him?"[89] In faith, one is called to a *stance* of faithfulness and loyalty. Anti-Climacus speaks of Christian endurance, and hence how a person "becomes *and continues to be* a Christian."[90] "In the New Testament faith is presented as having not an intellectual but an ethical character; it signifies the relationship of personality between God and man ... The apostle speaks of the *obedience* of faith. Faith is set to a test, is tested, etc."[91]

Kierkegaard develops the relational virtue conception of Christian faith in *The Gospel of Sufferings*, where he emphasizes self-denial, taking up the cross, and imitation. The stress is not on a *momentary* faith, an act renewed by sheer effort of will, but on discipleship as daily discipline: "As was the prototype, so must the imitation [*Efterfølgelsen*] also be, even though it is a *slow and difficult task* to deny oneself."[92]

The recurrence of faith as a "virtue" is seen in Kierkegaard's consideration that, while the Socratic (ethical, recollective) position sees that "knowledge (wisdom) is virtue," "Christian teaching is the opposite – that virtue is knowledge. From this comes the expression – to do the truth."[93] By "virtue is knowledge" Kierkegaard indicates here the

[87]   *JP* II, pp. 570–71.
[88]   *JP* II 1218 (*Pap.* IX A 482, n.d., 1848).
[89]   *PC* 202–03 (*SV* XII 186–87).
[90]   *PC* 199 (*SV* XII 184) (italics added).
[91]   *JP* II 1154 (*Pap.* XI² A 380, n.d., 1854–55).
[92]   *UDVS* 221 (*SV* VIII 309).
[93]   *JP* I 895 (*Pap.* IV C 86, n.d., 1842–43).

egalitarian theme that faith is not easier for the bright people, and that what is decisive is not "knowing," but "doing the truth." The Christian "virtue" of faith is in the doing.

CHRIST AND SALVATION

I want to step back from these reflections on faith as a "happy passion" in response to Christ in contemporaneity in order to draw out some implications concerning Kierkegaard's understanding of Christ and salvation, the "what" and the "how." At stake in these considerations of Kierkegaard's Christology and soteriology is not abstract theologizing, but clarification of *how* one "uses a picture," for I think Kierkegaard is often misunderstood on this score. This will allow us to distinguish his position from that of others with whom his thought is sometimes linked in Christology and soteriology, and augment what I argued in chapter 2 concerning the interplay between dogmatics and psychology, showing that there is not a contradiction, as alleged by Bohlin and others, between his dogmatic and existential thinking. I will now aim to show more precisely how Kierkegaard understands both the "what" of faith, Christ *extra nos*, and the "how" of faith's response, or "the logic of belief" and "the logic of coming to belief" in Frei's terms.[94] Christ is the logical and actual basis of Christian existence; at the same time the passional virtues – in this case, faith – are themselves the necessary subjective means for apprehending Christ.

(1) *Christ.* The Christ presented in Kierkegaard's thought is that of orthodox Nicene and Chalcedonian definitions.[95] Despite his suspicion of orthodoxy's tendencies to interpret Christianity as a doctrine or theory, he accepts the Chalcedonian understanding of Christ. Of interest is how Kierkegaard uses the Chalcedonian model. First, the Chalcedonian definition is important for him not in itself, or out of regard for tradition, but because it sums up what he perceives to be the Christian narrative of salvation, the "sacred history" of the divine love incarnate in a particular human being in order to redeem fallen humanity, worked out in Christ's life, death, and resurrection. The

---

[94] Frei, *Types of Christian Theology.*
[95] Compare David R. Law, *Kierkegaard as Negative Theologian,* 186n24, who rightly criticizes H. Roos' claim that (in Law's words), "Kierkegaard's position is a renunciation of the Chalcedonian formula." See H. Roos, "Søren Kierkegaard und die Kenosis-Lehre," *Kierkegaardiana* 2 (1957): 54–60.

focus of Christology is therefore on the story of Jesus Christ as unique and unsubstitutable savior who embodies divine love.

Second, however, Kierkegaard perceives how doctrines and narratives can be misread and abused. In *Practice in Christianity* Anti-Climacus points out that, whereas in ancient times the danger was either Ebionitism (denying Christ's divinity) or Gnosticism (denying Christ's humanity), "in the entire modern age, which so unmistakably bears the mark that it does not even know what the issue is, the confusion is something different and far more dangerous."[96] Either the danger is that

> the God–man has been made into that speculative unity of God and man *sub specie aeterni* [under the aspect of eternity] or made visible in that nowhere-to-be-found medium of pure being, rather than that the God–man is the unity of being God and an individual human being in a historically actual situation. Or Christ has been abolished altogether, thrown out and his teaching taken over, and finally he is almost regarded as one regards an anonymous writer: the teaching is the principal thing, is everything.[97]

Anti-Climacus here attacks not the abandonment of Chalcedonian doctrine, but its abuse. For speculative thought the Incarnation is, of course, central as the manifestation of the "unity of God and man." But the error of Hegelian thought is its translating the narrative of Christ as this particular human being into a "speculative unity" that both leads to contemplation and also falsifies the story by divinizing the human race. The difficulty of the modern age is that these dogmatic concepts can be set in another context that subtly undermines them. Christianity becomes a "doctrine" rather than an "existence-communication."

Third, therefore, what Kierkegaard adds to those dogmatic concepts is first a set of "metaconcepts" (the absolute paradox, the divine incognito, the impossibility of direct communication, the definition of "faith" in contrast to "knowledge") and also rhetorical strategies (like the two teachers and "the god's poem") that "seek to quicken awareness of the divine" by enticing, provoking, shocking. These metaconcepts do not replace the dogmatic concepts like "revelation," "sin," "faith," "Incarnation," but clarify their context of use.

---

[96] *PC* 123 (*SV* xii 115).

[97] *Ibid.* The former charge is directed against Hegelian thought of various stripes; the latter is directed specifically against H. L. Martensen's *Dogmatiske Oplysninger*, in which he speaks of Christianity as direct communication. See *PC*, Supplement, 330–31 (*Pap.* x⁵ B 54, n.d., 1849–50) and 399n90.

It is the objective content of the depiction of Christ, plus these other descriptive metaconcepts and rhetorical strategies, that shape the subjective qualifications of the response of "faith." This in turn rules out any theological stance that does not take seriously either that objective content or the subjective qualifications, anything that removes the *confrontation* between Christ and the potential believer, including any form of didacticizing that renders Christ's life into a teaching that is directly graspable or renders Christian faith into Socratic faith eliciting a truth within. The breadth of Kierkegaard's polemic here is striking, for it applies across the board to orthodox as well as liberal theology. It includes any orthodoxy that ignores the quality of the subjective response and reduces Christian faith to intellectual assent that neglects the paradox or assumes that the "divinity" is immediately recognizable. It also criticizes portrayals of Christ as an Enlightenment moral teacher, a Kantian moral archetype, an elicitor of insight (Schleiermacher), as the actual or ideal exemplification of the speculative unity of the divine and human (Hegelians left and right), or as someone who can be "known" by historical investigation alone.

Kierkegaard's distinction between Religiousness A and B, especially his delineation of the two teachers, also sets him apart from several contemporary theological options on Christology. As Robert C. Roberts, in my view correctly and perceptively, argues, Climacus' concerns apply not only to theologians such as Schleiermacher, but to Bultmann, and also John Cobb's process Christology. Each of them, he suggests, interprets Jesus as a Socratic teacher. Although they hold that Jesus alone is Redeemer, "what they have in common is thinking of redemption essentially as something that takes place in the consciousness of the 'believer,' or ... as essentially an insight (most likely with ethical consequences) that the redeemer helps the 'believer' to have."[98]

(2) *Salvation.* Roberts does not put it this way, but what Schleiermacher, Bultmann, and Cobb each have is a particularly strong emphasis on a "functional Christology" that interprets the significance of Christ (including, perhaps, Christ's divinity) in terms of human experience (as Roberts puts it, redemption as insight with ethical consequences). Ironically, Kierkegaard is quite different, for, despite his approach to Christian faith by way of subjectivity, his orthodox Christology begins

---

[98] Roberts, *Faith, Reason, and History*, 30. See also Evans, *Passionate Reason*, 29–31.

with Christ's identity as Redeemer and Pattern: Christ is divine and therefore able to save us. In short, Christology precedes soteriology.

In much modern Christian theology since Schleiermacher, this pattern of "Christology preceding soteriology" is altered, and two moves are made, in which "soteriology precedes Christology" results in a strongly functional Christology: (a) salvation is described primarily as an experience; (b) the priority is given to this experience of salvation as the logical ground for Christological affirmation. In Schleiermacher, for example, both moves are made. Christ alone is Redeemer, but salvation is an experience of Christ's redemptive activity as he assumes believers into the power of his God-consciousness. The experience of this God-consciousness then becomes the basis for attributing divinity to him.[99] In short, Christ saves, and therefore we conclude that he is divine. In the twentieth-century two classic proponents of "functional Christology," with a similar precedence of soteriology over Christology, are Paul Tillich and Rudolf Bultmann. For Tillich, "Christology is a function of soteriology,"[100] focusing on the power of the New Being communicated in the portrayal of "Jesus who is the Christ" (the one who saves). Bultmann too gives priority to soteriology over Christology, locating the significance of Christ's cross in its saving power.[101] It is the cross of Christ *because* of its saving power.[102]

At first glance Kierkegaard too appears to fit into this experiential model of soteriology governing Christology. Understandably, given his stress on subjectivity, a number of commentators read him this

---

[99] Friedrich Schleiermacher, *The Christian Faith*, section 100, ed. H. R. Mackintosh and J. S. Stewart (Edinburgh: T. & T. Clark, 1928), 425–28.

[100] Paul Tillich, *Systematic Theology*, ii, 150.

[101] Rudolf Bultmann, *Kerygma and Myth: A Theological Debate*, rev. trans. R. H. Fuller (New York: Harper & Row, 1961), 34–43.

[102] Classical Patristic and orthodox Protestant Christologies certainly have elements of a "functional Christology," never divorce Christology from soteriology, and may argue from soteriology to Christological affirmations: witness the Patristic affirmation that "what is not assumed is not healed" as the soteriological basis for affirming Christ's full divinity and full humanity; witness, too, in orthodox Lutheranism, Melanchthon's stress on the *beneficia Christi*: "To know Christ is to know His benefits." Yet even when, as with Athanasius, the classical tradition argues epistemologically from soteriology to Christology, the "ontological" pattern of these classical Patristic and orthodox Protestant functional Christologies is to proceed *from* Christ's identity as God incarnate: Christ is divine, and *therefore* able to save. By contrast, in Schleiermacher and much modern theology, with its Kantian "turn to the subject," Christ saves, and therefore Christ is divine. For an elegant, brief statement of this development in Schleiermacher and much modern theology, see Walter Lowe, "Christ and Salvation," in Peter C. Hodgson and Robert H. King, eds., *Christian Theology: An Introduction to Its Traditions and Tasks* (Philadelphia: Fortress Press, 1982), 210–12.

way. Certainly Kierkegaard is concerned to speak of how atonement is *pro me*, how the believer's life is shaped in the realization of the forgiveness of sins. But Kierkegaard does not interpret salvation solely in experiential terms, nor is soteriology the basis for his Christological affirmations.

Jeremy Walker, for example, says of Kierkegaard's doctrine of the atonement that if we are to understand it, we must recall his "fundamental assumption that 'the *situation* is inseparable from the God–Man.'"[103] From this Walker concludes that "the atonement itself is not to be understood as a theory or historical claim." But he goes on to say that when Kierkegaard uses the language of "substitution" and "vicarious satisfaction" we should take this seriously, but not as a doctrine of substitution. "In SK's works, substitution represents an experience, part of the way in which the believer experiences Christ. Substitution is part of the Christian's situation."[104]

Walker is correct in some ways. The atonement is not a theory or doctrine in the sense that it can be comprehended speculatively or that intellectual understanding of the teaching is sufficient or that it is a datum open to historical investigation. But Walker is clearly uncomfortable with Kierkegaard's use of substitution language and can accept it only if it "represents an experience, part of the way in which the believer experiences Christ."

Yet Kierkegaard uses the language of substitution and vicarious satisfaction in a more "realist" fashion, without feeling the constraint that Walker's reading imposes on him. Kierkegaard, of course, is concerned to draw out how the doctrine affects the believer's situation; "the *situation* is inseparable from the God–Man," and that is the consciousness of sin and despair. But this is not because atonement is simply an experience, or an experience that leads one then to affirm Christ as the God–man. Kierkegaard's logic of atonement and salvation is quite the opposite. The model rather is that of Christ's death itself being the atonement for sins, which then defines the believer's experience. Part of this is that faith is a response to an external *historical* event, "the appearance of Christ in his fullness," which "is not given and can never be deduced from the preceding consciousness – that is, the consciousness of sin and the assurance of

[103] Walker, *Kierkegaard: Descent into God*, 202, citing *PC* 81–82 (*SV* XII 79) in the Lowrie translation of *PC: Training in Christianity and the Edifying Discourse which 'Accompanied' It*, trans. with an introduction and notes, Walter Lowrie (Princeton University Press, 1944), 84.
[104] Walker, *Kierkegaard: Descent into God*, 202.

the forgiveness of sins."[105] This is also, however, a divine event, part of the sacred history, which then becomes applicable to human experience, altering the *situation* of the person whom Christ confronts.

In theological terms, Kierkegaard's understanding of Christ *extra nos* and of salvation *pro nobis* and *pro me* employs strikingly objective and realistic language, including forensic justification. The sacred history of the Redeemer's death – that it effects redemption – is not open to imitation, but has intrinsic meaning.

Neither is it that Kierkegaard uses Abelardian images alone (as might be concluded from "the god's poem"); he can also employ the Anselmian language of satisfaction and substitution with clear reference not to the believer's experience, but to Christ's life and death. His comfort with the language of substitution, with its predominance of a narrative-Christological framework over a soteriological-expressive framework, is evident in two 1851 entries from his journals on Anselm on the necessity of satisfaction:

> He shows the necessity of satisfaction not only from God's side, in order to satisfy God's honor, but also from man's side.
> Assuming that man could become saved by a compassionate act on God's part, but without satisfaction, man would still not be able to be saved. The fact that satisfaction was not made would continually torment him and disturb his bliss; or one would have to think that he did not even care if satisfaction were made or not, and that would indeed be wickedness.[106]

This passage indicates the place of satisfaction as a substitution, as it points to the *effect* of Christ's satisfaction on the believer, but it still focuses on the believer's experience. Yet the next entry makes the "objectivity" of satisfaction even clearer, for he defends Anselm against the criticism that his doctrine of satisfaction focuses on God's honor, and that "the fact that it is for man's salvation comes at the very end, almost tag-end."[107] Rather, Christianity is God's invention, God's interest, "the divine combat of divine passion with itself, so that in a sense we human beings disappear like ants (although it still is infinite love for us)."[108]

[105] *JP* II 1100 (*Pap.* III A 39, n.d., 1840).
[106] *JP* II 1423 (*Pap.* X⁴ A 211, n.d., 1851).
[107] *JP* I 532 (*Pap.* X⁴ A 212), n.d., 1851).
[108] *Ibid.* By contrast, David R. Law, *Kierkegaard as Negative Theologian*, 201, grants the presence of the satisfaction theory of atonement, but goes on to say that in Kierkegaard "we find nothing of Anselm's juristic terminology in his deliberations on the atonement." This is true in the sense that Kierkegaard does not dwell on the "juristic" image as such, but misses the substitutionary Anselmian aspects of Kierkegaard's thought on atonement.

Most striking, however, is a passage from *The Book on Adler*. Kierkegaard is wrestling with the concept of revelation, in reaction to Magister Adler's claim to a new revelation. Magister Adler's problem is that "he confounds the subjective with the objective, his subjectively altered condition with an external event."[109] The interesting contrast between romantic love and Christian faith that follows deserves to be quoted at length:

Love does not exist as something objective but comes into being every time a man loves, and it exists only in the lover; not only does it exist only *for* the lover but it exists only *in* the lover.

It is otherwise with every relation within the sphere of transcendence, and then again otherwise with the Christian concept of revelation. Christianity exists before any Christian exists, it must exist in order that one may become a Christian, it contains the determinant by which one may test whether one has become a Christian, it maintains its objective subsistence apart from all believers, while at the same time it is in the inwardness of the believer. In short, here there is no identity between the subjective and the objective. Though Christianity comes into the heart of never so many believers, every believer is conscious that it has not arisen in his heart, is conscious that the objective determinant of Christianity is not a reminiscence, as love is of the fact of falling in love, is not an apparently objective something which nevertheless is subjective, like love which as an objective something is an illusion and loving is the reality. No, even if no one had perceived that God had revealed himself in a human form in Christ, he nevertheless has revealed himself. Hence it is that every contemporary (simply understood) has a responsibility if he does not perceive it.[110]

No clearer statement of the "objectivity" of Kierkegaard's own understanding of "transcendence" and "revelation" in Christian faith, including the priority of Christ's work apart from its reception, could be found. The narrative of Christ *extra nos* is logically prior in Kierkegaard's vision of Christian faith.

It is more accurate to say that Kierkegaard sees salvation as having a subsequent experiential or subjective moment in addition to the objective moment, and it is his concern to elucidate that subjectivity. But Kierkegaard is not reducing the objective moment to the subjective moment, or making Christology dependent upon soteriology, or abandoning forensic justification. Hence, he speaks of "an Atoner who has made satisfaction for the whole race."[111] What Christ

109   *OAR* 168 (*Pap.* VII² B 235, p. 204).
110   *OAR* 168–69 (*Pap.* VII² B 235, p. 204–05).
111   *JP*IV 4038 (*Pap.* X² A 483, n.d., 1850).

suffered "was atonement for all, unconditionally for all."[112] But the objective moment (atonement made for the whole race) is completed by a subjective moment. What took place and was made actual in Christ in atonement is actual, but it does not acquire efficacy until something decisive also takes place in the believer, in the event of faith. Salvation is not *reduced* to experience (because of the logical priority and actuality of atonement), but soteriology includes human response and experience.

Kierkegaard's understanding can be illuminated by contrast to that of the later Karl Barth's *Church Dogmatics*. In contrast to Barth's soteriological objectivism, for Kierkegaard, the subjective moment's significance is this: coming to faith is decisive for whether salvation actually obtains in the case of any particular individual.[113] As Kierkegaard writes in his journal, "The question of man's eternal salvation is made commensurable with a decision in time by a relation to something historical occurring in time."[114] Unlike Barth, in locating an objective moment that is in some sense subordinated to a subjective moment Kierkegaard stands with a number of central orthodox theologians such as Augustine, Luther, and even Calvin.[115]

Salvation is not only *pro nobis*, but decisively *pro me*. The question of faith must therefore be addressed to the particular individual. Kierkegaard relates this objective atonement and satisfaction to the situation, as the "halt" addressed to the person who despairs. In this sense the atonement is, of course, not a mere theory or doctrine, it also addresses the person who despairs not only over the sin of weakness, but also the sin of despair; the situation is that "a man

---

[112] *JP*I 342 (*Pap.* x¹ A 587, n.d., 1849).

[113] George Hunsinger, *How to Read Karl Barth: The Shape of His Theology* (New York: Oxford University Press, 1991), 103ff. Hunsinger indicates how Barth's objectivism is a critique of the Augustinian stress on the "existential moment." That critique would obviously apply to Kierkegaard as well.

[114] *JP*IV 4922 (*Pap.* XI¹ A 296, n.d., 1854).

[115] In *Karl Barth's Critically Realistic Dialectical Theology: Its Genesis and Development, 1909–36* (Oxford: Clarendon Press, 1995), Bruce L. McCormack argues that, contrary to the "neo-orthodox" reading that sees the early Barth as a dialectical "Kierkegaardian existentialist" in contrast to the later Barth's discovery of analogy, Barth is actually dialectical throughout his career. McCormack says that Barth was never a "Kierkegaardian existentialist," since even in the second edition of *Romans* Barth was concerned not with how humans become Christian, but with how God could reveal himself without ceasing to be God. But if my reading of Kierkegaard's stress on the passion of God and the priority of Christology is correct, Kierkegaard is more "realist" than this contrast suggests, tempering the usual "dialectic versus analogy" view that pits Kierkegaard over against Barth. Yet the differences between them still obtain on the place of "becoming Christian" and also on their readings of the "soteriological moment."

doubts that the sin he committed out of weakness can be for-
given."[116] "The doctrine of the Atonement is essentially related to
this despair, the Atonement wants to halt this despair; only such a
person actually comprehends the Atonement – that is, feels a need
for it."[117] This is why Anti-Climacus speaks of the importance of
sin-consciousness as the gateway to Christian faith. It is only the
person in despair over sins who can hear the word of forgiveness of
sins. Sin-consciousness, Kierkegaard often insists, is the prerequisite
to faith; law precedes gospel. "Christianity presupposes that a man
has progressed so far that he has only one sorrow – sorrow over his
sins – and then it proclaims reconciliation"[118] "To become a
believer he must have passed by the possibility of offense."[119] "In
order to have faith, there must first be existence, an existential
qualification ... before there can even be any question about having
faith, there must be the *situation*."[120]

In summary, Kierkegaard's understanding of Christ and salvation is
concerned with how we "use the picture" of the Christian story. He
wends a way between two common options in modern Protestant
theology: the experiential, soteriological model with a functional
Christology (Schleiermacher, Bultmann, Tillich, Cobb), and the theological objectivism that rejects a decisive experiential moment as part
of salvation (the later Barth). Most important, the reason he stands
between these two is that he sees Christian faith as a story of passions
and loves: the divine passion embodied in a human life seeks "equality
with the learner," a passion that prompts response in either love or
offense.

In this chapter we have been concerned with how Christian faith for
Kierkegaard is best understood as a passional response to revelation. In
Kierkegaard's strategy of pursuing the way of subjectivity, he does not
end in theological subjectivism, but in a conceptual clarification of how
subjectivity is *shaped* in response to divine passion. Here too the
language of faith is used "referringly." His regard not only for the
"how," but also the "what" is evident in this journal entry:

In all the usual talk that Johannes Climacus is mere subjectivity etc., it has
been completely overlooked that in addition to all his other concretions he

---

[116] *JP*IV 4013 (*Pap.* VIII¹ A 497, n.d., 1847–48).
[117] *JP*IV 4016 (*Pap.* IX A 341, n.d., 1848).
[118] *JP*IV 4012 (*Pap.* VIII¹ A 473, n.d., 1847).
[119] *PC* 99 (*SV*XII 94).
[120] *JP*II 1142 (*Pap.* X⁴ A 114, n.d., 1851).

points out in one of the last sections [of *Postscript*] that the remarkable thing is that there is a How with the characteristic that when the How is scrupulously rendered the What is also given, that this is the How of "faith." Right here, at its very maximum, inwardness is shown to be objectivity. And this, then, is a turning of the subjectivity-principle, which, as far as I know, has never been carried through or accomplished in this way.[121]

The "how" of Christian faith is not subjectivism, anymore than is Religiousness A, but Christian faith has a further distinctively objective pole, a "what" to which faith is a response.

Yet Kierkegaard's concern, of course, is to show that this "what" is not an object for intellectual mastering and manipulation, but a Subject prompting passionate response in faith or offense. Wittgenstein is not always a good guide to Kierkegaard's thought (especially, I think, because Wittgenstein does not appreciate the role of doctrines in Christian faith or faith's interest in historical affirmations – Kierkegaard's "moment in time"), yet both of them explore how religious belief is something that does not stand in need of foundational justification, but becomes foundational when it is a way of life, when "the uses of a picture" "regulate for all" in a person's life.[122] Wittgenstein worried that we suffer from a "one-sided diet" of examples.[123] Kierkegaard's explorations of faith set Christian belief in the context not of rational demonstration or objective proofs of Christianity's truth. Both thinkers broaden the context of religious belief to include moral discrimination, caring, the passions of the heart, despair rather than doubt, faith and offense, uncertainty's risk and the resting that is trust.[124]

Kierkegaard and Wittgenstein explored religious faith as being like *love*, not speculation. In *Philosophical Fragments*, Climacus likens Socrates' passionate pursuit of the understanding for the paradox, the thought it cannot think, to love: self-love finds its limit, defeat, and fulfillment when it becomes love for another. In Climacus' "god's poem," the theme again is divine love. Wittgenstein too links faith and love when he writes:

But if I am to be REALLY saved, – what I need is *certainty* – not wisdom, dreams or speculation – and this certainty is faith. And faith is faith in what is needed by my *heart*, my *soul*, not my speculative intelligence. For it is my soul

[121] *JP*IV 4550 (*Pap.* x² A 299, n.d., 1849). See also Gregor Malantschuk, *Kierkegaard's Thought*, 307.
[122] Wittgenstein, *Lectures and Conversations*, 54.
[123] Wittgenstein, *Philosophical Investigations*, I, 593.
[124] Putnam, *Renewing Philosophy*, 154.

with its passions, as it were with its flesh and blood, that has to be saved, not my abstract mind. Perhaps we can say: Only *love* can believe the Resurrection. Or: It is *love* that believes the Resurrection. We might say: Redeeming love believes even in the Resurrection; holds fast even to the Resurrection. What combats doubt is, as it were, *redemption.*[125]

Wittgenstein also writes, "A proposition, and hence in another sense a thought, can be the 'expression' of belief, hope, expectation, etc. But believing is not thinking. (A grammatical remark.) The concepts of believing, expecting, hoping are less distantly related to one another than they are to the concept of thinking."[126] Faith in the Christian context is closer to "expecting," "hoping," and "loving." In the next three chapters we will explore further Kierkegaard's depiction of the relations between "faith" and "hope" and "love."

[125] Wittgenstein, *Culture and Value*, 33. Compare, of course, Paul's words in 1 Corinthians 13:7: "Love believes all things." We will return to this in chapter 6.
[126] Wittgenstein, *Philosophical Investigations*, I, 574.

CHAPTER 5

Becoming Christian II: suffering and following Christ in hope

Hope is the foster-mother of the Christian life.
*JP*II 1663 (*Pap.* II A 566, n.d., 1839).

It may seem odd to speak of Kierkegaard as a theologian of hope. While he writes extended treatments of faith and love, there is no discrete treatise on hope. But the conditions and possibilities of hope are a continuing concern to him, whether expressed obliquely in his concern with hope's opposite, despair, or expressed directly in depictions of patience, expectancy, repetition, and faith as oriented to the future, grounded in God as the source of endless possibility.

Of course, Kierkegaard's "hope" is not frivolous or lightminded; he presents a strenuous account of the shape of human and Christian hope. Hope is illuminated by its opposite, despair, and his primary passion is depicting hope in the midst of suffering. Indeed, the aim of hope is to address the situation of the sufferer.[1] Finally, he isolates a specific and demanding kind of Christian suffering in discipleship. Nonetheless, Kierkegaard's analyses of hope do not belie the passion; the tone of his discussions is at heart hopeful and even joyful. And it is because of the strenuous demands of Christian discipleship "following Christ" that the specific Christian accent to hope is so distinctive, for it is a hope in the midst of suffering, unavoidable and avoidable.

We will examine Kierkegaard's grammar of "hope" in the following way: first, we will look at expectancy and the origins of hope in a person's life; second, we will turn to despair as the enemy of hope, including an examination of despair as different forms of hopelessness, and also the diseases attending the relations of hope and recollection;

---

[1] See the preface to *The Gospel of Sufferings*: "These Christian discourses ... are not intended 'to fill an idle moment for inquisitiveness.' If, however, just one single sufferer, who perhaps is also going astray in many thoughts, should by means of them find a heavy moment lighter, should find in them a trail leading through the many thoughts, then the author will not regret his intention with them" (*UDVS* 215 [*SV*VIII 303]).

third, we will turn to hope and repetition; fourth, Kierkegaard's
dialectic of hope; fifth, we will turn to the various forms of suffering. All
of this is preparation for the sixth and final section, where we will focus
on the shape of specifically Christian suffering and following Christ in
hope, that is, the specific form of the Christian virtue of hope, including
discipleship as following the Pattern of the "suffering God" incarnate
in Christ, the special forms of Christian suffering in Kierkegaard's
version of *theologia crucis*, and the relations of hope to courage and
perseverance, to joy, and to humor, and, in a final coda and transition
to the next chapter, how hope and love are related. Here too, as in
chapter 4, we will see that there is a dialectic to hope just as there is a
dialectic to faith, that Christian hope is not undefined, but shaped in
relation to its objective correlative (Christ) as well as in its subjective
requirements as a relational virtue.

EXPECTANCY AND THE ORIGINS OF HOPE

In chapters 3 and 4 we noted some of the grammar of hope, in
Kierkegaard's exploration of capacities such as "expectancy" and
"faith." The very first of the *Eighteen Upbuilding Discourses*, for example,
develops the conceptual connections between "faith" and "expectancy" as immanent capacities of the religious life. Expectancy, as a
person's looking to the future, takes many forms, but faith's expectancy
is one particular way of looking to that future, an expectancy of victory
that gives strength to face the present moment.[2] And in *Eighteen
Upbuilding Discourses* this expectancy is developed to embrace patience
and the expectancy of an eternal, not just temporal, salvation.[3]
"Hope," like these other capacities, is rooted in the abilities people
have of seeing possibilities for themselves, envisioning a future. The
"self is a relation that relates itself to itself," as Anti-Climacus says in *The
Sickness Unto Death*.[4] As an active and concrete synthesis of the finite and
infinite, the temporal and eternal, necessity and possibility, a person is
continually in process of becoming, and to a greater or lesser extent is
consciously reflecting upon who one is and what one will become. The
expansive pole of the self (the infinite, eternal, and possible) are functions
of imagination; they are abilities that enable a person, as one journeys
through time, continuously to envision possibilities that inspire dread or

---

[2]   *EUD* 7–29 (*SV*III 13–34).
[3]   *EUD* 205–26, 253–73 (*SV*IV 95–113, 139–56).
[4]   *SUD* 13 (*SV*XI 127).

desire. We are destined, as it were, for expectancy, anticipation, dread, or hope. But the other pole of the self (the finite, temporal, and necessary) points to the givenness of what we bring to the moment, including the limitations of the past, one's talents and heritage and background, and the past decisions one has made.

From a Christian viewpoint, faith is the harmonious relation of these elements, as one moves through time and "rests transparently in God." Life is a gift and a task; one journeys trustingly from past through the present to the unseen future, shaping a life through commitment that relates imagined possibilities to the finite, making a concrete and particular life.

Like Samuel Johnson, Kierkegaard sees human beings not as thinking-machines, but as passional creatures; we are all attracted or repulsed by visions of what is possible. We live from hope to hope, moving from the past, through the present, and to the future.[5] Hope is therefore a human capacity, not necessarily religious or specifically Christian. Kierkegaard takes care to approach it in universal human terms.

DESPAIR AS HOPELESSNESS

Yet the enemy of expectation, anticipation, and hope is, of course, despair. In contrast to the harmonious relating of factors of the self, and resting transparently in God, despair, as analyzed in part 1 of *The Sickness Unto Death*, is disequilibrium. Despair as hopelessness takes different forms. We tend to think that despair, the loss of hope, is simply a loss of possibility, a lack of prospects, a closed future. That is indeed one of the forms of despair, which we will look at it a moment, but Anti-Climacus sees also that despair as hopelessness may also take the form of the "despair of the infinite" or the "despair of possibility," by which he means a despair in which one exaggerates the infinite and the possible. In this form, the imagination becomes "fantastic," unrelated to concrete life. In emotions, one may become sentimental, loving humanity in general, but not the particular person one sees. Or one may become fantastic in knowing, living in abstractions, lost in useless knowledge. Or one may become fantastic in willing, making great plans, but never carrying out the daily task necessary to realize

5   See, for example, *The Rambler*, *No. 196*, in Samuel Johnson, *Essays from the* Rambler, *Adventurer, and* Idler, ed. W. J. Bate (New Haven; London: Yale University Press, 1968), 221–25.

those plans. The self-deception involved here is that one flees the requirement of hope: that one live as a concrete individual, not in daydreaming. One may desire or crave a possibility, like "the knight who suddenly sees a rare bird and chases after it, because it seems at first to be very close" and then is lost, and "cannot find his way back to himself." Or one may have a "hope/fear or anxiety" by fixing in melancholy on one of "anxiety's possibilities," which too leads one deeper into anxiety.[6]

Of course, hopelessness reveals itself also in the other forms of despair that result from *fleeing* possibility, what Anti-Climacus calls the "despair of finitude" and "despair of necessity." This shows itself in the flight from the future, from possibility, from the requirement to make ideals and possibilities concrete. Here the person sinks into the finite and necessary. This too may be an unconscious hopelessness. Anti-Climacus' examples are perceptive critiques of the social pathology of despair, for the example of the despair of finitude he offers includes the conformist: "Surrounded by hordes of men, absorbed in all sorts of secular matters, more and more shrewd about the ways of the world – such a person forgets himself ... finds it too hazardous to be himself and far easier and safer to be like the others, to become a copy, a number, a mass man."[7] The socially conformed may appear successful, indeed, are apt to be successful. Such people will certainly entertain hopes (for advancement, etc.), but Anti-Climacus' point is that in terms of the basic project of becoming an individual self, they are in despair, without hope. This is a Christian diagnostic analysis that Anti-Climacus offers, and so measures hope against the standard of what a person should be, the standard of God's intent for persons. But even unconscious despair displays symptoms, in many cases, of its hopelessness: finding it "too hazardous" to be oneself, shrewdness reveals an underlying anxiety that supports such social conformity and "spiritlessness," a prudential willingness to keep silent, not to stand out from the crowd.

We need not continue with the details of Anti-Climacus' analysis of despair. The point to see is that despair, as the opposite of hope, takes many forms. In part 2 of *The Sickness Unto Death*, Anti-Climacus, as we have already seen, places his psychological analysis within a theological context, by defining despair as not only universal, but as equivalent to sin: "Sin is: before God in despair not to will to be oneself, or before

6 *SUD* 37 (*SV*xi 150).
7 *SUD* 33–34 (*SV*xi 147).

God in despair to will to be oneself."[8] Whether in passive collapse and self-hatred or in conscious, open defiance, hopelessness is a rejection of what a person is called to be before God.

Faith, however, is Anti-Climacus' cure for despair's hopelessness, since "Faith is: that the self in being itself and in willing to be itself rests transparently in God."[9] Thus, reflecting Romans 14:23 ("Whatever does not proceed from faith is sin"), Anti-Climacus gives his famous theological analysis of sin and faith: "The opposite of sin [i.e., of despair] is not virtue but faith."[10]

But, of course, the opposite of sin, if it is despair, is not only faith, but hope. Anti-Climacus phrases the cure in terms of faith, but it is obvious that faith is closely linked conceptually with hope. If faith points to the object of trust (God), God is the object of hope as well. Grammatically, if one does not trust in God, one cannot hope in God; conversely, if one does hope in God, faith's trust is impossible.

HOPE AND REPETITION

In *Either/Or* II Judge William addresses himself to the disorders of A's aestheticism of escaping genuine hope by noting that the remedy is not simply to direct hope to the future again, but to see how recollection *and* hope constructively relate to each other. He argues that "the healthy individual lives simultaneously in hope and in recollection, and only thereby does his life gain true and substantive continuity."[11] Hopeful, he or she does not wish to go backward in time, with the recollectors; but recollection – here the prosaic judge uses a musical analogy – "places a sharp on the note of the moment; the further back it goes, the more often the repetition, the more sharps there are."[12] In marriage, for example, a person gathers up past memories in the present moment of recommitment to marriage, which anticipates a future. Here again we see how hope is not simply oriented to the future, but "modulates" a "layered" self who builds upon the continuity given by the past, by recollection.

The musical analogy of modulating recollection into commitment leading to hope is a "harmonic" analogy. A more "melodic" analogy,

---

[8] *SUD* 81 (*SV* xi 193).
[9] *SUD* 82 (*SV* xi 194).
[10] *Ibid.*
[11] *EO* ii 142 (*SV* ii 129).
[12] *Ibid.*

pointing to the future of the self and not just to the increasing "harmonic depth," is found in "repetition." In repetition action and commitment are *themselves* hopeful, as they take one into the imagined future. Thus, the judge can say that "individuals do not live only in hope; at all times they have hope and recollection together in the present" and "hope hovers over it as a hope of eternity that fills out the moment."[13] "Achieving" it might be simply escape, a "self-creating" that "hopes" by rejecting a painful past, rejecting recollection. But in his "receiving" of oneself again, the split between recollection and hope is overcome. Hope is neither a fantastic wish for an imagined future, nor a melancholy inversion of painful memory. Both of these may be "willed." But the true hope, while it is willed (for it requires courage), at the same time is experienced as gift. Hope is not "possessed," but "received." Hope as a virtue like faith is not simply willed, and in that sense is not a just a habit or act, but in so far as it is received, is a gift. One can train oneself in hope, but more importantly one can train oneself to receive hope. For Kierkegaard the two are not contradictory.

THE DIALECTIC OF HOPE

So far we have looked at hope and despair as they surround the normal expectations that a person will experience, what Kierkegaard speaks of as "earthly hopes." But we need to examine Kierkegaard's contrast between "earthly hopes" and "hope based on the eternal," as an introduction to Christian hope. In a journal entry, Kierkegaard places the context for Christian hope by speaking of "how much living out of life" Christianity "presupposes in order rightly to be accepted." "But the dialectic of hope goes this way: first the fresh incentive of youth, then the supportive calculation of understanding, and then – then everything comes to a standstill – and now for the first time Christian hope is there as possibility."[14] He writes in another journal entry that "Hope is the foster-mother of the Christian life."[15] Why "foster-mother"? I think the point is the same; Christian hope has a history of human hope, and despair, behind it.

There are four stages in this dialectic of hope. First, as we have seen already, Kierkegaard finds the origins of hope in youthfulness, directed

----

[13]   *EO* II 142 and 143 (*SV* II 129).
[14]   *JP* II 1668 (*Pap.* VI B 53:13, n.d., 1845).
[15]   *JP* II 1663 (*Pap.* II A 566, n.d., 1839).

toward earthly, temporal expectations. And then follow disappoint-
ment and despair, in different possible forms.

The second stage of the dialectic of hope is "the supportive
calculation of understanding," which is not outright, conscious
despair, but the hidden despair that arises when one becomes sensible
and calculating. Here we find one of the most interesting aspects of
Kierkegaard's analysis of hope in his analysis of "calculation,"
"sagacity," and "shrewdness" as forms of despairing hopelessness. As
we have seen in examining *The Sickness Unto Death*, the despair of
finitude and of necessity may include an unconscious resignation, in
which one gives up youthful hopes, reins in expectations, and
calculates "probabilities."

Kierkegaard speaks much of this calculating, resigned reining in of
earthly hope. "Hope" becomes diminished as a person tailors his or
her life within a narrow range. One even advocates a narrowed
"hope" based on probabilities as wisdom. If faced with a serious illness,
one might say, "I should be hopeful, since I have a chance of survival."
This is, of course, actually a form of hidden, unconscious despair, for it
is based on calculation of the odds; it is a "quiet despair."[16] Hope is
not defeated, but merely worn down. A person becomes adept at
judging what is possible, and eventually settles for the probable.

Yet it is important to see that Kierkegaard is not advocating an
irrational hope in earthly things in contrast to the resignation of earthly
hopes. He does not simplemindedly understand hope as "believing
against the odds, whatever the circumstances." He realistically grants
that hope, *as long as it is earthly*, is subject to the calculations of
probability. Furthermore, earthly hopes can be tenacious in a spiritually destructive way. In *Purity of Heart*, he speaks of an "essential
sufferer," who may grasp earthly hopes, "misuse sagacity inwardly,"
pinning hopes on a possible end to suffering, remembering some story
of how this or that person hoped against hope, and was cured of dire
illness. But this too is sagacity, a sagacity that wrongly inflates earthly
hopes. "To sagacity it seems very sagacious 'not foolishly to give up an
earthly hope for a possible fantastic healing.'"[17] Such a person will say
that earthly hope should never be given up: "one must not take
suffering and life too much to heart ... it still might be possible, who
knows, etc."[18]

16   *SLW* 199–200 (*SV* vi 189–90).
17   *UDVS* 113 (*SV* viii 208).
18   *Ibid.*

The problem, however, is revealed in the third stage of the dialectic of hope, that because any earthly hopes are in the nature of the case subject to defeat, hidden despair, of whatever form, can come to full consciousness. In his well-known analogy in *The Sickness Unto Death*, Anti-Climacus offers a thought-experiment; he invites his readers to imagine for themselves some horror that is absolutely unbearable. Now if this horror occurs, then "collapse is certain" and "salvation is, humanly speaking, utterly impossible."[19] A person desires, perhaps, only to be left alone in despair. In Anti-Climacus' words,

When someone faints, we call for water, eau de Cologne, smelling salts; but when someone wants to despair, then the word is: Get possibility, get possibility, possibility is the only salvation. A possibility – then the person in despair breathes again, he revives again, for without possibility a person seems unable to breathe.[20]

In the words of the journal entry on the dialectic of hope, "everything comes to a standstill." And the question is posed sharply: can possibility and hope be regained?

This question sets the context for the fourth stage of the dialectic of hope, "eternal hope," and beyond that specifically "Christian hope." Anti-Climacus says, "At this point, then, salvation is, humanly speaking, utterly impossible; but for God everything is possible!"[21] Whereas experience is calculative, shrewd, and aware of the odds, leading to diminished hopes or else for hopes pinned on the earthly alone, there opens up an "eternal hope," a hope that is not based on "experience" or calculations of "sagacity." As Jeremy Walker has pointed out, Kierkegaard opposes two "frames" for understanding life, the frame of hope and the frame of experience, which are internally opposed.[22] Hope takes a different frame on life; one can "hope against hope," "by virtue of the absurd," not in the sense of an irrational earthly hope, but a hope *in spite of* a realistic appraisal of the odds against earthly hope.[23]

We can easily summarize some of the features of this hope for the eternal, and the shape of a life of hope. First, eternal hope opens up possibility, relieving the pressure of finitude and necessity that threatens

---

[19] *SUD* 38 (*SV* xi 151).

[20] *SUD* 38–39 (*SV* xi 151).

[21] *SUD* 38 (*SV* xi 151).

[22] Walker, *Kierkegaard: Descent into God*, 99. We will return to this in connection with the relation between hope and love, and again in the next chapter.

[23] *FSE* 82 (*SV* xii 365).

to suffocate a person. Second, hope is therefore future-oriented, but without, as we have seen, giving up one's past or "recollection." Third, hope is object-oriented, grounded not on earthly calculation, which can be supremely realistic, but on God alone as the source of possibility. Because God is the object of hope, this hope is not diffuse, but specific, and cognitively grounded. Hope depends logically upon the belief that God is present to help (Psalm 42:5). It is this belief that allows hope; conversely, hope strengthens the belief (faith) in God. This eternal hope is not limited by the earthly, for "there is still an expectation which cannot possibly be disappointed, for you do expect the resurrection of the dead ... you do hope finally to see your life transfigured in God – an expectation that God will work out everything for the best."[24] Fourth, eternal hope brings a person beyond the "resignation" of sagacity or despair. Instead of restraining one's hopes, or giving up hope altogether, hope is opened into broader prospects. One does not simply tolerate the future, dulling concern; hope allows one to welcome the future, to return to the finite world, as it enlivens concern. Fifth, hope is not a mood, but a character-trait and longterm attitude of a person. By its very nature, hope is not a mood, for it is not episodic, and perseveres in the face of despair and opposition. Kierkegaard's thought on hope is strongly Pauline, for Paul links hope closely to character: "We also boast in our sufferings, knowing that suffering produces endurance, and endurance produces character, and character produces hope, and hope does not disappoint us, because God's love has been poured into our hearts through the Holy Spirit that has been given to us" (Romans 5:3–5). Finally, this stress on endurance relates hope very closely to courage, for courage is recruited in order to maintain hope's endurance. Kierkegaard sees courage as providing the strength to continue in hope despite obstacles. Hence, in a journal entry, Kierkegaard writes of the "humble courage which dares to hope," in contrast to a proud despairing courage.[25]

In summary, the "eternal" is, for Kierkegaard, the only adequate grounds for a "hope" that can escape the defeat of despair. Given the threats of temporality and despair that undermine earthly hopes, the only possible means for surviving such calamities is to be grounded in a hope beyond the earthly. But this is far from escapism, or a diminution of earthly hope, for far from the "acosmism" and life-denial sometimes attributed to Kierkegaard, the eternal, as reflected

---

[24] *JP*II 1665 (*Pap.* III A 129, n.d., 1841).
[25] *JP*II 1664 (*Pap.* III A 217, November 15, 1840).

in hope, provides the standpoint from which one may hope *within* the world. As the Archimedean point for a life of hope, the "eternal" points to God as the source and ground of unending possibility within this world, as well as beyond. Because the prospects for a person's life are not limited to the temporal, one can live within the world in a "frame" of hopefulness.

Some suggest that, in his concern with the "eternal" as an aspect of the present moment and the temporal life, Kierkegaard's philosophy does not require an "objective salvation" or eternal life as "objective" or "resurrection" as a future event. But as one commentator has put it, "the object of one's belief makes a world of subjective difference."[26] Kierkegaard's understanding of salvation is not solely an existentialized "realized eschatology," with no concept of an afterlife; he speaks frequently of this life as a test, or death as the entry to an eternal happiness, and of the sobering thought not of an aestheticized immortality, but that "immortality is the judgment." For example, in "The Resurrection of the Dead Is at Hand – Of the Just and of the Unjust," one of the strongly Christian discourses in the series of "Thoughts Which Wound from Behind," the discourse gives appearance of a thoroughgoing realized eschatology, particularly since it speaks of resurrection as "immortality." But the futurist element comes to the fore in the link of resurrection with judgment: this life is a test, therefore *expect* a resurrection to future judgment.[27] While Kierkegaard is not one to allow speculation, the theme of expectation does not *reduce* talk of a Last Judgment to a belief that "regulates conduct." Part of the imaginative hold this picture has on a person is that one can see it not only as an "image," but as "something I *shall* experience," even if one is agnostic about the details.[28]

THE ANATOMY OF SUFFERING

We can expand on the "eternal hope" Kierkegaard sets forth by looking at a related dialectic, namely, the dialectic of suffering. Just as

---

[26] See the astute and subtle criticism of Harrison Hall (also mentioning Don Cupitt and D. Z. Phillips), in Gordon D. Marino, "Salvation: A Reply to Harrison Hall's Reading of Kierkegaard," *Inquiry* 28 (1985): 441–49, especially 447. Harrison Hall, "Love and Death: Kierkegaard and Heidegger on Authentic and Inauthentic Human Existence," *Inquiry* 27 (1984): 179–97.

[27] *CD* 210–20 (*SV* x 203–13). Compare *PC* 202 (*SV* xii 186), on Christ's second coming.

[28] See Ronald W. Hepburn, "Religious Imagination," in Michael McGhee, ed., *Philosophy, Religion and the Spiritual Life. Royal Institute of Philosophy Supplement: 32* (Cambridge University Press, 1992), 138–39.

there are earthly hopes and eternal hopes, so too there are earthly
sufferings and other more "eternal" forms of suffering. Suffering may
be a purely aesthetic category. A person living within the aesthetic
stage certainly knows suffering; the "rotation method" of the aesthetic
sphere of life is an intelligent attempt to avoid the suffering that is
caused not only by pain, but also by a surfeit of pleasure.

But as an ethical and religious thinker, Kierkegaard reflects upon
not only the universal forms of suffering that attend all human life.
He turns to the specific kinds of suffering that characterize ethical
and religious commitments. "Earthly suffering" is not to be neglected
or denigrated; it is weighty for human life, and also provides the
basis for spiritual advance. But Kierkegaard analyzes other forms of
suffering peculiar to an ethicoreligious life. As Simone Weil has
written, "affliction" (*malheur*) is not the same as simple suffering.[29]
For Kierkegaard as for Weil, affliction as a particular kind of
suffering throws light, in turn, on the particular kinds of hope that
are opened up in ethical and religious existence.

Kierkegaard is especially interested in this feature of ethicoreligious
suffering, namely, that suffering can be taken up into freedom. This is
seen first in that unlike much earthly suffering, it is often avoidable. A
person who holds to a difficult position out of ethical conviction can
escape the opposition and hatred of others simply by giving in to their
demands for conformity. Such a person may heartily wish to be
received back into the group, but nonetheless chooses to hold to her
position, and consequently chooses this avoidable suffering. Second,
unavoidable suffering too, if it is in the service of the good, can be
taken up into freedom, and thereby ennobled.

In both cases the hope that accompanies this suffering-in-freedom
will differ from "earthly hopes." An example of both of these aspects –
hope in the midst of avoidable and unavoidable suffering following
from willing the good – is expressed in an important passage on hope
and suffering in *Purity of Heart*. Here Kierkegaard discusses the willingness of a person to "will the good in truth," and points to the "dying
from" immediacy involved in the decisive hope that is willing to let go
of "double-mindedness" and "the consolations of temporality."[30] Here
a person does not *simply* "hope that all will turn out all right" – this is a
consolation of temporality – but rather one moves from "earthly hope
and sagacity" to an "eternal hope linked with decision." In willing the

29 Weil, *Waiting for God*, 117.
30 *UDVS* 112–15 (*SV* VIII 208–10).

good, childish hopes die, "but then – in death, in the decision of death, there is born a hope that does not die at birth, because it is born in death; *through this hope ... in the decision the suffering one is with the good!*"[31] "The person who acts wills to *do* everything for the good; the person who suffers wills to *suffer* everything for the good."[32]

But "can a person be said *to will* suffering?"[33] The answer is that as a person experiences suffering, one can indeed do more than simply undergo it. Suffering is not simply passive, nor is it of course desired; Kierkegaard, again, is not quietist. This is far from some forms of Pietism, and from Schopenhauer's advocacy of a quietist contemplation arrived at by moving through sufferings to an extinction of will.[34] Kierkegaard's point, rather, is that suffering *can* be chosen, and if so, it can be united with freedom. This suffering (*passio*) is not sheer passivity, for courage (*Mod*) and resistance (*Modstand*) are needed to confront *avoidable* suffering, and patience (*Taalmod*) is needed to confront *unavoidable* suffering.[35] Patience, as the virtue that responds to *unavoidable* suffering, "performs an even greater miracle" than courage, while the beauty of courage is that it "goes freely into the suffering that could be avoided."[36] Patience performs a greater miracle because, while in courageously willing the avoidable suffering one goes to the heart of ethical existence, it is in patiently willing the unavoidable suffering that even the constrictions of necessity become the occasion not for despair and suffocation, but for the exercise of freedom.

This is at the heart of Kierkegaard's understanding of suffering, for the problem that plagues him is how a person can survive the debilitating and numbing effects of suffering. Consider this example: a person suffering from an evil or unjust person may have exhausted all means of resistance, has acted so as "to *do* everything for the good," without success. Again, appearances to the contrary, Kierkegaard is not suggesting passivity in the face of evil, but is concerned with the problem of the person whose resistance and attempts to change the situation meet continual frustration. The difficulty is that, if action cannot change the situation, one is then tempted not only to anger, but to hopelessness. Kierkegaard's response to this, however, is to suggest

---

[31] *UDVS* 100–01 (*SV* VIII 198) (italics in original).
[32] *UDVS* 116 (*SV* VIII 211).
[33] *UDVS* 117 (*SV* VIII 212).
[34] For Kierkegaard's criticism of Schopenhauer's quietism, see *JP* IV 3877 (*Pap.* XI¹ A 144, n.d., 1854).
[35] *UDVS* 118 (*SV* VIII 212–13).
[36] *UDVS* 119 (*SV* VIII 213).

that even in the midst of powerlessness, even when one cannot effect a *change* for the good, *one is not simply a victim*. In choosing to endure the suffering, avoidable or unavoidable, one is still committed to the good; one can still be "single-minded" in devotion to the good, and so strive for "purity of heart." Spiritually speaking, what one gains is an understanding that the love of the good does not depend upon one's success, or in convincing others of the good. The devotion to the good is itself all that one is called upon to do.

Then there is, of course, the affliction that attends "spiritual trial" (*Anfægtelse*) such as endured by Abraham on the road to Mount Moriah, suffering treated more generally by Johannes Climacus in *Postscript*.[37] Here the suffering is not from guilt; "spiritual trial" is not "temptation" (*Fristelse*).[38] The spiritual trial arises from the situation that one is "in the sphere of the relationship with God"; "in temptation, it is the lower that tempts; in spiritual trial it is the higher."[39] It may even be, as with Abraham, that one is under the command of God, perhaps even commanded to break the ethical law. Central to this suffering is the uncertainty. One is condemned to sort out motives and pretexts in determining obedience. And one is under the rigorous requirement to "die from" the immediate, including all of the hopes of the promise of immediacy.

Suffering arises at the death of promise and of "earthly hopes"; new life arises from the ashes of those hopes. Just as Abraham's earthly hope for Isaac is given up, so too he nonetheless shows an eternal hope, beyond the calculations of the "understanding." In *Fear and Trembling*, Johannes de Silentio writes of Abraham that he is "great by that hope whose form is madness, great by the love that is hatred to oneself."[40] There is no clearer example in Kierkegaard's writings of the eternal basis of hope, a hope that goes completely against the grain of earthly calculations.

In the end, Kierkegaard stands in the tradition that sees suffering as "educative," part of God's upbringing. What is distinctive about his understanding of this educative suffering, however, is that he does not see "earthly" sufferings being a "school for character" that drive one to "the consolations of religion." Rather, as he puts it in a journal entry, he identifies much more strongly and starkly how the ethicoreligious

[37] *FT* 31 (*SV*III 83) and *CUP* 458–60 (*SV*VII 399–400).
[38] *CUP* 458 (*SV*VII 399).
[39] *CUP* 458–59 (*SV*VII 399).
[40] *FT* 16–17 (*SV*III 69).

life *itself* is a school of suffering, for "the more one gets involved with God, the greater the difficulties."[41] God's upbringing is a test; it is as if a person asks God to bring one up and "What does God do? He takes a stick, as it were, and begins to beat up the fellow. Alas, the poor wretch, he is completely bewildered by this. He had really believed himself to be the object of God's love – and now this dreadful beating."[42] In this, by the way, Kierkegaard thought that Luther was deficient, since Luther attributed such sufferings to the devil, whereas Kierkegaard sees their source in God's "upbuilding."[43]

One of Kierkegaard's concerns here is to guard against religious narcissism, in which God is "wish-fulfillment," a projection of a comforting "Father-figure" who delivers one from earthly difficulties. Kierkegaard seeks to eliminate that danger, in a radical fashion. Yet the believer sees that God's *intent* in testing and tempting is not that he or she should fail. "The believer, however, immediately interprets the matter inversely; he believes that God does it *in order that* he shall meet the test [*Prøven*] ... disciplined in faith ... [one regards] everything inversely, to remain full of hope and confidence when something happens which previously almost made him faint and expire with anxiety."[44] We need now to turn in more detail to that specific "inversion" that is Christian hope in the midst of suffering.

CHRISTIAN SUFFERING AND CHRISTIAN HOPE

Kierkegaard's descriptions of hope and suffering as sketched out thus far – the dialectical distinctions between the generally human and the ethicoreligious – are all "prologue" to the specifically Christian forms. It is to the last that we turn in this final section. Especially in his second authorship, prompted in part by the *Corsair* affair, but also his own more pronounced rethinking of Christian existence, the problems of specifically Christian suffering and hope take on greater force for his thought.

The polemical irony of this "prologue" is that Kierkegaard explores how much *precedes* Christian suffering and Christian hope, in order to show how far "Christendom" is from the distinctively Christian. The

---

41 *JP*II 1427 (*Pap.* x⁴ A 304, n.d., 1851).
42 *JP*II 1418 (*Pap.* x³ A 747, n.d., 1851).
43 *JP*II 1447 (*Pap.* xi² A 130, n.d., 1854).
44 *JP*II 1401 (*Pap.* x² A 493, n.d., 1850).

"purity of heart" to will one thing in voluntary suffering that is open to a Socrates requires no specifically Christian belief. Kierkegaard was particularly concerned to prevent the conceptual confusion, of which he found the clergy especially guilty, that resides in forgetting the distinctiveness of Christian suffering and Christian hope. The situation in "Christendom" had become one of leveling the distinctions, such that, as Anti-Climacus wryly notes in *Practice in Christianity*,

Authentic Christian suffering has been abolished, suffering "on account of the Word," "for righteousness' sake," etc., and on the other hand ordinary human sufferings have been dressed up to be Christian sufferings and then are made out to follow the paradigm – what a masterpiece of upside-downness! Even with respect to minor religious paradigms, it is customary to take them in vain. A man's wife dies. Then the pastor preaches about Abraham who sacrifices Isaac, and the widower is eloquently portrayed by His Reverence as a kind of Abraham, a counterpart to Abraham.[45]

The intent is not to diminish earthly forms of suffering; indeed, Anti-Climacus finds part of the confusion in "Christendom" to center around the patronizing belief that somehow "paganism" was un-familiar with earthly suffering, and that alleviating earthly sufferings is the main concern of Christianity.[46] In face of such demoralizing confusion and lack of conceptual rigor, Anti-Climacus (and Kierke-gaard) seek clarity concerning the peculiar shape and aim of Christ-ian suffering and hope, and hence the peculiar shape of Christian discipleship.

The suffering God

Near the end of his life, and during his attack on "Christendom," Kierkegaard published a sermon on "The Unchangeableness of God," based on one of his favorite texts, James 1:17–21: "Every good and every perfect gift is from above and comes down from the Father of lights, with whom there is no variableness or shadow of turning."[47] Kierkegaard often speaks of God's "unchangeableness," by which he means not Aristotle's unmoved Mover, but the constancy of God's eternity as the fixed point for a person's love and devotion.[48] In the

---

[45] *PC* 108 (*SV* xii 103).
[46] *Ibid.*
[47] *UG* 226–40 (*SV* xiv 281–94).
[48] Compare *JP* ii 1332 (*Pap.* iv a 157, n.d., 1843), *JP* iv 3838 (*Pap.* ix a 295, n.d., 1848), *JP* ii 1428 (*Pap.* x⁴ a 311, n.d., 1851).

prayer that opens the sermon, Kierkegaard writes, "Thou on the contrary art moved, and moved in infinite love, by all things."[49]

The unchangeableness of God is therefore God's constancy, and so is fully compatible with God's being affected. What Kierkegaard warns about, several years later, in other journal entries, is making all of this a "phantom-battle about the predicates of God," rather than about a relationship between two reconciled parties. The apparent contrast between God's unchangeableness and the change that God undergoes in atonement is "an anthropopathetic conception which cannot stand up under reflection." The solution to the apparent contradiction is that God is not an abstract unchangeableness, but is the Subject who encounters human beings.[50] God's constancy (unchangeableness) in atonement calls, rather, for one to recognize sin and reconciliation, that she or he has changed, has become a sinner, and that God, who has not changed, comes to reconcile – hence, it is human beings who must change.

Like Luther's *theologia crucis* before him and Bonhoeffer's similar stress on the cross after him, Kierkegaard holds that Christians meet God in the figure of Christ on the cross, and the God there known is the *suffering* God who loves sinners unto death.[51] Luther, like Kierkegaard later, contrasts a theology of glory, one that finds God *directly* in God's works, with the paradoxicality and hiddenness of the God who is hidden in the suffering Christ.[52] So too, Kierkegaard maintains the incognito of the Incarnation, that Christ is not directly *known*, but believed, to be divine. Kierkegaard does not deny the exaltation and glory of Christ; rather, he sees it dialectically, as exaltation in abasement. This is why he uses John 12:32 as the basic text for *Practice in Christianity, No. III*: "And I, when I am lifted up from the earth, will draw all to myself."[53] Finally, he also eschatologizes the exaltation of the theology of glory. The glory of Christ, directly perceived, will only be revealed hereafter: for the believer, Christ's "loftiness does not begin until his ascension to heaven, and since that time not one single word has been heard from him – thus every word he said was said in his abasement."[54] Hence, for the

---

[49] *UG* 227 (*SV* XIV 283). Compare too Climacus' discussion of God as "unmoved" yet needful in "the god's poem" in *Philosophical Fragments*, ch. 2.

[50] *JP* II 1348 (*Pap.* VII¹ A 143, n.d., 1846); *JP* II 1349 (*Pap.* VII¹ A 201, n.d., 1846).

[51] Paul Althaus, *The Theology of Martin Luther*, trans. Robert C. Schultz (Philadelphia: Fortress Press, 1966), 26; on specifically Christian suffering, compare Bonhoeffer, *The Cost of Discipleship*, 98.

[52] Althaus, *The Theology of Martin Luther*, 27.

[53] *PC* 145–262 (*SV* XII 135–239).

[54] *PC* 161–62 (*SV* XII 151).

believer, Christ "still exists only in his abasement, until he, something that is believed, comes again in glory."[55]

As we saw in chapter 4, the paradoxicality of the Incarnation is not an intellectual conundrum, but the paradox of the God who is revealed in lowliness, helplessness, and suffering. This too is a central theme in Luther.[56] It led Luther to affirm, in the words of one interpreter, if not a "patripassianism" (the suffering of the Father), then a "deipassionism," that *God* suffers in Christ's human nature.[57] Kierkegaard's language is similar in speaking of the suffering of God in Christ. In a journal entry of 1848 he writes, "Christ's suffering naturally cannot be comprehended, since the divine and the human have to be *believed* together, something only faith is capable of doing ... And now Christ's suffering: to have everything divinely in his power – and then nevertheless to will freely to suffer humanly, every moment divinely capable of changing everything."[58]

We can now place Kierkegaard's understanding of Christ as the suffering God a bit more precisely. The language in this journal entry may appear Nestorian, separating the two natures of Christ, the divine and the human, and predicating the suffering of the human, not the divine nature, of Christ. But the effect is not Nestorian, but quite the opposite: based on a Lutheran stress on the communication of idioms it is "deipassionate," allowing suffering to be attributed to Christ's *divine* nature. The divine and the human "have to be *believed* together," and hence "willing freely to suffer humanly" expresses the divine will, not simply the human will. Again the images of the depths of the sea and the heights of the sky come together, as they did in describing purity of heart: "At every moment Christ is God just as much as he is man – just as the sky seems to be as deep in the sea as it is high above the sea."[59]

---

[55] *PC* 31 (*SV* xii 29).
[56] Althaus, *The Theology of Martin Luther*, 230.
[57] Althaus, *The Theology of Martin Luther*, 197, on the *genus tapeinoticon.*
[58] *JP* iv 4610 (*Pap.* viii[1] A 579, n.d., 1849). Compare *SUD* 85 (*SV* xi 197), *PC* 138 (*SV* xii 129).
[59] *JP* i 284 (*Pap.* ii A 595, n.d., 1837). This is not the later kenoticism of Gottfried Thomasius; Kierkegaard holds rather to the orthodox Lutheran picture of Christ's possessing omnipotence, omniscience, omnipresence, etc., but that Christ chooses not to employ them. The lowliness is the kenotic self-emptying of God as incarnate and suffering in Jesus Christ. In terms of seventeenth-century Lutheran orthodoxy, Kierkegaard is closer to the kenoticism of the school of Giessen (Christ abstained from using these divine attributes altogether) rather than the *krysis* school of Tübingen (Christ used divine powers, but only in secret). For a concise statement of the issues between Tübingen and Giessen, see, for example, Heinrich Schmid, *Doctrinal Theology of the Evangelical Lutheran Church*, trans. Charles A. Hay and Henry E. Jacobs (Minneapolis: Augsburg, 1899), 390–93. For Thomasius, see Claude Welch, ed. and trans., *God and Incarnation in Mid-Nineteenth Century German Theology* (New York: Oxford University Press, 1965).

Kierkegaard's stress on the humanity of Christ is, then, not Nestorian, but, in classical terms, focuses on "the state of humiliation" rather than "the state of exaltation." This is why the "servant" language is so important for him. In the voluntary renunciation of divine powers, Christ's life is a continuing humiliation. The exaltation is a separate and later period, beginning with the ascension. In Christ, we see the divine–human love that *freely chooses avoidable suffering* incarnate in human nature. Not only did Christ foresee his suffering, but "Christ's suffering was a choice."[60] "He *wills* to be the sign of offense and the object of faith."[61] Hence, Christ, Anti-Climacus stresses, citing Hebrews 5:8, "himself learned from what he suffered, learned obedience."[62] His suffering was not accidental or episodic, but voluntary and lifelong.

It is the lifelong humiliation of Christ in the Incarnation that allows an adequate understanding of human suffering, not in a generalized theory of suffering, but in the particular fact of God's identification with suffering. This Christocentric approach to suffering thus provides the context for understanding both God's constancy and also human and Christian suffering. Kierkegaard holds together God's unchange-ableness as constancy together with suffering, and these are seen together (by the eyes of faith) in the concrete human life of Christ. More specifically, this constancy and suffering are both rooted in God's love. Love is central to what the believer sees in the cross of Jesus, for it is the love of God at work.

In *Practice in Christianity*, Anti-Climacus fills out the portrait of God's suffering love reaching out to suffering humanity; ironically, he illuminates thereby the specific pain of God's spurned love, because the divine love prompts offense. First, divine compassion reaches out to human suffering, but it is a reckless compassion that reaches out to *all* who suffer; such self-sacrifice is offensive to limited human com-passion that is always directed only to one's own group.[63] Second, however, divine compassion suffers the offense of rejection, since the divine compassion sees human suffering not only in externals, but in a deeper suffering, viz., the fact of sin.[64] Christ invites "the poor and

60   *JP*1 308 (*Pap.* VIII¹ A 344, n.d., 1847).
61   *JP*1 322 (*Pap.* IX A 59, n.d., 1848).
62   *PC* 182 (*SV*XII 169).
63   *PC* 57–59 (*SV*XII 55–56).
64   *PC* 60–61 (*SV*XII 57).

sick and suffering to come – and then to be able to do nothing for them, but instead of that promise them the forgiveness of sins."[65]

It is important to note here the narrative shape of Kierkegaard's portrayal of Christ. The narrative emerges from the fact that Christ is encountered only by way of a story of his life. In *Practice in Christianity*, Anti-Climacus stresses the narrative shape of Christ's life, its character as "sacred history," in contrast to Climacus' downplaying of that narrative.[66] Further, it is a "story of suffering," and lifelong suffering.[67]

There are two further factors at work behind this picture of Christ's suffering as key to confessing his divinity, and behind the stress on the theology of the cross as opposed to a theology of glory. First, as John Elrod has rightly argued, Kierkegaard's polemical point is crucial: he opposes the suffering God–man to all of the theologies of glory that were gaining political currency in his day, whether in the form of speculative theology's legitimation of reason, Golden Age Denmark's conservative church–state establishment, or Grundtvig's popularization of a nationalistic Christianity.[68] Especially obnoxious to him is the ecclesiastical form of the theology of glory: the false equation that identifies the established church with the "triumphant church."[69] Each of these abuses of the Incarnation results in a legitimation and deification of the established order. But if, as Kierkegaard argues, Jesus Christ is God incognito, is an offense to all claims to human glory, and is recognized only in faith, such direct cultural self-deification is impossible.

A second factor behind this portrayal of Christ's sufferings is Kierkegaard's reading of the New Testament on "offense." *Pace* Elrod, there is considerable biblical support for the centrality of the "offense" against Christ by his contemporaries; in *Practice in Christianity*, the extensive biblical references to the use of "offense" in the gospels are not accidental or mere window-dressing.[70] Anti-Climacus is rather providing a solid exegetical foundation for his emphasis on offense. This is crucial strategically, since at the heart of his claim is that a theology of glory is totally at odds with the New Testament portrayal of Christ.

---

[65] *PC* 61 (*SV* XII 57).
[66] *PC* 33, 168 (*SV* XII 31, 157).
[67] *PC* 168 (*SV* XII 157).
[68] Elrod, *Kierkegaard and Christendom*, 213, 74.
[69] See, for example, *PC* 211–24 (*SV* XII 194–206).
[70] Elrod, *Kierkegaard and Christendom*, 213, writes: "Even though one may find [in the New Testament] direct references to Christ as an offense to reason in only a few passages..."

There is one further point that must be emphasized: suffering is central to Christ's earthly life, and, furthermore, Christ's suffering as the incarnate one is qualitatively *unique*. Anti-Climacus, in *Practice in Christianity*, specifies, typically, a distinction between two forms of Christ's sufferings. First are his public, external sufferings, "how he was mocked, scourged, and crucified."[71] Second, Christ's unique suffering follows from his identity as the God–man: "the suffering of inwardness, suffering of soul, or what might be called the secret of the sufferings that were inseparable from his life in unrecognizability from the time he appeared until the very last."[72] Affirming as he does that Christ possessed a consciousness of divinity, Kierkegaard sees in the concealment of this the peculiar suffering that attends the unrecognizability of divinity and the need for indirect communication and faith to apprehend Christ's identity. At the heart of this suffering is "his concern and grief that his suffering is an occasion for offense."[73] The pain of Christ is that his divine love is hated. This unique suffering indicates again that the suffering of Christ is the suffering of God; it is unique because it is divine suffering, in the midst of the incognito, not allowing direct self-revelation.

Taking up one's cross: from "dying to the world" to discipleship

We turn now from the suffering of God in Christ incarnate to the human correlate and response. Christian suffering is a specific response to Christ; it is defined by his suffering. Christian existence in suffering and in hope is "Christomorphic," formed after Christ as the Pattern or Prototype (*Forbilledet*) for the believer. As Bradley Dewey rightly argues, Christ is "attractive" to the believer, beyond offense, and despite the repellent features of his death as a call to discipleship.[74] The "attractiveness" is not aesthetic, but is the call to "Come, follow me," which paradoxically promises life, for it is the promise of forgiveness and of communion with Christ that lures one into faith and sustains one in the midst of discipleship's suffering. At the heart of this is not only the Moravian Pietistic understanding of communion with the risen Christ, but also the Pauline concept of being "in Christ" in participating in his suffering and humiliation.[75]

71　*PC* 136 (*SV* xii 127).
72　*PC* 136–37 (*SV* xii 127).
73　*PC* 138 (*SV* xii 129).
74　Dewey, *The New Obedience*, part 2, ch. 4.
75　Dewey, *The New Obedience*, 138–39.

In the later literature, Kierkegaard's concern with Christian existence as "taking up one's cross" deepens. First, he presents the
possibility of hope to a person no matter the extent or depth of one's
suffering, since the suffering God at the heart of the Christian gospel
allows a discipleship that gives meaning to suffering, "taking up one's
cross" in imitation of Christ. As with Luther, so too with Kierkegaard,
the proper *response* to the God who is hiddenly revealed in the cross is
that the believer does not strike a bargain with God, but responds as
one called to suffer.[76] The Christian meaning of life, he writes in his
journal a year before his death, is "to suffer ... only in suffering can the
eternal come into contact with the temporal in time: only in suffering
can spirit come in contact with worldliness in worldliness."[77]

"Dying from the world" includes "letting go" of the objects of
desire.[78] Again, however, Kierkegaard distinguishes between Christian
"dying from" and Schopenhauer's pessimism, the "gloomy Indian view
that to live [*at leve*] is to suffer."[79] On the contrary, Christianity is based
upon an Old Testament affirmation of existence:

Christianity does not declare that to exist is to suffer. Quite the reverse, and
therefore it is erected directly upon Jewish optimism, utilizes as foreground
the most intensified lust for life which has ever attached itself to life – in order
to introduce Christianity as renunciation and to show that to be a Christian is
to suffer, including having to suffer for the doctrine.[80]

Second, Christian suffering is a specific form of "Christomorphic"
imitative renunciation in which one follows Christ's own path. Already
in an early journal entry from 1834, he writes: "Christ's whole life in all
its aspects must supply the norm for the life of the following Christian
and thus for the life of the whole Church."[81] Just as Christ had to
"learn obedience," so too, for Christian existence, "to be a human
being, to live here in this world, is to be tested; life is an *Examen*
[examination] ... and the greatest examination a human being has to
take, to which his whole life is assigned, is to become and to be a
Christian."[82] For this reason, one must begin, not with the exalted
Christ in glory, but with where he began, in lowliness, not loftiness:
"where should *we* begin? Because he is now on high, can we therefore

---

[76] Althaus, *The Theology of Martin Luther*, 27.
[77] *JP*IV 4712 (*Pap.* XI¹ A 377, n.d., 1854).
[78] *FSE* 78 (*SV*XII 362).
[79] *JP*IV 3881 (*Pap.* XI¹ A 181, n.d., 1854).
[80] *Ibid.*
[81] *JP*I 273 (*Pap.* I A 28, November 26, 1834).
[82] *PC* 183 (*SV*XII 170). Compare *JP*I 481 (*Pap.* IX A 51, n.d., 1848).

also begin with loftiness; that is, because he inherited loftiness, can we therefore also take it in advance?"[83] The disciple, the follower, must tread the same path Christ walked. Is it that "he (Christ) has suffered and now the rest of us will have it easy"?[84] This finally becomes the model for Christian discipleship as well.[85]

Here such images as "journey," "pilgrimage," "cross-bearing," "follower of Christ" become central. Christ is the "Way," and "to follow ... means to walk along the same road walked by the one whom one is following ... to *follow Christ* means to take up one's cross," as a daily task, to continue "to *carry one's cross*."[86] It is "*to walk the same road* Christ walked in the lowly form of a servant," and "*to walk by oneself*" in self-denial, following Christ who "is no longer visibly walking ahead."[87]

Third, as several scholars have recently pointed out, there is an important development of Kierkegaard's thought on specifically Christian suffering from the Climacean writings to the later literature, including the writings of the Christian pseudonym Anti-Climacus. John Elrod and Merold Westphal argue that Climacus focuses on suffering as specifically a religious "dying away from immediacy" in Religiousness A, a concealed suffering that is part of "hidden inwardness." Hence, "earthly sufferings" are relativized and even dismissed as "merely outward," and thus spiritually unimportant. Particularly in the Climacean writings, the contrast is not between "unavoidable/avoidable sufferings," but between "outer/inner." Elrod rightly puzzles over "how Climacus can so casually dismiss the pain inflicted upon the individual by both natural causes and human agency external to himself," seeing this as "misfortune," without religious significance.[88] Westphal cites Climacus' portrayal in *Postscript* of Acts 5:40–42 (the flogging of the apostles); Climacus sees this not as a case of religious suffering, but mere misfortune.[89]

---

[83] *PC* 182 (*SV* XII 169).

[84] *JP* IV 4711 (*Pap.* XI¹ A 357, n.d., 1854).

[85] *PC* 34–35 (*SV* XII 32).

[86] *UDVS* 219, 221, 222 (*SV* VIII 307, 308, 309).

[87] *UDVS* 223, 219 (*SV* VIII 310, 307).

[88] John William Elrod, "Climacus, Anti-Climacus and the Problem of Suffering," *Thought* 55:218 (September 1980): 306–19; the quotation is from 312.

[89] *CUP* 452–53 (*SV* VII 393–94). Merold Westphal, "Kierkegaard's Phenomenology of Faith as Suffering," in Hugh J. Silverman, ed., *Writing the Politics of Difference, Selected Studies in Phenomenology and Existential Philosophy* 14 (Albany: State University of New York Press, 1991), 62–63.

In the later writings, including *The Gospel of Sufferings* and Anti-Climacus' *Practice in Christianity*, the same passage from Acts indicates the problem with Climacus' "hidden inwardness," and points to the decisive quality of Christian suffering: that it is voluntary and avoidable.[90] In *Practice in Christianity*, Anti-Climacus writes that Christian suffering is not simply enduring the world's ills, but that "what is decisive in Christian suffering is voluntariness and *the possibility of offense for the one who suffers*."[91] Later in the same book he writes: "To suffer in a way akin to Christ's suffering is not to put up patiently with the inescapable, but it is to suffer evil at the hands of people because as a Christian or in being a Christian one wills and endeavors to do the good: thus one could avoid this suffering by giving up willing the good."[92] It is not that Anti-Climacus dismisses inwardness, since this suffering requires inwardness.[93] Nonetheless, Westphal argues that "the inward journey developed in the pseudonymous writings is *aufgehoben* in the outward journey developed in the 'second' authorship under the heading of the imitation of Christ." One must go beyond Religiousness B's "self-sufficiency of inwardness, which must ... be overcome."[94]

I think that Elrod and Westphal are correct, although the latter misses the extent to which the *voluntariness* of suffering is present already in such writings as *Purity of Heart*. We will pursue the social and political aspects of this further in chapter 7. For now, the point to see is how Kierkegaard increasingly moves in his "second literature" from the "hiddenness" of religious suffering in Climacus' *Postscript* to a stress on the voluntariness *and* the public character of suffering, both of which mark specifically Christian suffering. One can trace out a deepening of Kierkegaard's reflections on the shape of Christian suffering, a deepening that follows from several factors: his own experience of public ridicule in the *Corsair* Affair (Elrod), the faltering of the logic of hidden inwardness (Westphal), and also his closer attention to the New Testament portrayal of discipleship.

In the later literature, Kierkegaard by no means gives up the Climacean ideal of "dying from the world." Rather, he amplifies and fills it out, expanding it from the "hidden inwardness" of Religiousness

---

90   *Ibid*. See also Merold Westphal, "Kierkegaard's Teleological Suspension of Religiousness B," in Connell and Evans, eds., *Foundations of Kierkegaard's Vision of Community*, 110–29.
91   *PC* 109 (*SV* XII 104) (italics in original).
92   *PC* 173 (*SV* XII 161).
93   Elrod, "Climacus, Anti-Climacus and the Problem of Suffering," 313n4.
94   Westphal, "Kierkegaard's Phenomenology of Faith as Suffering," 64, 67. Westphal argues that Kierkegaard's Religiousness B (as defined by Climacus) gives way to a "Religiousness C."

A toward a specifically Christian discipleship. Already in Climacus, "dying from the world" is not withdrawal from the world, or a lack of concern for the finite world, but a stance in which one seeks to follow Christ in not being anxious for worldly matters, not being dominated by the world. As John Elrod points out, this "dying from the world" is a suffering that is (a) not simply the suffering called for in the choice to abandon an aesthetic existence, (b) neither is it the suffering of learning inattentiveness to one's own needs in love of neighbor. Beyond that, Kierkegaard stresses that Christian existence is a continual suffering, a kind of living death, since (c) Christian suffering mirrors Christ's in that the Christian cannot make voluntary grasping of this suffering understood; it is an offense to the practical reason that still calculates advantages and disadvantages.[95] It is like being told that one wins by losing.

Suffering, indeed, becomes one of the central marks of the Christian life. This has several important implications. First, in the later literature, the sufferings of misfortune *can* have ethicoreligious significance. As Westphal puts it, "for those who have progressed to ethico-religious subjectivity, it is not the pain of misfortune as such that dehumanizes our life, but rather the inability to interpret that pain in any but aesthetic categories."[96] As we have seen, universal human suffering is reinterpreted when it is raised into the sphere of freedom; when one *wills* to endure suffering in patience, or struggle against it in courage, the possibility opens that one is no longer dehumanized as a victim. Suffering is not thereby ended, but it is gathered into the sphere of one's active response. One moves from victim to (in whatever degree) master of suffering.

Second, as we have seen, avoidable, voluntary suffering (i.e., in contrast to misfortune) is more and more linked with "suffering for the doctrine," "suffering for the truth" of Christian faith.[97] It is the suffering that results from any Christian attempt to do the good and to live the truth.[98]

Third, this suffering is not an accidental feature of Christian existence, but is entailed by it. If one gets involved with God, one *will* suffer for the truth. This, by the way, is the problem with seeing "religion as refuge." It is true as far as it goes, but it does not capture

[95] Elrod, "Climacus, Anti-Climacus and the Problem of Suffering," 316.
[96] Westphal, "Kierkegaard's Phenomenology of Faith as Suffering," 66.
[97] On "suffering for the doctrine," see for example *JFY* 169 (*SV*xii 440).
[98] *PC* 173 (*SV*xii 161). Compare *PC* 109 (*SV*xii 104) where voluntariness is linked with "spiritual trial."

the increasing emphasis in Kierkegaard's writings on the way in which involvement with God (the *suffering* God) calls one to endure opposition from the world. Yet as Bradley Dewey rightly argues, for Kierkegaard Christian suffering is inevitable, but it is not commanded *per se*. The commandment to the believer is not "go and suffer." Rather, given the world's opposition, following the pattern will lead to opposition and suffering.[99] Behind the careful exegetical analysis of "offense" in *Practice in Christianity* lies Anti-Climacus' desire to affirm the possibility of offense as foundational to New Testament Christianity. Christ's persecution is thus not historically accidental, as is the persecution of other historical figures; it expresses what the truth *has* to suffer (John 14:6).

Again the question arises: Does Kierkegaard simply romanticize suffering, legitimizing *ressentiment*? The language of "sacrifice" and "suffering" is subject to immense abuse. Is it theologically appropriate to stress so much the suffering of Christ as the model of discipleship? It is striking, however, how aware Kierkegaard is of the psychological and ethical dangers of this model, and he approaches it cautiously. This is seen specifically in his struggles with the ethical justification for allowing oneself to suffer at the hands of others. In the 1847 essay "Has a Human Being the Right to Allow Himself to Be Put to Death for the Truth?," one of the *Two Ethical-Religious Essays* published in May 1849 under the pseudonym "H. H.,"[100] Kierkegaard first strongly distinguishes between Christ's death and the martyr's, for, while Christ's death is justified as effecting atonement, the latter is problematic in bringing guilt upon the persecutors. Further, Christ's suffering itself is not romanticized as a model for imitation; indeed, the cross is not edifying or attractive, but repellent. In an 1847 journal entry, Kierkegaard writes,

When I consider the death of Christ, the sight (regarded as the prototype) is scarcely upbuilding or edifying. (1) There is little edification in seeing that the holy and innocent one has to suffer in this way, consequently that the world is so corrupted. (2) What upbuilding is there for me (the guilty) in the innocent one's suffering in this way? But it [the upbuilding] is the atonement. Therefore, at the same time that he thrusts me away from himself as if to say: What fellowship is there between you and me? – at the same time he draws me to himself by the atonement.[101]

---

[99] Dewey, *The New Obedience*, 144–45.
[100] *Two Minor Ethico-Religious Essays* (*SV* xi 47–109). See Kirmmse's perceptive discussion of these essays in *Kierkegaard in Golden Age Denmark*, 330–39.
[101] *JP*1 304 (*Pap.* viii¹ A 83, n.d., 1847).

Nonetheless, Kierkegaard gradually develops a cautious justification of Christian suffering as imitation of Christ. Significantly, however, he locates the decisive justification of such suffering not simply in the intent of the sufferer, but in the social setting. The necessary efficient cause of the suffering, as it were, is not the sufferer, but the world; being what it is, the world inevitably persecutes the truth. Thus, while suffering for the good (including Christ's crucifixion) certainly requires the agent's willingness to suffer voluntarily, this does not mean that such a person seeks death. As Kierkegaard writes in his journal:

> one pretends as if Christ himself and God's providence ordained it this way [that Christ was crucified] ... [T]hat Christ was willing to sacrifice his life does not at all signify that he sought death ... Christ's willingness to offer his life simply means a conception of the world as being so evil that the Holy One unconditionally had to die ... If you will unconditionally risk everything for the good – then you will be persecuted, unconditionally persecuted.[102]

In other words, the justification of such martyrdom, whether for Christ or the follower, is located not in a desire to suffer, but in the state of the society against which one protests for the sake of the good.

Hence, Kierkegaard does not rush to embrace a romanticism of imagined suffering, but considers that the call to discipleship is purged and purified in the rigors of actual suffering. The danger of *imagining* discipleship is replaced by *living* the ideal of discipleship. Here Kierkegaard strives to avoid both the distancing of romanticism and the extinction of the imagination in Christian discipleship. The ideal is not extinguished, but lives; yet it lives in actuality, not in sheer possibility.

There is one final danger in romanticizing Christian suffering; as Stanley Hauerwas has written, when suffering is used for purification, we may simply increase our self-fascination. The image of the suffering God can be abused by the victim (and in this the victim is even more deeply victimized) to legitimize passivity or self-hatred.[103] It seems to me, however, that Kierkegaard's distancing of Christ's suffering from the follower also seeks to curb that final danger of lethargy and self-hatred by delivering the disciple from self-fascination. If the vision of the suffering God can be abused, becoming a warrant for narcissistic self-absorption, the distance of the ideal can also deliver the sufferer,

---

[102] *JP*i 305 (*Pap.* viii¹ A 145, n.d., 1847).
[103] Hauerwas, "The Significance of Vision," 43. Hauerwas cites Iris Murdoch's novels as explorations of the abuse of suffering.

not only in forgiving sins (in faith), or in identification with suffering, but in giving the sufferer a point of *attention* that delivers one from the degradation of self-absorbed suffering. It is in that sense that the cross, and the way of taking the cross, can heal and open one to possibility. In taking the role of victim and substitute, God breaks the cycle of victimization, including the victim's pain. It is to that possibility that we now turn.

Hope, courage and perseverance, joy, and humor

In Kierkegaard's inverse dialectic, suffering does not stand alone, nor is the suffering Christ the warrant for self-destructive narcissistic pain. Suffering is rather a coin with an obverse face, the other side of the dialectic: the themes of hope, courage and perseverance, joy, and humor in the midst of Christian suffering.

The Christocentric focus here is crucial too. Dietrich Bonhoeffer, in a strongly Kierkegaardian strain, writes in *The Cost of Discipleship*: "Such grace is *costly* because it calls us to follow, and it is *grace* because it calls us to follow *Jesus Christ*. It is costly because it costs a man his life, and it is grace because it gives a man the only true life."[104] For Kierkegaard too the strenuousness of discipleship is allayed by a strong sense of the presence of the risen Christ.

As we have seen, often Kierkegaard stresses the absence of the exalted Christ who is prototype and pattern: Christ is not visibly ahead of one on the way of discipleship; one walks alone.[105] Yet, Kierkegaard affirms presence and absence together. Christ is present in two ways, as helper and as goal of the journey. The opening prayer of the first discourse of *The Gospel of Sufferings* sounds the themes of discipleship as following the prototype, but also affirms the presence of Christ as helper: "You who yourself once walked the earth and left footprints that we should follow; you who from your heaven still look down on every pilgrim, strengthen the weary, hearten the disheartened, lead back the straying, give solace to the struggling."[106] Second, Christ is the goal of the journey and thus the object of hope for the Christian pilgrim:

But there is still one final blessed joy contained in the thought of following Christ. Admittedly, as has been shown, he does not walk along with the

[104] Bonhoeffer, *The Cost of Discipleship*, 47.
[105] *UDVS* 223 (*SV* VIII 310).
[106] *UDVS* 217 (*SV* VIII 305).

follower, nor is he visible before him, but he has gone *ahead*, and this is the follower's joyful hope: that he is to follow him ... [believing that Christ] went ahead *in order to prepare a place for the follower.*[107]

Because the risen Christ is not only prototype but helper along the way and the goal of the way, Christian imitation and suffering can be eminently hopeful. As we have seen, central to Kierkegaard's hope is its "eternity": because hope is oriented to God, it is never defeated. This is given a more Christological focus in *The Gospel of Sufferings*, where Kierkegaard writes:

The Apostle Paul declares (1 Corinthians 15:19), "If we hope only for this life, we are the most miserable of all." This is indeed the case, because if there were no eternal happiness in a life to come, the person who for Christ's sake renounces all the world's goods and bears all its evils would be deceived, dreadfully deceived ... If, however, there is an eternal happiness in the life to come, then he, the miserable one, is still the richest of all ... There is only one eternal hope on this earth: to follow Christ into heaven.[108]

Relevant here is Kierkegaard's third discourse in *The Gospel of Sufferings*, an extensive meditation on 2 Corinthians 4:17: "our hardship, which is brief and light, procures for us an eternal weight of glory beyond all measure."[109]

Finally, the "presence" is also that of the Holy Spirit. Johannine as well as Pauline in tone, Kierkegaard stresses the presence of the Holy Spirit, who brings "hope against hope." After the death of immediate hopes is "the hope of the life-giving Spirit ... against the hope of the understanding."[110]

The "absence" theme – now "absence within presence" – brings us to the importance of perseverance and courage. "Where courage is not," Samuel Johnson writes, "no other virtue can survive except by accident."[111] Certainly, where courage is not, hope is impossible. Kierkegaard can now say that specifically Christian hope requires perseverance and courage. Christian faith builds upon the virtue of courage, but also shapes courage in specific ways. Part of this is the realism of Kierkegaard's understanding of discipleship, which leads him to reflect in his journals on the need for an increase in courage as

---

[107] *UDVS* 227 (*SV* viii 314). The Scriptural reference is John 14:2.
[108] *UDVS* 228–29 (*SV* viii 315–16).
[109] *UDVS* 308 (*SV* viii 387).
[110] *FSE* 82–83 (*SV* xii 366).
[111] As cited by C. S. Lewis, *Surprised by Joy*, 161.

difficulties mount.[112] There is no escape from the burden of suffering, but suffering is not the final word.[113]

Because Christian life for Kierkegaard is a pilgrimage, perseverance is necessary. Due both to the uncertainty of the road and the fact that one never arrives at the goal in this life, hope and perseverance are always required. Kierkegaard's interesting reflections on the "road" metaphor in the fifth discourse of *The Gospel of Sufferings* stress that it is not that one road is easy and another road is hard; rather, "it is not the road that is hard but that hardship is the road."[114] The crucial question is not *what* road one travels, or whether the road will get easier, or whether one should have taken a different road, but *how* one walks and perseveres in the chosen road. "The sufferer perseveres and walks ahead in hardships on the road of perfection."[115] The comfort in the thought is that one does not complain that some have it easier, or that one is simply a victim of misfortune, since hardship is the way for every road.

In the first discourse of *The Gospel of Sufferings*, Kierkegaard extends the "grammar" of courage to include perseverance and, at first glance surprisingly, links courage with meekness. He plays with the linguistic similarity between courage (*Mod*), high-mindedness (*Høimod*), and patience (*Taalmod*). The crucial clue, however, is that "gentle courage" (*sagte Mod*) brings to mind the meekness (*Sagtmodighed*) to which Christ summons his followers: "Learn from me, for I am meek and lowly of heart."[116] "Courage [*Mod*] makes a noise, high-mindedness [*Høimod*] holds its head high, patience [*Taalmod*] is silent, but meekness [*Sagtmod*] carries the heavy weight lightly."[117]

The seventh discourse in *The Gospel of Sufferings* picks up the theme of courage [*Frimodighed*], and emphasizes especially the suffering a Christian undergoes from the world's opposition.[118] The text is Acts 5:41, on the apostles' rejoicing, after their flogging by the council, that they had been deemed worthy to be scorned for the sake of Christ's name.[119] As we

---

112 See his appreciative remarks on Seneca in *JP* IV 3907 (*Pap.* x³ A 31, n.d., 1850) and 3912 (*Pap.* x³ A 601, n.d., 1850). This doubtless reflects also Kierkegaard's reflections on his own need for courage after the publication of *Practice in Christianity*; see Malantschuk's note in *JP* IV, p. 638.
113 Bradley R. Dewey, "Kierkegaard on Suffering: Promise and Lack of Fulfillment in Life's Stages," *Humanitas* 9:1 (February 1973): 21–45; see 44.
114 *UDVS* 292 (*SV* VIII 373).
115 *UDVS* 297 (*SV* VIII 377).
116 *UDVS* 239–40 (*SV* VIII 326).
117 *UDVS* 240 (*SV* VIII 326).
118 *UDVS* 321 (*SV* VIII 398).
119 *UDVS* 328 (*SV* VIII 404).

have seen, this discourse is a good example of what Merold Westphal
has noted, that Kierkegaard in his later literature finds a place for
earthly sufferings. Further, as Bruce Kirmmse puts it, we see here
"one of SK's principal cultural-political assessments prior to the
'attack on Christendom.'"[120] Kierkegaard dwells extensively
throughout these discourses on the "reversal" of Christian existence,
and this is especially evident in this final, culminating discourse on
persecution and the courage it calls forth. The courage (*Frimodighed*)
that a believer learns in persecution is an "open-hearted courage."[121]
As Kirmmse argues, this concept links two important concerns of
Kierkegaard in this discourse: the problem of judging others that
arises from confessing Christianity in Christendom and the tendency
of modern culture to deny the integrity of individuals.[122] For our
purposes, the point to see is that the suffering of persecution is the
motivation for a courage that reverses the world's shame and scorn
into honor: "*This reversing is the reverseness of open-hearted courage.*"[123] Most
important in this discourse is Kierkegaard's answer to this problem:
how a victim of persecution can see her or his "weakness" as a
strength. The answer is that submitting to persecution can become a
manifestation of strength, not weakness; suffering for the sake of
righteousness is not "renouncing one's power," but learning a new
power. Indeed, the sufferer *takes power from the ridiculing world*: this
open-hearted courage "is able to take power from the world and has
the power to change scorn into honor, downfall into victory!"[124] The
victory won by this courage is not simply the hope for eternal life;
rather, the witness to the truth "is victorious while he is living;
suffering, he is victorious while he is still alive – he is victorious on the
day of suffering. If all human opposition mounts up, yes, if a world
rises up against him, he is the stronger."[125]

This leads us to the related aspects of Christian existence in hope:
humor and joy. Johannes Climacus had already expounded upon
humor as the confinium of the religious sphere and the incognito of
religious existence.[126] In *The Gospel of Sufferings*, Kierkegaard develops

---

[120] Kirmmse, *Kierkegaard and Golden Age Denmark*, 300.
[121] The Hongs translate *Frimodighed* as "bold confidence." Bruce Kirmmse favors "open-hearted
courage," Kirmmse, *Kierkegaard and Golden Age Denmark*, 301.
[122] Kirmmse, *Kierkegaard and Golden Age Denmark*, 301.
[123] *UDVS* 330 (*SV* viii 406), altered from the Hongs' "bold confidence."
[124] *UDVS* 331 (*SV* viii 407), altered to reverse the last phrase; see *UDVS* notes, 418n139, and
UDVS 332, line 3.
[125] *UDVS* 331 (*SV* viii 407).
[126] *CUP* 505–25 (*SV* vii 439–58).

the more specifically Christian understanding of joy, focused on the "reverseness" of Christian existence that finds joy in the midst of sufferings. Joy's relation to suffering is the theme also of part 2 of *Christian Discourses*, inaccurately but tellingly entitled in the older English translation "Joyful Notes in the Strife of Suffering."[127] The epigraph, Psalm 49:4, sets the mood of music-making: "I will incline my ear to a proverb; I will solve my riddle to the music of the harp." In an unused preface, the joyful "notes" (*Stemninger*) are musical notes: "That most valiant of nations in antiquity (the Lacedæmonians) prepared for battle with music – in the same way these are notes [*Stemninger*] of triumphant joy, which tune one [*stemme*] for the struggle, and instead of discouraging [*forstemme*] a person in the struggle will rather keep him in perfect tune [*velstemt*]."[128]

The second discourse of "Joyful Notes" specifically links hope and joy with affliction.[129] Affliction bereaves of hope, but "it is affliction which recruits hope."[130] Affliction "does not *bestow* hope, but it *recruits* it."[131] Like a jet of water propelled by an unseen pressure, hope is recruited by the pressure of affliction. This does not mean the end of affliction, but that affliction "converts itself into hope."[132] Hope, again, is never defeated, even in the midst of suffering, for hope is eternal. Finally, hope's eternity in the midst of affliction puts a perspective on what is truly fearful: not affliction, but sin. The discourse ends: "In life there is only one danger which decisively brings with it destruction, that is sin; for sin is [a person's] ruin. Affliction – yes, though it were more terrible than any man ever has experienced – affliction recruits hope."[133] Hope allows one to "breathe," in contrast to despair's suffocation. Christian existence is always "on the way," a "warfare," but it is also necessarily hopeful and even joyful. Looking to Christ, the Christian's existence mirrors joy in the midst of suffering.

---

[127] *CD* 97–163 (*SV* x 99–160). The Danish title is "Stemninger in Lidelsers Strid," or "Moods in the Strife of Sufferings," rather than "joyful notes." In a journal entry, Kierkegaard indicates that while *The Gospel of Sufferings* leaves the suffering indefinite, "Joyful Notes in the Strife of Suffering" keeps in mind "innocent suffering – in order to approach sin." *JP* v 6101 (*Pap.* VIII¹ A 504, n.d., 1848).

[128] *JP* II 2201 (*Pap.* VIII¹ A 503, n.d., 1848).
[129] *CD* 111–18 (*SV* x 111–18).
[130] *CD* 111 (*SV* x 111).
[131] *CD* 115 (*SV* x 115).
[132] *CD* 117 (*SV* x 117).
[133] *CD* 118 (*SV* x 118).

Coda: hope and love

Christ is the object of both faith and of hope; hope also calls forth love. Kierkegaard treats both themes in *Works of Love*, in the parallel sections in part 2, "Love *Believes* All Things and Yet Is Never Deceived," followed by "Love *Hopes* All Things and Yet Is Never Put to Shame."[134] The theme of the second section, which is a commentary on 1 Corinthians 13:7 and Philippians 1:20, is that "no one can hope unless he also loves" and hopes for the other person's good.[135]

Hope is not for the self alone, but is directed, like love, to one's neighbor. "Love, which is greater than faith and hope, takes upon itself the work of hope or takes hope upon itself as the work of hoping for others."[136] Hope never despairs of another person, but in love "continually keeps possibility open with infinite partiality for his possibility of the good."[137] If one loves the neighbor, then one hopes for the neighbor's good. Hope, in short, is not solely individual, but, linked with love, is deeply social in its implications.

Elsewhere in *Works of Love*, Kierkegaard speaks of "hope thinking" in forgiving another. If love hides a multiplicity of sins, then God, or any lover, forgives and so *forgets* sin. Hope engages in a final dialectical reversal; in contrast to the aesthete's strategy of manipulating forgetting in order to avoid hope, Christian love, in forgiveness, employs forgetting in a work of love: consigning another's sin to oblivion. Hope comes into play, not by creating something by thinking it, but by hopefully forgetting it, in an exercise of "*hope* thinking."[138]

Finally, in suffering hope finds resources for joy and love, giving meaning for eternity, but also for the task of the present moment. In *The Gospel of Sufferings*, Kierkegaard weaves together these themes:

The joy, then, is that it is eternally certain that God is love; more specifically understood, the joy is that there is always a task. As long as there is life there is hope, but as long as there is a task there is life, and as long as there is life there is hope – indeed, the task itself is not merely a hope for a future time but is a joyful present.[139]

---

[134] *WL* 213–30 and 231–46 (*SV* ix 216–34 and 235–51), respectively.
[135] *WL* 239 (*SV* ix 243).
[136] *WL* 233 (*SV* ix 237).
[137] *WL* 237 (*SV* ix 241–42).
[138] *WL* 275 (*SV* ix 282).
[139] *UDVS* 279 (*SV* viii 362).

The believer can therefore say, "Whatever happens to me, there is something to do, and in any case there is always a task; hopelessness is a horror that belongs nowhere if a person will not presumptuously give himself up."[140]

Grounded in the belief that God is love, hope is possible; hope leads naturally to the final and highest Christian virtue of love, to which we must now turn.

[140] *UDVS* 280 (*SV* viii 362).

CHAPTER 6

Becoming Christian III love and imitating Christ in works

If there were no spring at the bottom, if God were not love, then there would be neither a little lake nor a man's love. As the still waters begin obscurely in the deep spring, so a man's love mysteriously begins in God's love.

Works of Love, 27 (*SV* IX 13–14).

Love is not a feeling. Love is put to the test, pain not.

Wittgenstein, *Zettel*, 504.

The epigraph from Wittgenstein can help us approach Kierkegaard's extensive reflections on the third and culminating virtue of love. "Love" is not shapeless, anymore than are faith and hope; love too has a "grammar." Like Wittgenstein's notion that grammar "shows differences" as well as the "family resemblances" between uses of a concept, Kierkegaard's reflections on love, as on faith and hope, show a similar dialectical interest in making distinctions. Love is analyzable as a human passion, and his literature, beginning even with his dissertation on *The Concept of Irony* and, of course, his portrayals of romantic love (especially in literature) and married love in *Either/Or*, contain extensive treatments of human love. Kierkegaard is one of the great philosophical and theological thinkers on the love (pathological or healthy) that binds humans together. As indicated in the epigraph above from *Works of Love*, Kierkegaard sees divine love as the source and ground of human love. Christian love is specifically definable in terms of God's love and human love as a response of "neighbor-love."

THE DIALECTIC OF OPPOSITION

The first impression that a reader receives in turning to Kierkegaard's understanding of Christian love is the contrasts between natural love and Christian love. The dialectic appears to be one of stark opposition

186

between erotic love and friendship on the one hand, and Christian love on the other hand. In the next section, I want to question that standard interpretation, arguing that the dialectic of opposition, while certainly present, is only part of the picture. First, however, it is important to outline the differences between natural love and Christian love, differences that Kierkegaard believes to be crucial.

Kierkegaard places in opposition natural human love (*Elskov*, in Danish) and Christian love (*Kjerlighed*). The former, which includes all "worldly" attachments, is based upon aesthetic principles: attraction, inclination, pleasure. Such "poetic" love is enchanted with the *object* of love as desirable. Such love is also discriminatory; it distinguishes between the desirable and undesirable. At bottom, Kierkegaard argues, these loves are self-love, disguised forms of self-affirmation in which the beloved is desired as a projection of oneself; "acquisitive-ness" is thus at the heart of all worldly loves.

Christian love, by contrast, regards the other person as the "neighbor," loved not by virtue of special attractiveness, but simply as "the Other."[1] Christian love is therefore profoundly egalitarian. The Christian does not see the other person in terms of likeness or attractiveness to oneself. Predilection and preference are both excluded as the basis of love; proximity alone is the criterion of another person being the "neighbor."[2] Furthermore, duty is the positive quality that replaces inclination and attraction as the basis of love; the basis for seeing the person as "the Other" is recognizing, first, that loving one's neighbor is a duty; second, the basis of that duty is that one sees that person not solely in a "two-way" relationship, but in a "three-way" relationship, with God as "the middle-term." In loving another person, one "refers" that person to God, sees that person as a creature of God.

Another important element in Kierkegaard's understanding of Christian love is the relation between law and gospel, a relation that is, as we will see in the next section, open to possible misunderstandings. Following a Lutheran understanding of law and gospel, Kierkegaard sees love as manifested in two forms: first, as law, which places love under duty rather than inclination, and in the strenuousness of its demand drives one to repentance by showing how far our natural loves

---

[1]   *WL* 37 (*SV* ix 25).
[2]   Kierkegaard's stress on the equality of regard in Christian love raises questions concerning the place, if any, of preferential relations. See Gene Outka, "Equality and Individuality: Thoughts on Two Themes in Kierkegaard," *The Journal of Religious Ethics* 10:2 (Fall 1982): 171–203, and Gene Outka, *Agape: An Ethical Analysis* (New Haven; London: Yale University Press, 1972).

are from the requirement; and second, as gospel, the good news that the demand of the law has been fulfilled in Christ, and that by faith a person can then freely do the works of love.

As we will see, however, this immediately raises some questions concerning both Kierkegaard's estimation of natural loves, and also how he conceives of the relation of law and gospel in Christian existence. It is to these issues we need now turn.

EROS AND AGAPE; LAW AND GOSPEL

The relation of *eros* and *agape* is complex. There is much of the dialectic of opposition in Kierkegaard's analysis of love, or *eros* versus *agape*. He pushes again and again at the distinction between earthly love and spiritual or Christian love, inclination versus the duty to love, the preferential element of romantic love and friendship versus the call to love the neighbor as oneself, the narcissism of self-love versus the self-sacrifice of love for another. Over against reciprocity in love, he lauds too the renunciation of earthly love and exalts disinterest in the return of love from another.

Kierkegaard is therefore understandably often seen as a precursor of Anders Nygren's *Agape and Eros*, which treats these two forms of human love largely antithetically, *eros* as the love of desire, need, preference, and finally self-assertion and "acquisitiveness," and *agape* as the self-giving love that typifies Christian love.[3] Nygren too relentlessly pushes the antithesis between *eros* and *agape*, with Christian love as superior; for Nygren, Luther is the hero who clarifies (in opposition to the alleged confusions of *eros* and *agape* in the medieval "*caritas*-synthesis") the virtues of Christian love over against all natural affection, whether of friendship or erotic love.

Is this stark opposition of *eros* and *agape* valid? Karl Barth, in contrast to Nygren, sees this distinction as having limited, but only limited, validity. He is especially concerned that Christian love, while "superior" to *eros*, does not need to measure itself by *eros*, and he cites Kierkegaard as one who, before Nygren, also relentlessly pushes the contrast between *eros* and *agape*. Here is Barth's final critical judgment of Kierkegaard's theology of love:

If only the final impression left by this book [*Works of Love*] were not that of the detective skill with which non-Christian love is tracked down to its last

---

[3] Anders Nygren, *Agape and Eros*, trans. Philip S. Watson (New York: Harper & Row, 1969).

hiding-place, examined, shown to be worthless and haled before the judge!
... it is disturbing to see from the example of Kierkegaard how easily
reflection on this antithesis can be deflected from Christian love and find
itself rivetted even by way of opposition (and the more firmly because
inimically) to erotic love. It is even more disturbing to see how ... in *agape* we
have to do with a superior and triumphant human action, and in *eros* with
one which is inferior and already routed – and this for the simple reason that
the former has its basis in the good being and action of God, and the latter in
the corruption of man.[4]

While I question whether Barth is correct to see Kierkegaard's
conception of *agape* as "triumphant human action," Barth correctly
notes a weakness in Kierkegaard's opposition of *eros* and *agape*, what
Sylvia I. Walsh has called "a certain ambivalence toward natural
love," for, although Kierkegaard "says that Christianity is not opposed
to natural inclination as such, only to the selfishness in it, yet he does
not seem to recognize any ability on the part of natural love to love
unselfishly."[5]

Part of the difficulty in Kierkegaard's tendency to contrast *eros* and
agape is not only his dialectic of opposition, but also his theological
understanding of law and gospel. Barth is partly correct in seeing in
Works of Love an "unlovely, inquisitorial and terribly judicial character,"
a Kantian "naked commandment: 'Thou shalt,'" which not only
condemns *eros*, but "impresses because it provokes, and then suddenly
becomes as such a saving power and the source of all good counsel."[6]
Theologically, from Barth's perspective, Kierkegaard is guilty of two
errors: first, he sees law apart from gospel, law as judgment; the law
commands love, but thereby reveals the hidden elements of selfishness
in *eros*, what Walsh correctly calls the inability "on the part of natural
love to love unselfishly." Second, and more seriously, Barth charges
Kierkegaard with seeing law, the commandment to love, *as such* having
saving power. The commandment "Thou shalt love" then shows the
higher way of *agape* that fulfills the law. Barth, by contrast, allows grace,
and the God of grace, to be the source of both *eros* and *agape*, despite
the provisional opposition between them.[7] For Barth, grace – rather
Jesus Christ – is the ground of gospel and law, in contrast to the
Lutheran law – gospel distinction; indeed, gospel precedes law; the

---

4 Barth, *Church Dogmatics*, IV, part 2, 747.
5 Sylvia I. Walsh, "Forming the Heart: The Role of Love in Kierkegaard," in Bell, ed., *The Grammar of the Heart*, 248.
6 Barth, *Church Dogmatics*, IV, part 2, 782.
7 Barth, *Church Dogmatics*, IV, part 2, 749.

structure is one of "gospel – law – gospel" rather than the traditional Lutheran "law – gospel." The command "Thou shalt love" for Barth is therefore "not an abstract demand but a direction which points to an inescapable conclusion in the form of a future ... Thou wilt love."[8] The imperative of love is grounded in the indicative of God's grace in Jesus Christ.

I cite Barth because one of his criticisms is sound, while another is not. First, I think that Barth is deeply wrong on the second point, in seeing Kierkegaard holding to the command and duty of love *in itself* having salvific force. Law for Kierkegaard functions in *Works of Love* as preparatory for gospel, but law is never confused with gospel. Despite all of his emphasis on the *works* of love, he does not fall into a works-righteousness, but maintains the priority of grace and Lutheran solafideism. Second, however, Barth is correct on the first point, in that Kierkegaard uses the law – gospel distinction to criticize natural love as disguised forms of self-love, as condemned by the law. And Kierke-gaard's insistent contrast of law and gospel is at the heart of this problem. More precisely, Kierkegaard sees the "law" as in itself bringing a critique of natural love; by calling upon one to love unreservedly, without regard to the loveliness of the neighbor, and out of duty, natural loves are indeed hauled into the court and found wanting. This explains why Barth can see *Works of Love* as a consistent critique of *eros*.

Granting all of this, two comments are in order. First, the *rhetorical* force of *Works of Love* is crucial for correctly understanding it; the dialectic of opposition is indeed offensive, and it would be a serious misreading to make this text inoffensive. The offensiveness functions to lead the reader to self-examination, to weigh the quality of one's love, to prompt one to seek and give forgiveness.[9] If this is "law," it is a proper function of the law. Second, in addition to the dialectic of opposition, there is nevertheless, as Walsh points out, another element in Kierkegaard's thought on love, one that I believe Barth misses completely in his critique of Kierkegaard: the way in which *agape* overcomes the dialectic of opposition and hence overcomes the dichotomy between *agape* and *eros*. Walsh writes:

By interpreting Christian love as a spiritual quality that is brought to our normal love relations rather than as a separate form of love, Kierkegaard

8   Barth, *Church Dogmatics*, IV, part 2, 782.
9   I am indebted to an unpublished paper by Timothy Polk for insights into the dangers of "removing the offensiveness" in *Works of Love*.

shows us a way of affirming the unity of love and of overcoming the dichotomy between *eros* and *agape*, human and divine love, sensuous and spiritual love, that has been fostered by much classical thought as well as by such recent thinkers as Anders Nygren.[10]

If Walsh is correct (and I believe she is), then Kierkegaard, despite his opposition of law and gospel, is actually somewhat closer to Barth's understanding of the relation of *eros* and *agape*. Granted that Barth accurately identifies how Kierkegaard's grammar of love erroneously becomes a dialectic of opposition between *eros* and *agape*, stressing the reversal that Christian love brings to *eros*, finally Kierkegaard has room for a dialectic of unity that allows not an elimination of *eros*, but a transformation of *eros*. *Agape* is not a love that eliminates and condemns the erotic, but in dethroning *eros* embraces and transforms it.

The theological basis for overcoming this dichotomy of *eros* and *agape* is crucial: for all of the opposition of law and gospel in Kierkegaard, there is *pace* Barth another theme: gospel and grace are the basis of *all* human love. *Agape* is certainly not for Kierkegaard a "superior and triumphant human action" apart from grace, a Kantian triumph of duty, but neither is the basis of the duty to *agape* simply the "naked commandment: 'Thou shalt love.'" *Agape* arises from the love of God, in a manner similar (albeit not identical with) the way that Barth grounds law and gospel in Jesus Christ. Crucial to understanding *Works of Love* is the *divine* basis for human love; God's love is likened to "the hidden springs" that feed a quiet lake.[11] Thus Kierkegaard can affirm so strongly the unity of love, *eros* as transformed by *agape*, that from the Christian standpoint *all* love relations are grounded in God's love. In his chapter on "love is the fulfilling of the law" (Romans 13:10), Kierkegaard employs the usual "law – gospel" distinction, but, when God is seen as the "middle term" relating two persons in love, this sets a perspective on natural love in which friends and lovers see one another not only in their individual needs and preferences, but also as neighbor, embraced by God, and as determined to return their love to God. "*Worldly wisdom thinks that love is a relationship between man and man. Christianity teaches that love is a relationship between: man – God – man, that is, that God is the middle term.*"[12] Hence, again quoting Walsh, God (and therefore love) "forms the proper object of love relations precisely by putting the focus of those relations on helping one another learn *to love*

10 Walsh, "Forming the Heart," 248.
11 *WL* 27 (*SV* IX 14).
12 *WL* 112–13 (*SV* IX 104) (original italics).

rather than seek to be loved in and through the relation."[13] By keeping the focus on how one rightly loves, *eros* is not dismissed, neither does the love for God replace *eros; eros* is embraced within a concern with "how" one loves. The passion of *eros* is not condemned as simply narcissistic, but is surrounded by a love for one's beloved as neighbor.

Kierkegaard's vision of love is thus open to a more "holistic" interpretation; at least, the dialectic of unity tempers the undeniable dialectic of opposition in *Works of Love.* Divine love is the source of human love. *Agape* embraces *eros.* Again, the central theological vision underlying Kierkegaard's thought on Christian love is that all are created by God, and are invited to be on the way toward love of God and neighbor, in which natural loves are transformed but not eliminated.

One final indication of this holistic understanding of love's unity is seen in the affirmation of what Walsh calls the "spontaneity" of love that completes and even surpasses duty. Despite his suspicions of the natural abilities of *eros*, including the fragility of erotic love's spontaneity that can easily become habit, Kierkegaard's vision of the creative, free divine love as the basis of human love, embracing and transforming *eros*, directing human love back toward God, allows the spontaneity of *eros* not only to be redeemed, but to complement the duty to love. In this part of Kierkegaard's grammar of love, one loves not from duty against inclination, but duty actually engenders a desire that defeats "habit"; one loves from a desire to love others that no longer needs to be *commanded.* Here is, as Walsh notes, "the apotheosis of Kierkegaard's thought, the final insight that unites duty and inclination, passion and reflection, law and love in his understanding of the Christian life."[14] (We will return to the dialectic of unity when we turn to "imitation" in the next section.)

THE PRIORITY OF DIVINE LOVE

Turning to the specific shape of Christian love, we need to see first the source of Christian love in God and Christ, and then Christian love as response to divine love. The aim throughout will be to show the "holistic" understanding of love Kierkegaard proposes, especially in *Works of Love,* and how God's love embraces and directs and fulfills

---

[13] Walsh, "Forming the Heart," 237.
[14] Walsh, "Forming the Heart," 246. See *WL* 49–57 (*SV* ix 37–46).

human love. Contrary to Barth's interpretation, Christian love is not autonomous, but radically dependent upon God's love as its source, object, and goal.

First, Christian love finds its origin and goal in God's love. Howard and Edna Hong speak rightly of *Works of Love* as proceeding from an indicative ethic, motivated by the love of God for every person.[15] The Christian virtue of love is theocentrically defined; it moves from the primacy of God as creator, lover, and forgiver, rather than from any finite social or individual basis for ethics. As already noted, central for Kierkegaard is the image of God's love likened to "the hidden springs" that feed a quiet lake: "If there were no spring at the bottom, if God were not love, then there would be neither a little lake nor a man's love. As the still waters begin obscurely in the deep spring, so a man's love mysteriously begins in God's love."[16] The divine love has priority, temporally and logically, in God as creator, who intends love between humans as "God's eternal – though veiled – witness of Himself as Creator."[17] The human's love for God is distinct from, albeit logically related to, love for neighbor.[18] But he does not conclude from this, as do others, that it is incorrect to speak of "love for God." In contrast to others, Kierkegaard never reduces *agape* to human relations, so that if one loves other people, then one has exhaustively "loved God." Kierkegaard distinguishes love for God as "unconditional *obedience* and ... *adoration*."[19] Again, the divine love, given and returned, has priority and is irreducible to human relations.

The divine love as the prior ground of Christian love is seen also in Christ's atoning love. "It is indeed God in heaven who through the apostle says, 'Be reconciled'; it is not man who says to God: 'Forgive us.' No, God loved us first."[20] While the Christological element is not at first glance structurally or formally central to *Works of Love*, it is materially central, and evident in many ways throughout the book.

---

[15] See Howard and Edna Hong, "Translator's Introduction," *WL* 15, who see an imperative ethic at work in *Purity of Heart, Either/Or*, I, *Postscript*, and "parts of *Fear and Trembling*," in contrast to the "indicative ethic" of *Works of Love*.

[16] *WL* 27 (*SV* IX 13–14). This is why Barth, in the quotation above, is mistaken in thinking that Kierkegaard understands *agape* as "a superior and triumphant human action."

[17] Paul Müller, *Kristendom, etik og majeutik i Søren Kierkegaard's "Kjerlighedens Gjerninger,"* 2. oplag. (Viborg: C. A. Reitzels Forlag, 1983), 83; in English, *Kierkegaard's* Works of Love: *Christian Ethics and the Maieutic Ideal*, trans. C. Stephen Evans and Jan Evans (Copenhagen: C. A. Reitzel, 1993).

[18] See Outka, *Agape*, 46. Compare 216–17: Barth's critique of Brunner on this.

[19] *WL* 36 (*SV* IX 23).

[20] *WL* 310 (*SV* IX 320).

Here too, the pattern is one of Christ's "presence within absence." The prayer addressed to God as the source of love with which Kierkegaard opens *Works of Love* sets the tone and mood of invocation and prayer. Addressing Christ, Kierkegaard writes, "How could love properly be discussed if You were forgotten, You who made manifest what love is, You, our Saviour and Redeemer, who gave Yourself to save all!"[21]

This still leaves open the question of how Kierkegaard understands the relation between divine grace and human love. Although in chapter 4 we have already addressed the relation of human freedom and grace in faith, it is worth turning to again as we consider love, since love – so self-evidently a longterm disposition – raises (especially for Protestants) the question whether one may speak of love as a "possession" or "characteristic" of a person. Gene Outka summarizes four models that Christian moral theologians have proposed for understanding this relation: "agape as a human virtue ... may be the instrument of invading grace; it may be infused by grace; it may be acquired irrespective of grace; it may be elicited by grace."[22] The first three do not describe Kierkegaard's conception. First, given Kierkegaard's concerns to safeguard the integrity of human freedom, he does not (in contrast to Nygren) see love in terms of the first model, what Outka calls grace as "an *invasive* reality."[23] Neither does Kierkegaard employ the Thomistic category of infusion or the Pelagian category of "acquired virtue." The model that comes closest to Kierkegaard is that of elicitation: grace (the divine love as *agape*) elicits the human response of *agape*. Outka's summary of elicitation places it in contrast to the other three:

Grace elicits rather than invades in that the agent must actively respond, not just passively receive. Grace elicits rather than infuses in that nothing fundamentally non-human is introduced as an extension of given human powers. The creaturely response considered in itself is never more than creaturely. Elicitation also differs from acquirement in that virtue is evoked and sustained from without; it is not simply self-activated and self-directed. The agent is drawn to do what he cannot do by himself. The relation between grace and human love may be called interpersonal, but it is also asymmetrical.[24]

---

21 *WL* 20 (*SV* ix 8). Note that the form of the prayer is Trinitarian, beginning with the "God of Love," proceeding to Christ, and then invoking the Holy Spirit. On Christ's presence in the midst of absence in *Works of Love*, I am indebted to discussion with Timothy Polk and Lee Barrett.

22 Outka, *Agape*, 149.

23 *Ibid.*

24 Outka, *Agape*, 151.

While Outka does not discuss Kierkegaard in this connection, this fourth model of elicitation describes Kierkegaard's understanding of grace and human love. Despite the "well-spring" image, Kierkegaard does not state an *identity* between divine and human love. Human love is rather modeled upon Christ as an "imitation," a distinctively human love. What supports most strongly an "elicitation" understanding of grace and human *agape* is Kierkegaard's central image of love as "loving forth" (*elske op*).[25] We will discuss this image of "loving forth" more fully in a bit, in connection with love's imaginative vision; for now the point to see is that Kierkegaard envisions the divine love in personal terms, as an encouragement and upbuilding and drawing forth of love as a human response to prior divine love, engendering free and genuine human activity. Omnipotence, again, is not a curb to creaturely freedom, but its support, for "The greatest good ... which can be done for a being, greater than anything else that one can do for it, is to make it free. In order to do just that, omnipotence is required."[26]

The "elicitation" of human love leads to a complementary element in Kierkegaard's understanding of *agape*: human love as imitation.[27] Christ as Pattern is central to *Works of Love*. The redemptive love in its self-giving ("You ... who gave Yourself to save all!") is also the Pattern who "made manifest what love is" in the form of *agape* as self-giving love for neighbor. Christ is, of course, the one who gives the love command.[28] But imitation is not condemnation. Kierkegaard's understanding of love is not, as Barth charges, sheer abstract demand or imperative, but is based upon the concrete realization of love in the life of Christ.

This concrete realization of love in Christ's life is especially apparent in the chapter on "Love Is the Fullfilling of the Law."[29] Kierkegaard explores this by detailed comment on the quality of Christ's love; throughout the chapter the pattern of Christ's life is constantly invoked in order to give material content to the pattern of Christian love. Christ's own love is "the fulfilling of the law," but he was also "the end

[25] *EUD* 61 (*SV* III 279).

[26] *JP* II 1251 (*Pap.* VII¹ A 181, n.d., 1846).

[27] Elicitation and imitation can go together, as indicated in Outka's treatment of Barth; see Outka, *Agape*, 238. Both themes, elicitation and imitation, stress the non-identity of divine and human love, in contrast to a Thomistic infusion model that can speak of the divinization of human capacities.

[28] *WL*, part 1, chapter 2: "You Shall Love," 34–98 (*SV* IX 21–89).

[29] *WL*, part 1, chapter 3. A, 99–136 (*SV* IX 90–129).

of the law" (Romans 10:4) in that "Christ became the law's destruction because he was what it demanded."[30] At the same time, the law now exists in Christ as demand only in its perfect fulfillment.[31]

"Following the Pattern" is therefore more than a "new law" as condemnation. The prayer that opens *Works of Love* is again the key to understanding here, for it includes the words: "You who are love, so that one who loves is what he is only by being in You!"[32] Gospel not only follows, but embraces law; both law and gospel, indeed, are simply different forms of love. From the strictness of the law's demand ("Thou *shalt* love") one is led to the gentleness of forgiving one's neighbor. It is love as relationship, the middle term, that fulfills the law.[33] The Christian life is joyful gratitude in performing the works of love.

As Paul Müller has shown clearly, *Works of Love* exhibits in its form and structure the centrality of divine grace. The first part shows the function of the law, including the duty to love one's neighbor and the impossibility of fulfilling that law. The second part of the book shows the grace of God in Christ as it works in a person's life. Love is then *shown* in action, as the practice of the gospel. What the shape of that Christian love is we will see in the next section.

To sum up: God and Christ are the necessary source and origin, as well as pattern, of love. As with faith and hope, so too with love: it is a gift from God and not, as Barth interprets Kierkegaard, a human self-achievement. As we saw in the chapter on faith, to speak of these as virtues is, within the Protestant and specifically Lutheran understanding, not to attribute them finally to human rather than divine activity. It is not that whereas justification is the imputation of Christ's "alien righteousness" to the believer, sanctification, Luther's "proper righteousness," including the fruit of faith, hope, and love, is human self-creativity. All is gift of God. On the final page of *Works of Love*, Kierkegaard writes that "Certainly we do not say, nor is it our thought, that a person ultimately earns grace. O, what you learn first of all in relating yourself to God is precisely that you have no merit at all."[34] As a relational virtue nurtured from the depths of divine love, human love

---

30   *WL* 106 (*SV* ix 97).
31   *Ibid.*
32   *WL* 20 (*SV* ix 8). Paul Müller, *Kristendom, etik og majeutik*, 84; see also ch. 5, "Lovens fylde."
33   *WL* 112–13 (*SV* ix 104).
34   *WL* 353 (*SV* ix 364).

is "bound" within a larger history of God's prior love. Speaking of the heart that loves God as a "bound heart" rather than a "free heart," Kierkegaard writes of love as a response to God:

The free heart has no history ... But the heart bound infinitely to God has a prior history ... that eternal love-history is begun far earlier [than one's experiences of love]. It began with your beginning, when you came into being out of nothing, and just as you do not become nothing, so your history surely does not end at the grave.[35]

LOVE AS HUMAN RESPONSE

Grounded in divine love's grace, Christian love is also human response. Specifically shaped in the response to God and to Christ as Redeemer and Pattern, it is love for God and love for neighbor (Matthew 22:37–40) conceived as task as well as gift. While one continually in faith has recourse to God's love and grace, rather than any self-reliance, love is still a human "work." In this regard, Kierkegaard shifts the emphasis from faith to works, albeit still within the context of Lutheran solafideism. In his foreword to *Works of Love*, Kierkegaard writes that "these are *Christian reflections*; therefore they are not about *love* but about the *works of love*."[36] It is "works" that spring from faith and show forth love. In the same prayer that opens the book, Kierkegaard invokes the "Spirit of Love" to set the reader to a task, to "remind us of that sacrifice of [Christ's] love, remind the believer to love as he is loved, and his neighbour as himself!"[37]

The bulk of *Works of Love* is concerned with the grammar of that love, its logic and implications. "Love is not a feeling," writes Wittgenstein. The same is true for Kierkegaard, who writes that "nowadays we have wanted to make love into an unseen something ... To say that love is a feeling and the like is really an unchristian conception."[38] Wittgenstein continues, "Love is put to the test, pain not." Love can be tested because it is a disposition and passion, enduring through 'time; "love abides." Kierkegaard's *Works of Love* presents an extensive grammar that examines and tests the quality of human love in light of divine love.

[35] *WL* 149 (*SV* ix 143).
[36] *WL* 19 (*SV* ix 7).
[37] *WL* 20 (*SV* ix 8).
[38] *JP* iii 2423 (*Pap.* xi¹ A 489, n.d., 1849).

Love as disposition: hidden and recognizable

The reader of *Works of Love* is called to be concerned not with "testing" the presence of love, but with being loving. But "being loving" means seeing love as "hidden" and yet also "recognizable." Kierkegaard insists on the hiddenness of love, for love that is not hidden, but is directly recognizable, eradicates "spirit," and reduces human beings to the externals of their behavior. At the same time, Kierkegaard is increasingly suspicious of the dangers and evasions of a hidden interiority that finds it convenient to seek refuge in the depths of "inwardness," evading the demands of action.

Kierkegaard's reflections on the "recognizability" of love developed over time. *Postscript* emphasizes religious existence as "hidden inwardness with humor as its incognito."[39] However, Kierkegaard increasingly alters his understanding of religious and specifically Christian existence away from an "ethics of interiority" to an affirmation both of the external action (as well as the "internal attitude" and hidden motivation) and also the sociality (ethics is directed to others). As Louis Dupré notes, *Works of Love* is a waystation in the development of Kierkegaard's thought on the relation of the internal and external. In *Works of Love*, in the chapter on "Love Is a Matter of Conscience," he still rejects any role for Christianity in bringing about external change; he writes that "Christianity has never wanted to conquer in a worldly way," "Christianity has not wanted to hurl governments from the throne in order to set itself on the throne," or "to change the shape of the world."[40] Christianity rather alters the world by making love a matter of conscience instead of simple inclination. Indeed, it is a person's making love a matter of conscience that marks love's "hidden inwardness." But, as Dupré points out, in this same chapter of *Works of Love* Kierkegaard begins to break down the opposition of inner and outer, for he defends "his ethics of interiority against the charge of indifference toward others," since the Christian seeks to draw the other person as neighbor into the absoluteness of one's God-relationship.[41] None the less, the vocabulary is still largely that of "interiority." As we will see in the next chapter, Kierkegaard moves beyond this position in *Works of Love* to a more strenuous critique of the religion of "hidden inwardness" after 1847, allowing more stress on the "external

---

[39] *CUP* 505–12 (*SV* vii 439–45).
[40] *WL* 136–37 (*SV* ix 130–31).
[41] Dupré, *Kierkegaard as Theologian*, 160.

realization of Christianity" in the social world.[42] Yet already in *Works of Love*, the language of *Postscript*'s "hidden inwardness" begins to be augmented by the language of the "works of love." Hence, he speaks of how deeply the need for love is grounded in the need and longing for community.[43]

Another important element in *Works of Love* that indicates a greater concern for "externality" is the theme of chapter 1, that "Love's Hidden Life" is "Recognizable by Its Fruits."[44] This is the most important shift in *Works of Love*, for it marks a move to a more full-bodied "dispositional" way of speaking of love, one that includes actions as well as intentions, the outer as well as the inner. Kierkegaard captures this dispositional way of speaking of love – the manner in which love is a virtue received and also an active task – in making a distinction in *Works of Love* between love "proceeding from the heart" and love "forming the heart." Discussing how love is recognizable from its fruit, he writes that "Love, to be sure, proceeds from the heart, but let us not in our haste about this forget the eternal truth that love forms the heart."[45] In Danish, the distinction is between "*fra Hjertet*" (proceeds from the heart) and "*sætte Hjertet*" (forms the heart).[46] The contrast that Kierkegaard makes, using again his vocabulary of "the eternal," is between the "transient excitements of an inconstant heart" and "forming a heart in the eternal sense."[47] "Forming a heart" combines the elements of "inwardness" ("love proceeds from the heart," there is a "hidden life" of love that finds its source in God) with "behavior" ("the *works* of love"); the first discourse unites these elements in its title: "love's hidden life and its recognizability by its fruits."[48]

We need to pause a moment to look at both the "inner" and "outer" aspects of love. This vocabulary provides Kierkegaard with the language for construing love as an active virtue, since it indicates the

---

[42] Dupré, *Kierkegaard as Theologian*, 164.

[43] *WL* 153 (*SV* IX 147–48).

[44] *WL* 23–33 (*SV* IX 9–20). For the charge that Kierkegaard's ethics is acosmic, focused on individual self-development alone, see Louis Mackey, "The Loss of the World in Kierkegaard's Ethics," in Thompson, ed., *Kierkegaard: A Collection of Critical Essays*, 266–88.

[45] *WL* 29 (*SV* IX 16). See Walsh, "Forming the Heart."

[46] See the Hongs' note in *WL* 359n10, which also cites *JP* II 1995 (*Pap.* VII[1] A 205, n.d., 1846).

[47] *WL* 29–30 (*SV* IX 16).

[48] *WL* 23 (*SV* IX 9). Contrast Kierkegaard's place for the works of love in contrast to Anders Nygren's stress on love as received; Nygren shares a Protestant fear of any sense of "works-righteousness" or spontaneity in relation to God. See Outka, *Agape*, 49. Kierkegaard is aware of the danger, but fears more any hidden interiority that ignores (what Luther himself recognized) that the life of faith bears the fruit of love.

interrelationship between the "inner" elements of attitude, intention, motive and action; yet Kierkegaard does this without losing the "outer" elements of action and behavior. His descriptions of the hiddenness and recognizability of love lend themselves to an understanding of love in virtue-terms; his interest is not only in describing the intentions of an agent, but also the agent's action.

Let us look a bit more closely at the "inner" aspect, the "hiddenness" of love. There are several important reasons why Kierkegaard wants to maintain the "hiddenness" of love, insisting on love's "incognito." (1) Forming of the heart, relying on the hidden depths of love, is the essential *condition* for the fruit of love. Kierkegaard's interest in stressing the hiddenness of love is not to affirm an essential privacy to love, in the sense that only the subject can logically know whether he or she loves, but rather to make the point that love is seen *indirectly*. This correlates to the hiddenness of God, as well as the hiddenness of God's presence in Christ, whose being and love are believed, not demonstrated; so too, human love is hidden in that it is not directly visible to the natural eye, but "love is believed."[49] The invisibility of love is directly related to the "how" of love's manifestation. "There is no deed, not a single one, not even the best, of which we dare to say unconditionally: he who does this thereby unconditionally demonstrates love. It depends upon *how* the deed is done."[50] "One can perform works of love in an unloving, yes, even in a self-loving way, and when this is so, the works of love are nevertheless not the work of love."[51] Love "forms the heart" in "hiddenness."

(2) Beyond these aspects of "inner" intention and motive as crucial to a work of love, Kierkegaard sees love as dependent upon the lover, not the object of love. If the object of one's love rejects that love, this does not negate the fact that one does love. This is another reason that Kierkegaard sees Christian love as "eternal." This is especially clear in the chapter in part II on "The Work of Love in Remembering One Dead," wherein the independence of love from the object of love is most clear: one's love does not depend upon attractiveness, response, or reciprocity.[52]

(3) A related aspect of the hiddenness of love is that in Christian love one is concerned not with external actions alone, or with whether love

49 WL 32 (SV ix 19–20).
50 WL 30 (SV ix 17).
51 Ibid.
52 WL 317–29 (SV ix 327–39).

is returned by another person, but with one's inward relationship with God. Kierkegaard opposes consequentialism. In loving another person "in God," God (or love) becomes the true object of one's love.

None the less, love is not private; it is recognizable by its fruits in the "reduplication of the eternal" in the temporal.[53] Kierkegaard's image for love is the fruit of the tree, "for figs are not gathered from thorns, nor are grapes picked from a bramble bush" (Luke 6:44).[54] While no act is by definition, in itself, a loving act, the disposition of love is not private, but is apparent in the works that proceed from a loving disposition. Kierkegaard speaks of love as "needy," yet rich and overflowing, in its "need" to be recognizable.[55] A love that is never manifest in works is a "self-contradiction."[56] Here is the important shift from a religion of pure "hidden inwardness" to a greater recognition that love must be manifest in works. The goal is not the consequentialist one of having others see one as loving; this makes another person's appreciation the criterion for a work of love. Yet neither is the inner intention sufficient. Kierkegaard steers between consequentialism and acosmism: the goal is that the works of love be done so that they *may* be recognized.[57]

Love as vision

To understand how the heart is shaped by love, we need to see further how love is a matter of nurturing one's imagination and vision to enable the works of love. This is apparent already in the opening discourse. Kierkegaard writes "Believe in love! This is the first and last thing to be said about love if one is to know what love is."[58] There are two points here: first, as we have seen, although love is recognized by its fruits, love is hidden, both in its source in God's love and in the inwardness of the individual. This is spoken against a practical or "shrewd" person who will insist on never being deceived by what one cannot see with the eyes; but such a person is deceived, for to "cheat oneself out of love is the most terrible deception."[59] Second, to

53 Louise Carroll Keeley, "Subjectivity and World in *Works of Love*," in Connell and Evans, eds., *Foundations of Kierkegaard's Vision of Community*, 96–108.
54 *WL* 23 (*SV* ix 9).
55 *WL* 28 (*SV* ix 14).
56 *WL* 28 (*SV* ix 15).
57 *WL* 31 (*SV* ix 18).
58 *WL* 32 (*SV* ix 19).
59 *WL* 23 (*SV* ix 10).

"believe in love" calls one from "the morbid, anxious, shrewd mean-heartedness which in petty, miserable mistrust insists upon seeing the fruits."[60] The governing principle is the old Platonic axiom that "like is known only by like": love is known by love.[61]

To "believe in love" means to "see" from the standpoint of love rather than mistrust. Already in one of the 1843 upbuilding discourses entitled "Love Will Hide a Multitude of Sins," Kierkegaard spoke of Christian love as a way of seeing. Love "does not depend, then, merely upon what one sees, but what one sees depends upon how one sees; all observation is not just a receiving, a discovering, but also a bringing forth, and insofar as it is that, how the observer himself is constituted is indeed decisive."[62] Mistrust and envy easily see evil in others, but "love hides a multitude of sins" for "the eye has the power to love forth [*elske op*] the good in the impure."[63] The Danish word *opelske* (literally, "to love forth") means "to raise, cultivate, encourage," and Kierkegaard's play on the word appears again in *Works of Love*, where it is "used along with *opbygge* [to build up] and *opdrage* [to draw upward, to bring up, to educate; cf. Latin *educere*, to lead out, to lead forward]."[64] "The eye has the power to love forth [*elske op*] the good in the impure." Love's vision "loves forth" the good. Love is "blind" in not seeing evil, but is an active "seeing" that "upbuilds" in lovingly drawing out the good. Love's vision also shapes the lover; it allows the "fruit of the spirit" of Galatians 5:22–23. In the early upbuilding discourse Kierkegaard continues that

when quarreling, malice, anger, litigation, discord, factionalism live in the heart, does one then need to go far to discover the multiplicity of sin, or does one need to live long to bring it forth all around one? But when joy, peace, patience, gentleness, faithfulness, kindness, meekness, continence [Galatians 5:22–23] live in the heart, no wonder then that a person, even if he stood in the middle of the multiplicity of sin, would become a stranger, a foreigner, who would understand only very little of the customs of the country; if an explanation were required of him, what a covering of a multitude of sins this would be![65]

This theme of vision is central also in *Works of Love*, where Kierkegaard writes (again on how love hides the multiplicity of sin) that in mistrust,

---

60 *WL* 32 (*SV* IX 19–20).
61 *WL* 33 (*SV* IX 20).
62 *EUD* 59 (*SV* III 277).
63 *EUD* 61 (*SV* III 279).
64 This helpful note is in *EUD* 508n100.
65 *EUD* 61–62 (*SV* III 279).

one's eyes are sharpened, yet one's "vision is narrowed more and more so that infected he sees evil in everything," even where there is no sin.[66] Jeremy Walker is again helpful here by saying that mistrust and love are each conceptual schemes or "frames" by which a person sees the world. In mistrust, one is unable to see the real good and truth that may be before us in another. This is an epistemic defect in worldly shrewdness (for one is unable to see the good that is really present). But it is also "condemnable on intrinsic grounds, that is, morally," for one tragically loses the capacity to see the good that one can see only within that framework.[67]

Kierkegaard is chipping away again at the common notion that, epistemically, we first determine the "objective facts" about another person, and that, when this task is (easily) accomplished, our evaluation and judging naturally follow. Yet this is not the case; our "frames" determine what it is that we see in one another; they carry with them the ability to recognize what is present in another. This is not to say that there is not good or evil in another person, "really there," but is simply to say that what we can see in another person is determined to a large extent by what we are willing to see. This too is Kierkegaard's point in speaking of the "inwardness" of love, his refusal to reduce love to external acts. Let us return to Kierkegaard's example of opposing "mistrust" and "love." "Mistrust," in its "shrewdness" – ironically in its very interest not to be deceived by another person – is blind to what is good in another person. So too, although "love is blind," it is also capable of seeing the good that is present in another, the good that mistrust refuses to see. Iris Murdoch illuminates this in her well-known example of a woman's judgment of her daughter-in-law: from believing that her son married "a silly vulgar girl," the woman gradually alters her *vision* of the girl. The woman realizes that she is old-fashioned and certainly jealous, and she says to herself, "Let me look again." And if, Murdoch adds, the daughter-in-law is absent or dead, the change is not the woman's behavior, but in her mind, or as Kierkegaard would put it, her "spirit." The girl "is discovered to be not vulgar but refreshingly simple, not undignified but spontaneous, not noisy but gay, not tiresomely juvenile but delightfully youthful, and so on."[68] The alteration is brought about by the woman's imaginative transformation of her vision of her daughter-in-law; employing the standpoint of love

[66] *WL* 267 (*SV* ix 273).
[67] Walker, *Kierkegaard: Descent into God*, 92.
[68] Murdoch, "The Idea of Perfection," in *The Sovereignty of Good*, 17–18.

rather than mistrust, she comes to see the girl differently, and certainly, in her newfound judgment, believes that she comes to see her daughter-in-law more fairly and truly. Simone Weil writes that the love of neighbor is first of all being attentive to another person: "The soul. empties itself of all its own contents in order to receive into itself the being it is looking at, just as he is, in all his truth. Only he who is capable of attention can do this."[69]

Kierkegaard's opposition of mistrust and of love as different conceptual points of view is deliberately stark. This raises again in another context the question of truth. Does love see truly? Or is the frame of love naive? In Murdoch's example, is the woman indeed seeing the girl truly, or is she self-deceptively sacrificing her critical discernment in this new judgment of her daughter-in-law? Kierkegaard would answer that while mistrust in its desire to "see things as they are" believes itself to be undeceived, the frame of love is never deceived. How can this be?

Two comments are called for here. First, love is not naive; the point is rather that love sees evil, but does not judge. Let us sharpen the question by changing the example from Murdoch; let us say that the daughter-in-law is vicious, cruel, and heartless. Kierkegaard points out that "it would be weakness, not love, to delude the unloving person into thinking that he was right in the evil he did; it would not be reconciliation but treachery which would strengthen him in the evil."[70] Appearances to the contrary, there is no room in Kierkegaard's understanding for a sentimental love that ignores sin and evil; that would in fact be incomprehensible from a thinker who, as we have seen, has such a profound understanding of the extent and depth of human sinfulness.

This clarifies the related issue of what Gene Outka has termed "the question about the blank check," whether *agape* requires submission to exploitation and moral evil. As Outka says, for all of his stress on Christian love as self-sacrifice, and "perhaps not always consistently," Kierkegaard draws back from such a conclusion (in contrast, Outka points out, to Nygren).[71] Not only is there a legitimate *self-love*, conceived as "loving oneself in the right way,"[72] but, again, precisely out of love of *neighbor*, one may have to resist a person's moral evil and exploitation. The criterion again is the distinction between "treachery"

69 Weil, *Waiting for God*, 115.
70 *WL* 312 (*SV* IX 321). Compare Walker, *Kierkegaard: Descent into God*, 109.
71 Outka, *Agape*, 21–24. Compare 274–79, on self-regard and self-sacrifice.
72 *WL* 39 (*SV* IX 26).

that wrongly condones, ignores, or fails to resist evil, in contrast to love's attempt at "reconciliation."[73]

Second, because love is not naive but is open-eyed, "love believes all things [1 Corinthians 13:7] and yet is never deceived."[74] Love recognizes the evil in another person when it is there, but love renounces judgment, leaves it to God.[75] Love is not naive, but rather handles the recognized evil by *hiding* it: "Not to discover *what nevertheless must be there*, insofar as it can be discovered, means to hide."[76] Love also restrains a person from sinning oneself: "The person who reduces sins surely hides a multitude of sins, and hides it doubly by not sinning himself and by keeping another from it."[77] In a striking image in *Works of Love*, Kierkegaard writes of the love that is not embittered: Christ before his condemners did not return their glances of contempt; he "discovered nothing; out of love he hid the multiplicity of sins."[78] The pattern bids the Christian walk "between ridicule and pity," unharmed, for "ridicule and contempt really do no harm when the one scorned is not injured by *discovering*, that is, by becoming embittered."[79] By silence,[80] or by finding mitigating explanation,[81] or finally by forgiveness,[82] love hides the multiplicity of sins.

Most importantly, love is never deceived because it never stops loving.[83] This "open-eyed" love that "hides the multiplicity of sins" does not ignore sin or evil in another, but in leaving judgment to God finally and most importantly shares in God's love for the offending person, for one never *gives up* on another person. This is love's *hope*. Love unites with faith (love *believes* all things and yet is never deceived) and, as we saw at the end of the last chapter, love unites with hope (love *hopes* all things yet is never put to shame).[84] Just as love believes all things, including the offending person's "possibility of the good," love

---

[73]   *WL* 312 (*SV* IX 321). Outka, in criticizing Reinhold Niebuhr's stress on self-sacrifice as the essence of *agape* states the need for "recourse to some additional principle, such as justice" (275). Kierkegaard addresses this issue indirectly in *WL* 312 (*SV* IX 321), which seems to require an understanding of justice as mutual regard as the heart of reconciliation.

[74]   *WL* 213–30 (*SV* IX 216–34).

[75]   *EUD* 57–58 (*SV* III 275–76).

[76]   *WL* 263 (*SV* IX 269) (italics added).

[77]   *EUD* 63 (*SV* III 281).

[78]   *WL* 267 (*SV* IX 274).

[79]   *WL* 268 (*SV* IX 275).

[80]   *Ibid.*

[81]   *WL* 271 (*SV* IX 278).

[82]   *WL* 273 (*SV* IX 280).

[83]   *WL* 223 (*SV* IX 226).

[84]   These are the respective titles of *WL*, part 2, chapters 2 and 3, 213–46 (*SV* IX 216–51).

is never deceived because it is "open-eyed" love.[85] Without ignoring evil, love "hides" the multiplicity of sins, *in light of a larger imaginative vision of the other person*, one that "hopes in love" for them "that the possibility of the good means more and more glorious advancement in the good from perfection to perfection *or resurrection from downfall or salvation from lostness* and thus beyond."[86] Vision allows this love and hope for another. "Christianity procures vision,"[87] and "Christianity's hope is the eternal."[88] The logical assumption that allows love to hope for a person's *ultimate* possibility of good is again the thought of the *eternal*. The Christian is called to see that person not only as she or he is in the present moment, but in a vision of the possibility that this person may indeed be perfected in the good, in time or in eternity.

The maieutic form of love

Christian love, we have seen, shapes the lover, and allows the lover a new vision of the other person, seeing others in forgiveness rather than mistrust. In this love there is offered the possibility of "presupposing the presence of love in all others," seeing others according to the truth, that is, according to the divine plan of love, in contrast to "deceiving" oneself out of love by adopting an attitude of shrewdness and mistrust. We have seen also that this is a matter of "belief" for Kierkegaard as well as hope, and have responded to the charge that the strong emphasis on "self-denial" results in a "blank check" for victimization.

This brings us to another central point for Kierkegaard. One of Kierkegaard's central points in the second part of *Works of Love* is Christian love as self-revelatory.[89] Love's presence or absence is *revealed* in human lives, and in love (or its absence) a person reveals himself or herself. This means that the form of the discourse must reflect the content. In speaking of love, we are speaking not about an abstract quality, but about how particular persons reveal themselves in their attitudes and works of love. Hence, reflections *about* love are insufficient; the entire discourse of *Works of Love* must rather be maieutic, focused on shaping and eliciting the *lover's* capacities. As Paul Müller has emphasized, at the heart of *Works of Love* is a maieutic of

[85]　*WL* 237 (*SV* ix 241–42).
[86]　*WL* 237 (*SV* ix 242) (italics added).
[87]　*WL* 232 (*SV* ix 236).
[88]　*WL* 233 (*SV* ix 237).
[89]　Kirmmse, *Kierkegaard in Golden Age Denmark*, 313.

communication; the goal is not to lead one to become adept at reflecting about love, but rather to arouse the reader to become loving.[90] The structure and content of *Works of Love* is maieutic in that it leads the reader ever again *from* either objective reflection about love in the abstract, or the equally (or even more) attractive possibilities of judging others' lovelessness, back *to* the question of whether and how the *reader* loves. The *reader's* concern should always be with whether one's own love is at work, not with the fruit or "results" of love; in loving another person, in God, one finally learns her or his own identity as a lover or non-lover. In choosing to see oneself and others in the frame of love rather than in mistrust, one chooses to be a particular kind of person, a loving person.[91]

This "reflexive" goal of love is not, however, an egocentric goal, since it is oriented first to God and secondly, to return to an earlier theme, it is oriented to the maieutic task of "loving forth" love in others. In this maieutic goal, the role of self-denial becomes clear, for self-denial expresses love's wish not to "seek its own" (1 Corinthians 13:5) but the good of the other. In self-denial the lover wishes not to appear as the great benefactor, leading the other person to feel in debt; the loving person seeks to disappear, to allow the other person to stand alone in her or his individual God-relationship.[92] The lover "seeks not its own," but willingly and lovingly becomes a tool in the divine task of bringing another person to love, to "stand alone" before God.

Kierkegaard's vision of Christian love, I have argued, is therefore "holistic" rather than fragmentary; it unites divine and human love, *eros* and *agape*, duty and inclination, self and others, rooting all of love in the love of God. In a lovely article, Martin Andic has recently shown how God's love ("the eternal") maieutically "loves forth" in two related ways: God's love is "redoubled" in one's own "inwardness," but this love is in turn "reduplicated" in one's love for another person. God's love and one's love for others are united, preserving the individuality yet interrelation of human lovers, the "confidence" of truth and of intimacy, grounded in God's love. A lover maieutically gives to others the love one acquires from God in inwardness, and so too one acquires from God what one gives to another (such as forgiveness).[93] Paul

---

[90] Müller, *Kristendom, etik og majeutik.*
[91] Kirmmse, *Kierkegaard in Golden Age Denmark*, 314.
[92] *WL*, part 2, chapter 4: "Love Seeks Not Its Own," 247–60 (*SV* ix 252–66).
[93] Martin Andic, "Confidence as a Work of Love," in George Pattison, ed., *Kierkegaard on Art and Communication* (New York: St. Martin's Press, 1992), 166.

Müller uses a similar image of wholeness, the "unbreakable circle," to describe *Works of Love*, uniting self-love, the love of one's neighbour, and love of God as the safeguard of every love relationship.[94]

As we have seen, part of that growing holistic vision of love includes its social implications, something of which Kierkegaard was keenly aware from the outset of *Works of Love*; he writes in his journal:

Despite everything people ought to have learned about my maieutic carefulness, in addition to proceeding slowly and continually letting it seem as if I knew nothing more, not the next thing – now on the occasion of my new upbuilding discourses [*Upbuilding Discourses in Various Spirits*] they will probably bawl out that I do not know what comes next, that I know nothing about sociality. You fools! Yet on the other hand I owe it to myself to confess before God that in a certain sense there is some truth in it, only not as men understand it – namely, that when I have first presented one aspect sharply, then I affirm the other even more strongly.

　Now I have my theme of the next book. It will be called:
　　　　　　　　　　　"Works of Love."[95]

Kierkegaard began the project of *Works of Love* with the question of sociality in mind. If *Works of Love* did not complete the development of Kierkegaard's social thought, it marked an important transition in his thinking, allowing a greater appreciation both of external action and sociality in love of neighbor. We will trace out that development further in the next chapter.

<hr>

[94]　Müller, *Kristendom, etik og majeutik*, 87.
[95]　*JP* v 5972 (*Pap.* viii¹ A 4, n.d., 1847).

CHAPTER 7

Witness in faith, hope, and love

Christianity is *praxis*, a character-task.

*JP*IV 3864 (*Pap.* X⁵ A 134, n.d., 1853).

Even if faith, hope, and love are not simply internal, but actively manifested in individual action, and even if faith struggles, hope recruits courage in oppression, and love reaches out maieutically to the neighbor, this still does not touch the question of the social and political implications of these Christian virtues. Does Kierkegaard's understanding of these passions of Christian faith give one resources for critique of one's society? Another way to put this is: does the religious imagination simply strive to *endure* and *attend*, or does it do more?[1] Can we stand outside of our social worlds and critique the images of the age? And how does one Christianly justify a stance of opposition?

The common interpretation of Kierkegaard is that his religious thought does not address these problems, that despite his critique of institutionalized self-deception (chapter 1) he is radically individualistic, not only acosmic in his alleged ethics of inwardness, but cut off from the political world. Given his frequent references to the contrast between Christianity and politics, his hatred of "the crowd," his concern with the individual, his respectful regard for the monarchy, Kierkegaard is often labeled a conservative. He is viewed, as Bruce Kirmmse says,

as having had no politics at all, or, what amounts to the same thing, as having embraced a nostalgic, traditionalist, and irrational authoritarianism, a misty reverence for hierarchy and monarchy which was completely irrelevant to the emerging social and economic realities of his times. Kierkegaard has thus been enlisted in the Cold War, and his views have been described, on the one hand, as a stout Christian refutation of "the doctrines of political

---

[1] See Sabina Lovibond's worries about Iris Murdoch on this score, and her broader concerns about how moral imagination can transcend and critique experience, *Realism and Imagination in Ethics*, 190.

liberalism" which insist upon the "divine right of majorities to govern wrong," and as a typical irrationalist excrescence of bourgeois society, on the other. The "Marxists" and the "conservatives" both agree in their portrait of Kierkegaard's politics, but merely assign opposite evaluations to it.[2]

The common interpretation of Kierkegaard as asocial has great difficulty accounting for the final years of Kierkegaard's life, especially his "attack upon 'Christendom'" (1854–55), which is either dismissed as psychological aberration, or as the result of "slippage" from his earlier period.[3] Kierkegaard's attack is indeed ferocious, his rhetoric is extreme, at times stark in its opposition of Christianity and worldly life. At the end he condemns marriage and procreation themselves as a contribution to the amount of original sin in the world. He criticizes Paul as well as Augustine and Luther on grace. On his deathbed, he refuses communion from any priest of the established Danish church. Theologically, one recent commentator sees Kierkegaard's attack as an assertion of radical individual ethical autonomy, a clear break not only with established Christendom, but with orthodox Christianity and with grace.[4]

Thanks to the work of a number of recent writers, however, the social dimensions of Kierkegaard's thought are being re-evaluated, leading both to criticism of the standard interpretation of Kierkegaard as asocial, and also to more nuanced readings of his final attack.[5] Bruce H. Kirmmse's *Kierkegaard in Golden Age Denmark* demonstrates convincingly that Kierkegaard's thought, while originally conservative, shifted gradually to a complete opposition to the conservative establishment of which he was a member. By the time of the "attack upon Christendom" in the last year of his life, Kierkegaard is shown to be anything but a conservative; according to Kirmmse, "he called for nothing less than the total dismantling of the traditional aristocratic–conservative synthesis

---

2   Kirmmse, *Kierkegaard in Golden Age Denmark*, 3, 487n1 and 2. The first quotation is from Walter Lowrie, *Kierkegaard*, 365–66; for the Marxist approach Kirmmse cites Georg Lukács.

3   Kirmmse, *Kierkegaard in Golden Age Denmark*, 3–4.

4   Anthony Rudd, *Kierkegaard on the Limits of the Ethical*, 164, 168, 169.

5   Important here in addition to the work of Bruce Kirmmse is Kresten Nordentoft, *Kierkegaard's Psychology* and *Hvad Siger Brand Majoren?: Kierkegaards Opgør med sin Samtid* [*What Says the Fire-Chief?: Kierkegaard's Settling-Up with His Times*] (Copenhagen: G.E.C. Gad, 1973), Johannes Sløk, *Da Kierkegaard Tav: Fra Forfatterskab til Kirkestorm* (Copenhagen: Reitzel, 1980), John Elrod, *Kierkegaard and Christendom*, Merold Westphal, *Kierkegaard's Critique of Reason and Society*. An illuminating volume of essays is Connell and Evans, eds., *Foundations of Kierkegaard's Vision of Community*. See also the essays in *International Kierkegaard Commentary: Volume 13: The Corsair Affair*, ed. Robert L. Perkins (Macon, GA: Mercer University Press, 1990) and *International Kierkegaard Commentary: Volume 14: Two Ages*. Note also the suggestive essays of Michael Plekon listed in the bibliography.

known as 'Christendom' or 'Christian culture,' which was the time-
honored and comfortable marriage of the 'horizontal' element of
traditional society and the 'vertical' element of religious transcendence."[6] In similar manner, the "attack on Christendom can only be
understood intelligently, not as an aberration, but as a response to the
social and political developments of Kierkegaard's time."[7] His reactions to the revolutions of 1848, the rise of the lower classes, and the
development of liberalism and democracy were not defensive or
fearful. Rather, his political and social thought is grounded, Kirmmse
argues, in an otherworldly Christian vision, combined with a political
and social vision that is best seen "as variants of liberalism and
populism."[8]

Of interest for our purposes, and requiring a bit more explication, is
Kirmmse's description of the development of Kierkegaard's social and
political thought as a Christian reflection on *boundaries*: the boundaries
between the public and private, between politics and religion.[9] In
maintaining the boundaries, Kierkegaard is not anticommunal, but is
consistently suspicious of modern attempts to sacralize the secular
order. He opposes the claim of politics to achieve human happiness
and even salvation, whether in the establishmentarian conservative
union of church and state, or in N. F. S. Grundtvig's populist attempts
to unite Christianity and the state.[10] His thought develops into a
theological reflection that increasingly finds in Christian discipleship
the Archimedean point for social religious witness and action, one that,
grounded in the individual, issues in a public call to one's contemporaries.

Kierkegaard's concern to reassert the boundaries still involves
dualism, his strong insistence upon the reality of the world of spirit in
contrast to this world of appearance. Because of the reality of the world
of spirit and the Christian's obligation to God, Kierkegaard reflects
extensively on how these two realms relate in the current situation of
believers. As Kirmmse argues, in a number of his later books, such as
*Upbuilding Discourses in Various Spirits, Christian Discourses, Practice in
Christianity*, and *The Sickness Unto Death*, Kierkegaard reflects upon two
different models of how the Christian relates to society, hinging upon

6 Kirmmse, *Kierkegaard in Golden Age Denmark*, 3.
7 Kirmmse, *Kierkegaard in Golden Age Denmark*, 4.
8 *Ibid.*
9 Kirmmse, *Kierkegaard in Golden Age Denmark*, 5.
10 Michele Nicoletti, "Politics and Religion in Kierkegaard's Thought: Secularization and the
   Martyr," in Connell and Evans, *Foundations of Kierkegaard's Vision of Community*, 186.

how one understands Matthew 6:33–34, on "seeking first [God's] kingdom and his righteousness." Does this mean simply a "prioritarian" stance, in that one gives God priority, or does it mean another stance not envisioned in the traditional Lutheran two-kingdoms understanding, that of the believer's active opposition to the social and political realm, even to martyrdom? Is the Christian called to be a good "citizen," giving priority to God while living in an integrated way in society, or is one also called to the additional role of "saint," or "martyrdom"?[11] It might not be possible simply to prioritize the two kingdoms, indeed, the demand may be that one is not simply citizen but prophetic witness, perhaps to martyrdom: the principle of God *rather than* Caesar (Acts 5:29) allows a radical and vocal critique of the social world.[12] While he alters a Lutheran "two-kingdoms" understanding in making ample room for Christian protest, ironically it is precisely that dualism of the absolute relation to the absolute that provides the impetus for prophetic action and witness. Again, as in the dialectical relation of the eternal and temporal, the inner and outer, the active and passive, so here is a dialectic tensive and yet holistic. In its dualism, it is tensive; in its expansiveness in embracing the social world, it is holistic.

What increasingly impresses itself upon Kierkegaard's mind, however, is the manner in which the Christian relates these dynamic elements in living as an individual within the social world. The question is *how* one does this, and that is a question of moral imagination. As Kirmmse shows, the *absoluteness* of the demand of Christianity over the conscience of the individual emerges with greater force in his thought. But what is the source of this absoluteness? It is in part, but importantly, his imaginative reflection on the gospels' portrayals of Jesus' life that gives him the standpoint for radical critique, from which he concludes that a believer may well be called not simply to grant priority to God over Caesar, but may in addition be called to active opposition.

Kierkegaard is sensitive to the ethical ambiguities and spiritual temptations involved here. Part of his exercise of moral and Christian imagination, focused around the figure of the outsider or prophet, is in determining its ethical justification. Just as Abraham had to wrestle in fear and trembling with the question of his motives in leading Isaac to Mount Moriah, and just as the Christian must reflect upon the ethical

---

11 Kirmmse, *Kierkegaard in Golden Age Denmark*, 376–78.
12 Kirmmse, *Kierkegaard in Golden Age Denmark*, 422.

justification for suffering at the hands of others, so too the Christian who contemplates the role of "saint" or "martyr" must also examine whether his or her motives are not really self-serving. When is a desire for prophetic witness a self-deceived desire for either self-glorification or senseless gesture?

Kierkegaard wrestles with the theological foundations for rethinking the role of "witness," "prophet," and "martyr," beyond that of the "citizen." Gradually he clarifies for himself the ethical and Christian possibility and appropriateness of the public stance of opposition to the established order in the name of Christianity. Of interest to us here is the shape of faith, hope, and love, including the figure of the "witness to the truth" in that imaginative moral refiguring. This is particularly crucial given the solitariness of the witness, the lack of support or even understanding from the environment. In the face of opposition, how does one defend taking up such a role against one's own community? To address these questions, we will examine Kierkegaard's transition from "hidden inwardness" to "public stance," and even social opposition. Then we will return to Christ as Pattern, and see how the role of the witness socially *manifests* rather than contradicts a life of faith, hope, and love.

FROM HIDDEN INWARDNESS TO PUBLIC STANCE

Central to Kierkegaard's development is his transition from a religion of "hidden inwardness" to a public role for the Christian. We have already seen Kierkegaard's move from inward suffering to outward suffering, and his thought on love being "inversely recognizable" by its fruits. By the time he writes *Practice in Christianity*, he can speak of "hidden inwardness" very critically. His major concern is that "if everyone around defines himself as being a Christian *just like* 'the others,' then no one, if it is looked at this way, is really confessing Christ."[13] Such an inwardness is "so to speak, behind a jammed lock: it is impossible to find out whether all these thousands upon thousands actually are Christians, for they all are that, so it is said, in hidden inwardness."[14]

The critique of "hidden inwardness" also stems from his reflection on the church. In *Practice in Christianity*, Kierkegaard writes that "hidden inwardness" is precisely the form of spirituality that characterizes

[13] *PC* 219 (*SV* xii 201).
[14] *PC* 220 (*SV* xii 202).

"established Christendom." "In established Christendom we are all true Christians, but this is in hidden inwardness."[15] The pretext, Kierkegaard points out, is that all of these Christians keep their Christianity secret out of humility; they fear being honored and esteemed for their extraordinary inner spirituality. By contrast, in the church militant "being a Christian was recognizable by the opposition one suffered."[16] Bourgeois Christianity thereby succeeds in making spiritlessness and worldliness the mark of spirituality, providing a convenient means for avoiding opposition from the world! Kierkegaard's understanding of "inwardness" is more sensitive to the social duplicity that self-deceptively uses "hidden inwardness" as an excuse for cowardly silence, which he describes as "the silence of death": "Established Christendom, where all are Christians but in hidden inwardness, in turn resembles the Church militant as little as the silence of death resembles the loudness of passion."[17]

In his increasingly pointed critique of "hidden inwardness," Kierkegaard never abandons "inwardness," and certainly never reduces Christian existence to mere "observability"; one cannot identify a Christian simply by observing outward behavior.[18] Rather, he develops further the implications of "inwardness," implications that lead him away from "hidden inwardness" to an appreciation of how faith is manifest in works and hence also in the public sphere. The stage is thus set for a relation between the private and the public, and for a strong consideration of a religious role with political implications.

Kierkegaard also rethought his role as "poet" in this new light. He never adopted the prophetic mantle *for himself*: "I am not what the age perhaps demands, a reformer – that by no means, nor a profound speculative spirit, a seer, a prophet; no (pardon me for saying it), I am in a rare degree an accomplished detective talent."[19] He explicitly rejects the title of "witness" in favor of the title of "poet" and "Socratic gadfly." In the "attack," he says that

I am not a Christian ... The only analogy I have before me is Socrates. My task is a Socratic task, to revise the definition of what it is to be a Christian.

15   *PC* 216 (*SV* xii 198).
16   *PC* 217 (*SV* xii 199).
17   *PC* 214 (*SV* xii 196).
18   Dewey, *The New Obedience*, 219n52.
19   *KAUC* 33 (*SV* xiv 46).

For my part I do not call myself a "Christian" (thus keeping the ideal free), but I am able to make it evident that the others are still less than I.[20]

So too, in contemplating that he might become a "sacrifice" at the hands of the established order, he says that "suppose that quite literally I were to become a sacrifice: I would not even in that case be a sacrifice for Christianity, but because I wanted honesty."[21] "Prophet," like "apostle," assumes *authorization* and *authority* in delivering a revelation from God. Evident in his critique of Magister Adler, Kierkegaard labored to distinguish the qualifications of "apostle" from that of "genius." Kierkegaard also insisted upon conformity of life to message, a conformity he did not claim for himself. Behind this is his desire not to obscure the issues with red herrings; he chose rather to fight out the issues in terms of what the Christian *ideals* themselves demanded. Yet the Socratic role resembles the prophets, to say nothing of Christ. Pseudonymity thus comes to serve him in a new way in the later writings.[22]

Hence, Kierkegaard is again, and for new reasons, a kind of poet, rather than a "prophet" or "witness to the truth" or "hero of faith." In *For Self-Examination* (1851), he writes under his own name that

there are among us some who claim to be Christian in the strictest sense of the word, to be that in contrast to the rest of us. I have been unable to associate myself with them. For one thing, I think that their lives do not meet the standard ... For another, I am too far short of being a Christian to dare to associate myself with anyone who makes such a claim ... I am ahead only in the poetic sense – that is, I am more aware of what Christianity is, know how to describe it better.[23]

Kierkegaard sees his task rather as a poet who points to "heroes of faith"; unlike the heroes of faith and witnesses to the truth, whose "restlessness" "aims at reforming things as they are," the poet's different kind of restlessness has to do with "inward deepening."[24] The poet works for inward deepening by presenting the hero of faith and witness to the truth in order to make clear the contrast between their lives and our lives.[25] The standard by which he judges "Christendom" to be rebellion is that of the "ideal" of "New Testament Christianity."

20 *KAUC* 282–83 (*SV* xiv 351–52).
21 *KAUC* 40 (*SV* xiv 55).
22 Elrod, *Kierkegaard and Christendom*, ch. 7.
23 *FSE* 21 (*SV* xii 311).
24 *FSE* 21 (*SV* xii 312).
25 *FSE* 22 (*SV* xii 312).

Without claiming that he himself fulfills the ideal, he nonetheless presents himself (again, in the guise of human honesty) as someone who can at least *state* the ideal in its purity.[26] It is in this sense that Kierkegaard points to, if he does not embody, the role of "witness to the truth," who presents the ideals as the standard for existence. As poet and gadfly pointing to the truth, he indicates at once the ideal (Christ) and the shape of a life in response to that in faith, hope, and love.

THE PATTERN AND THE RESPONSE

Imitatio Christi

The imagining involved in critical scrutiny of existing institutions involves one in what Wittgenstein called "seeing a new aspect."[27] For Kierkegaard, the themes of Christianity as "the absolute," of "contemporaneity with Christ," and the necessity of identification with his humility and suffering as the "sign of offense," developed with such precision and force in *Practice in Christianity*, generate a vocabulary and transcendent criterion that allows social critique.[28] Although the "prioritarian" model of the Christian as "citizen" is maintained in this book, the alternative model of witness to the truth is there developed in detail in light of Kierkegaard's understanding of Christ.[29] We already saw in chapters 4 and 5, on faith and hope, how *Practice in Christianity* contrasts Christ and the world. But Christ's call is also to opposition to society, including the willingness to suffer as witness and martyr. The suffering is avoidable, is "suffering for the doctrine." But the very act of suffering is now an affront to the world. This Christ identifies with the social outcasts, with the suffering, and with "the poor and lowly of the people, the workers, the manual laborers, the cement mixers, etc.!," those scorned by the elitist world.[30] He "comes into collision with an established order."[31]

The model of Christ as sign of offense to the established order is directed first of all at the established church, attacking the portrayal of a triumphalist Christ who is the warrant for a triumphalist church. The

---

[26] This again gives the lie to the view that only *practitioners* of a faith can understand it.

[27] Lovibond, *Realism and Imagination in Ethics*, 194–200.

[28] On "contemporaneity" see especially *PC* 62–66 (*SV* xii 59–63); on offense *PC* 81–144 (*SV* xii 78–134).

[29] Kirmmse, *Kierkegaard in Golden Age Denmark*, 399.

[30] *PC* 58 (*SV* xii 55).

[31] *PC* 85 (*SV* xii 81).

believer rather is "situated between [Christ's] abasement, which lies behind, and his loftiness – that is precisely why he is said to draw to himself."[32] The church's existence is not a triumphal celebration of his victory, as if "we have only to join up with him and share the victory with him."[33] The church rather is called to a time of struggle in imitation of Christ the prototype. Kierkegaard likens the time of the church to a "parenthesis or something parenthetical in Christ's life; the content of the parenthesis begins with Christ's ascension on high and ends with his coming again."[34] In this "parenthesis" – identical with "contemporaneity" with the suffering Christ – the church is called to "an examination period":

The examination period begins with his ascension; it has lasted for eighteen hundred years and may last eighteen thousand. But (and this belongs to the intervening period as an examination) he is coming again. When this is so, then any direct adherence to him in order to profit from his victory as a matter of course is more impossible than in relation to any other person.[35]

It is not, again, that Christ is not "elevated" or "victorious," but that this elevation is an aspect of eternity, whereas the church is called to imitate Christ in time, and therefore the suffering Christ in time.

The polemical force of *Practice in Christianity* was directed against any attempts at "the deification of the established order," which is ironically "the secularization of everything."[36] In opposition to this, Kierkegaard asserts again an imaginative prophetic "dualism" of God and humanity – "the infinite qualitative difference between God and man."[37] Discipleship opposes society's self-deification, for Christ is the model for the struggling church, to whom one responds in offense or in faith's indirection, rather than in a "direct" intuitive, cultural, or speculative "knowledge" of God.

Faith, hope, and love in prophetic witness

Witness to the truth: faith

How then can one justify the role of witness as an exercise of faith, hope, and love? The answer is that the struggling, suffering Christ

---

[32] *PC* 153 (*SV* xii 143).
[33] *PC* 201 (*SV* xii 185–86).
[34] *PC* 202 (*SV* xii 186).
[35] *Ibid.*
[36] *PC* 91 (*SV* xii 86).
[37] *PC* 140 (*SV* xii 130).

provides the imaginative model for such witness. And this discipleship is the only way of relating to the truth of Christ. "Christ is the truth," but "to *be* the truth is the only true explanation of what truth is."[38] It is not a matter of belief (alone), but of modeling one's own life after his example.

> One can ask an apostle, one can ask a Christian, "What is truth?" and in answer to the question the apostle and this Christian will point to Christ and say: Look at him, learn from him, he was the truth. This means that truth in the sense in which Christ is the truth is not a sum of statements, not a definition etc., but a life.[39]

The witness to the truth is one whose life *shows* his or her belief, including a willingness to *suffer* for the doctrine. Kierkegaard sees "witness to the truth" in broader terms than Christian; it can be part of an ethical requirement to stand for a conviction, as when in *Purity of Heart* he speaks of the requirement to be "willing to suffer all" for the truth, as "witnesses to the good and the true."[40]

But "witness" is central to understanding the proclamation of Christianity, for Kierkegaard is convinced that this concept highlights a central necessity of Christian proclamation: the integration of one's speech, life, and belief. As he writes in his journal, "A witness is a person who directly demonstrates the truth of the doctrine he proclaims," and the problem with "Christendom" is "that Christianity is not proclaimed by witnesses but by teachers."[41] This integration of speech and life in witness to the suffering Christ Kierkegaard thinks extremely difficult: "let this venturing to preach that there is joy in suffering insult be met with insults, and then we will see what becomes of the speaker."[42]

The polemic against the professors and the clergy finds its source in the conviction that they fall so far short of the standard of the "witness." In a scathing journal entry from 1850, Kierkegaard writes of the properly Christian order: first, the apostles ("with a special quality"); second, the witnesses ("whose lives express what they teach and are marked by sufferings 'for the sake of the Word'"); and finally "what could be called teachers of religion, or what are presently called

---

38 *PC* 205 (*SV* xii 189).
39 *Ibid.*
40 *UDVS* 90 (*SV* viii 188).
41 *JP* iv 4967 (*Pap.* x³ A 5, n.d., 1850).
42 *JP* iv 4972 (*Pap.* x³ A 677, n.d., 1850).

pastors whose conception of Christianity essentially is that it is a doctrine," and who (satirically)

are again ranked among themselves according to their true rendering of the doctrine (orthodoxy), a certain imaginative fervor in respect to conviction (this fervor is nevertheless esthetic, for if it were existential, "witnesses" would necessarily result), according to penetration and depth in reflecting on the doctrine, according to imagination, feeling, artistry in presenting the doctrine eloquently, etc.[43]

In *For Self-Examination* – several years before H. L. Martensen's funeral sermon praising Bishop Mynster as a "witness to the truth" – Kierkegaard gives a careful description of some of the other characteristics of the "witness to the truth."[44] Echoing Luther, "faith is a restless thing," and it is first of all describable; one can examine this "given actuality" of the hero of faith or witness to the truth. In opposition to the "crowd," such a witness is solitary, like Luther, for true reformation can only come, Kierkegaard writes, from individuals, not from the "public." Furthermore, he or she will be beset by "spiritual trial" (*Anfægtelse*), not enjoying the call to be a witness, but actually terrified of the responsibility. "There is not one of those called who has not preferred to be exempted, not one who, as a child begs and pleads to be let off, has not pleaded for himself, but it does not help – he must go on."[45]

Nonetheless, although the "witness" (unlike the "citizen") speaks *against* society, the "witness" is not a private role; this role *unites* the private and public realms and is in the best interests of the community. "Witness" creates space for the meeting of the private and public realms, for in this figure private responsibility and public accountability embrace. First, it is only an individual who can take *responsibility* for his or her action; the witness points to the absoluteness of individual responsibility over the collective. Second, in the act of witnessing to the truth, one stakes oneself in a public manner that is *accountable* before others. In reflecting on the public role of the individual, Kierkegaard throughout the later 1840s and 1850s develops the vision of the individual, personal, act that has public implications.[46]

Kierkegaard's final attack upon acculturated Christianity was prompted by social responsibility as well as devotion to the truth:

43   *JP* iv 4971 (*Pap.* x³ A 570, n.d., 1850).
44   *FSE* 19–20 (*SV* xii 310–11).
45   *FSE* 20 (*SV* xii 310).
46   I owe this way of putting it to Jack Schwandt.

offense at what he considered to be the complete collective amnesia found in the church assumes that the witness identifies with the community. The issue was that the church (and "Christian culture") forgot the activities of (in Wittgenstein's sense) "using the picture" of Christ to shape discipleship. While using the language of Christ as the pattern and model, the community emptied it of content. So the attack was launched as a direct maieutic, a Socratic reminder of how the picture had been used ("New Testament Christianity") and should be used, what the actions are that constitute "following the Pattern" of Christ.

At the very outset of the 1854–55 "attack" is a stark and insistent presentation of the contrast between two forms of "witness" and "imitation," imitating Christ and imitating the ecclesiastical figures of the established church. Kierkegaard wrote the first broadside in the attack, the _Fatherland_ article of December 18, 1854, in the previous February, immediately after Martensen's sermon on the Sunday prior to Bishop Mynster's funeral. Martensen, who anticipated appointment to the bishopric, based his sermon on Hebrews 13:7 ("Remember those who had the rule over you ... and considering the issue of their life, imitate their faith");[47] from this text Martensen urged those present "'to _imitate_ the faith of the true guide, the genuine witness to the truth'" (i.e., Mynster).[48] Given Kierkegaard's extensive reflection on what it is to be a "witness to the truth," he drafted this response, contrasting Mynster as a "witness to the truth" and the true character-istics of such a witness. In contrast to Mynster, Kierkegaard charges, stands Christ; Christianity has to do with "dying from the world, by voluntary renunciation, by hating oneself, by suffering for the doc-trine."[49] The genuine "witness to the truth" is the one whose life reflects his or her belief, whose life involves "suffering for the doctrine," one who "in poverty witnesses to the truth – in poverty, in lowliness, in abasement, and so is unappreciated, hated, abhorred, and then derided, insulted, mocked."[50] Bishop Mynster's preaching "soft-pedals, slurs over, suppresses, omits" the decisively Christian, and "thereby implicitly condemn[s] as an exaggeration the true Christian preaching (by a suffering witness to the truth)."[51] So the issue is simply which

---

[47]   _KAUC_ 21 (_SV_ xiv 29).
[48]   _KAUC_ 5 (_SV_ xiv 5) (italics added).
[49]   _KAUC_ 5 (_SV_ xiv 6).
[50]   _KAUC_ 7 (_SV_ xiv 8).
[51]   _KAUC_ 5 and 6n (_SV_ xiv 6 and 7n).

pattern one follows: Christ as Pattern, or Mynster as pattern; in exasperation Kierkegaard writes of Mynster: "to represent this man – God in heaven! – before the congregation as a pattern, before a Christian congregation, and therefore as a Christian pattern!"[52]

The Pattern shows the way, and the ways diverge; if Mynster is a pattern, "the 'way' has now become a different one, not that of the New Testament: in humiliation, hated, forsaken, persecuted, condemned to suffer in this world – no, the way is: admired, acclaimed, crowned with garlands, accorded the accolade of knighthood as the reward of a brilliant career!"[53] But "what Christ, what the Apostles, what every witness to the truth desires as the only thing ... is imitation – the only thing humanity has no taste for, takes no pleasure in."[54]

The world's opposition: hope and courage

As we saw in chapter 5, Kierkegaard is convinced that truth and the good are always persecuted in the "world." The suffering of hidden inwardness yields to the requirement that one publically witness to the truth. The believer can avoid this suffering simply by collapsing before the power structure. Yet one endures the suffering despite the world's opposition. What he comes to emphasize now is that specifically Christian suffering is marked by collision with the world; Christian existence is not simply an inward detachment from worldly concern, but actual hostility, opposition, and persecution.[55] The witness to the truth will meet opposition: "All attack him, hate him, curse him."[56]

Against the truth, the world deifies itself, violating the boundary between politics and religion. Because self-deification is always self-deception, the world is in falsehood. The world is not a neutral medium, much less a glad hearer of truth. Grounded as it is in self-interest, it is actively hostile toward the good. Hence, the world is by definition based upon a lie. This was impressed upon Kierkegaard, of course, in his reflections on Socrates. In his conflict with the newspaper *Corsair* Kierkegaard had occasion to appreciate the misunderstanding and opposition of the world on a personal level, and during the attack he expected (unrealistically) that he might be arrested and even martyred. Most importantly, he sees this opposition in Christ,

---

52   *KAUC* 21 (*SV* xiv 29).
53   *Ibid.*
54   *KAUC* 264 (*SV* xiv 329).
55   Elrod, "Climacus, Anti-Climacus and the Problem of Suffering," 316–17.
56   *FSE* 20 (*SV* xii 311).

whose life was the truth, and who also was hated and slain by the world.

Kierkegaard's critique here is deeply social, as is clear for example in *Two Ages: The Age of Revolution and the Present Age: A Literary Review* (1846), which analyzes the social conditions of modern bourgeois life: the victory of the "herd," superficiality, lack of passion, the devaluation of language, leveling and *ressentiment*.[57] Over against the Truth, society fashions and dictates its own norms of "truth." The "offense," as we saw in chapter 4, is an acoustic illusion; what Kierkegaard sees more clearly later is that the world, as part of what Merold Westphal calls "the noetic effects of sin," sets up its own defenses against God and the truth.[58]

Interestingly, some of Kierkegaard's most searching portrayals of the world's opposition to the truth are to be found in *Works of Love*. We saw in the last chapter that *Works of Love* presents a holistic portrayal of love, one that seeks to redeem natural love and to relate the love of self, of neighbor, and of God, yet we saw too how the dialectic of opposition is also important in that book. Nowhere is this clearer than in the treatment of the opposition of Christian love by the world, the response of the world to the individuated love of the Christian, and the way that the world reverses eternal values. In the midst of a book that deals with the duty of love to neighbor and thus with the social dimension of Christian existence, Kierkegaard at the same time does not neglect, but indeed highlights, that the response of the world to neighbor-love and to the truth is not a comfortable communitarianism, but the opposition of offense and rejection. If one loves others, one will not receive love and gratitude from them in return. He criticizes Christian sermons that misleadingly give the impression that if one has "faith, love, and humility," and labors "with self-renunciation to develop a Christian consciousness," "the youth must certainly believe that if he accomplishes what is demanded or honestly works to accomplish it, it will go well with him in the world."[59] Invoking 1 John 3:13 ("Do not wonder, brethren, that the world hates you"), Kierkegaard describes "a double danger" in true Christian striving: not only is there the danger "in man's inner being, where he must strive with himself," but if one passes through this danger, there is also the striving "*outside of man with the*

57   *TA* 60–112 (*SV* VIII 57–105).
58   Westphal, *Kierkegaard's Critique of Reason and Society*, 108; on ideology critique, 117.
59   *WL* 185 (*SV* IX 182–83).

world."[60] Kierkegaard further contrasts the "purely human conception of self-renunciation" with the "Christian conception of self-renunciation": in the first, the promise is "give up your selfish desires, longings, and plans – and then you will become appreciated and honoured and loved as a righteous man and wise," but the latter is "give up your selfish desires and longings, give up your arbitrary plans and purposes so that you in truth work disinterestedly for the good – and submit to being abominated almost as a criminal, scorned and ridiculed for this very reason."[61] Here the Christian meets the world's offense and puzzlement, for "willing to be forsaken in this way is regarded by the world as stupidity and insanity ... The world looks upon self-renunciation only with shrewd practicality and therefore honours only the self-renunciation which prudentially remains in worldliness."[62] The difficulty one faces in learning Christian self-renunciation is to renounce the expectation of being honored.

Yet Kierkegaard continues that, faced by such opposition and hatred, one should never abandon hope or its correlative virtue, courage. The world's opposition affects the Christian dialectic of the virtue of courage; "it was with this in mind that the old church fathers said: The virtues of paganism are glittering vices."[63] Human self-renunciation has a notion of danger and of courage that are "mutually given"; there is agreement about the danger and the honor. But Christian courage *redefines* the danger and thus redefines the courage; it must "struggle to get permission to call dangerous that which the contemporaries are not willing to call danger."[64]

In a journal entry in 1854 Kierkegaard reflects further on the peculiarity of "Christian courage" in contrast to the courage shown in classical paganism. "Christian courage"

is one person holding out alone, as a single individual, against the opposition of the numerical (and this corresponds to the fact that the truth was in one person, in Christ, in opposition to the whole race), is conceptual heterogeneity, character heterogeneity with the numerical; Christian courage increases in proportion to the number, and the longer the opposition is endured the more inward the courage becomes.

---

[60]   *WL* 186 (*SV* ix 183) (italics added).
[61]   *WL* 188 (*SV* ix 185).
[62]   *Ibid.*
[63]   *WL* 189 (*SV* ix 186).
[64]   *WL* 189 (*SV* ix 186–87).

Paganism, with the single exception of Socrates, "did not really know this kind of courage," since it assumed that "the numerical constitutes the concept." Christianity, however, is spirit, and therefore postulates "the single individual against number." And in words that one feels were meant to steel himself to the task of attack, he confesses, "Alas, how human to want rather to give in and be himself the one who is living a lie. But precisely right here is the Christian battle, the Christian courage, both with regard to the impulses of fear and of compassion."[65]

More and more dominant in Kierkegaard's later writing is this theme of how Christianity heterogeneously redefines concepts, including concepts like hope. The source of that redefinition and subsequent clash is twofold. First, the world's hatred directed toward the Christian is yet another form of the "acoustic illusion" that is offended at Christianity, yet unwittingly that offense is prompted by the revelation itself, for the revelation redefines the concepts in its judgment on the world. Second, that clash is *social*, for it involves a redefinition of the concepts – the shared goals, plans, hopes, and vision – that make a community into a community.

The "community" versus the "herd": love

Kierkegaard's attack on "Christendom" was not an attack on the community *per se*. It was a personal act addressed *to* the community, calling the community to accountability. If in the end Kierkegaard advised leaving "the priests," it was not out of hyperindividualism or anti-ecclesiasticism, but because the church so flagrantly subverted its own ideals, no longer even aware of having subverted them.

The issue for Kierkegaard was this: what is the condition for a "community" to be a community rather than a "herd," the "mass," the "crowd," the "public," a mere collection of units? It is not sheer numbers alone, a *vox populi, vox Dei*. Rather, the condition for community is that each individual is related to an idea or ideal that is then the basis for sociality. This, again, is the importance of Kierkegaard's *Two Ages*, in which he approvingly contrasts the passionate "age of revolution" of the previous century with the present "spiritless" age. The book is an important contribution to Kierkegaard's thought on the relation between the individual and community. Whereas the former age of revolution had a proper understanding of how "individuals"

---

[65] *JP*III 2987 (*Pap.* XI² A 89, n.d., 1854).

related to one another in an appropriate sociality, the present age "levels" all differences in a "herd":

When individuals (each one individually) are essentially and passionately related to an idea and together are essentially related to the same idea, the relation is optimal and normative. Individually the relation separates them (each one has himself for himself), and ideally it unites them. Where there is essential inwardness, there is a decent modesty between man and man that prevents crude aggressiveness; in the relation of unanimity to the idea there is the elevation that again in consideration of the whole forgets the accidentality of details. Thus the individuals never come too close to each other in the herd sense, simply because they are united on the basis of an ideal distance.[66]

As Michael Plekon has argued, when Kierkegaard wrote these lines in 1845–46, about the time he was completing *Postscript*, they still reflected an essentially conservative outlook, although one in transition.[67] What is of interest to us, however, is not the politics, but the essential possibility of *community* that they open up. Sociality is not illegitimate for an "individual," but the "community" in the modern age can no longer be based on traditional class structures, or reduced to the "herd."[68] The basis of social interaction in community is rather the presence of the idea or the ideal.

So too, scattered throughout his journals are similar contrasts applicable to the church. Kierkegaard's critical remarks on the "congregation" are sometimes misinterpreted because they are taken out of the context of Grundtvig's elevation of the term as part of his populist attempt to unite church with Danish culture. In contrast to this, Kierkegaard in a late entry contrasts "congregation" with the "public," specifying that the "individual" is the "middle term" in any true congregation that distinguishes it from the formless public; and that "middle term" is further defined as the individual's relationship to God and the possibility of offense.[69]

But is the role of witness, or even a poetic gadfly directly attacking the community, an exercise of love? Kierkegaard's concern with the "middle term" reflects his interest in the proper conditions for relationship. In Augustinian fashion, social relations are grounded not in abstract rights, but, as we saw in chapter 6, in the essential "middle

66   *TA* 62–63 (*SV* VIII 59).
67   Michael Plekon, "Towards Apocalypse: Kierkegaard's *Two Ages* in Golden Age Denmark," in Perkins, ed., *International Kierkegaard Commentary: Volume 14: Two Ages*, 19–52, especially 19–21, 47–50.
68   For other journal entries on the "herd," see *JP* III 2922–3010.
69   *WL* 357n2 (*Pap.* X⁵ B 208; the entry does not appear in *JP*).

term" of the God-relation. Love is the basis for sociality, for in love, one is related to another person on the basis of that "middle term" that preserves the two lovers as individuals. Community is not based upon submerging individuals; this is the inhumanity that refuses to recognize that the individual is the locus of ethical responsibility and of the God-relationship. Any other view is inhuman, just as inhuman as what Kierkegaard sees as the Hegelian view of the meaning of history residing at a level of sociality above the significance of individual lives.

Neither are individuals atomistic. The essential sociality of love as a virtue is evident particularly in the important discourse that opens part 2 of *Works of Love*, "Love Builds Up."[70] This is crucial in indicating Kierkegaard's understanding of love as not only active (discussed in chapter 6), but social. The topic is how "love builds up by presupposing that love is present" in another,[71] and Kierkegaard begins by contrasting the two ways that a person can "possess a quality": "The qualities a man can possess must be either qualities he has for himself, even if he makes use of them in relationship to others, or qualities for others." Wisdom, power, talents, knowledge are examples of qualities for oneself; a wise person, for example, can have wisdom without attributing wisdom to another person. But love is a "quality for others," for one cannot possess it without "presupposing that love is present in others." "Love is not an exclusive characteristic, but it is a characteristic by which or in virtue of which you exist for others."[72] In a touching passage he continues,

When you praise [someone] as a loving person, you mean that love is a characteristic which he possesses, which it is, too, and you feel yourself built up by him, simply because he is loving, but you do not detect the true explanation, that his love means he presupposes love in you and that you are built up precisely by this, that precisely by this is love built up in you.[73]

Love, as the fruit of faith, binds persons together; as a "quality" it is by definition "for others." The "character" that Kierkegaard envisions at the heart of Christian existence is by necessity a love that relates to others. The basis for sociality is, therefore, not Grundtvig's vision of shared national identity, or the conservative aristocratic vision of community, or association based upon rights as such; the basis of sociality, in more truly classical Augustinian fashion, is love.

70 *WL* 199–212 (*SV* ix 201–15).
71 *WL* 210 (*SV* ix 213).
72 *WL* 211 (*SV* ix 214).
73 *Ibid.*

But perhaps this describes the "citizen" but not the "witness"? Can the role of witness truly exhibit love of neighbor? Yet, as we saw above in discussing hope in facing the world's opposition, the works of love are often rejected, met with the "acoustic illusion" of offense; so too, the work of the witness to the truth, despite the fierceness of the witness' attack, may *indirectly* and *hiddenly* manifest love for others. In particular, as we saw in chapter 6, while it may be loving to "hide" the neighbor's sin, it may also be unloving to hide that sin; the justification of the confrontational role of witness in the specifically Christian context hinges on this possibility.

It is in developing this justification of the witness' role that Kresten Nordentoft, and other commentators after him, have argued that central to understanding the later Kierkegaard's thought, including the Kierkegaard of the attack, is that, despite his indisputable talent for "revealing, tearing down, dissecting, and reducing," that is, the power of the "negative" element in his maieutic, culminating in the final attack, Kierkegaard still sees the eternal basis of love in "the fundament" of things, beneath alienation and beneath guilt, in a basic optimism.[74] In *Works of Love*, Kierkegaard writes that the aim of love is "to aid one or another human being to become his own."[75] "The lover presupposes that love is in the other person's heart, and by this very presupposition he builds up love in him – from the ground up, insofar as in love he presupposes it present as the ground."[76] Love is basic to each human life, and to believe it is present, to see another person from the standpoint of love, is "the sprout in the grain"[77] that supports the Christian's basic optimism. Nordentoft argues that the "fundament" of the human being is not guilt, but the forgiveness of sins, and the presence of love.[78]

In *Practice in Christianity*, Kierkegaard reflects on how Christianity appears to be harsh, even a horror and madness. Indeed, over against the false comfort of much Christian preaching, which sees Christianity as "gentle teachings, the sublime and the profound, about [Jesus as] a friend, etc.,"[79] "Christianity is the *absolute*"

[74] Nordentoft, *Kierkegaard's Psychology*, 376.
[75] *WL* 260 (*SV* ix 266).
[76] *WL* 206 (*SV* ix 208).
[77] Nordentoft, *Kierkegaard's Psychology*, 376–86; see *WL* 207 (*SV* ix 210); the Hongs' translation reads, "like the germ in a kernel of grain."
[78] Nordentoft, *Kierkegaard's Psychology*, 365.
[79] *PC* 68 (*SV* xii 65).

whereby God "wills to transform human beings."[80] But here too the
ground of the transformation is God's love: "It is out of love that
God so wills it, but it is also *God* who wills its, and he wills as he
wills. He wills not to be transformed by human beings into a cozy –
a human god; he wills to transform human beings, and he wills it
out of love."[81]

In support of this interpretation, it is significant that in August of
1855, in the midst of the final phase of his attack, Kierkegaard
published the little discourse, originally delivered in 1851, that we
have already looked at in chapter 5, "The Unchangeableness of
God." Returning to one of his favorite texts, James 1:17–21, it speaks
of the contrast between God's changelessness as constancy and
human inconstancy. In the opening prayer, God is praised as "O
Thou who in infinite love dost submit to be moved" even by the
need of the sparrow. And to this constancy is contrasted the muta-
bility of human beings, with the admonition from James to be swift
to hear, slow to speak, slow to wrath, and to relate oneself to God in
fear and trembling. But at the conclusion of the discourse, echoing
Works of Love, is the final image of the wayfarer who returns to a
spring after years of wandering, and it speaks of God as a spring who
is "always to be found unchanged," who indeed follows the traveler
"on his way." "And whenever any human being comes to Thee, of
whatever age, at whatever time of the day, in whatever state: if he
comes in sincerity he always finds Thy love equally warm, like the
spring's unchanged coolness, O Thou who art unchangeable!"[82] The
coda in the attack, published only three months before his death,
points to God's love as the beginning and end of the journey of *homo
viator*.

Even at the end, despite the undoubted extremity of his attack,
Kierkegaard does not abandon God's love as the "fundament."
Neither does he abandon grace or even Lutheran solafideism; with
God's love at the beginning and end, the late Kierkegaard is not, as
recently asserted, a break with Christian orthodoxy, or an abandonment of grace in a loveless call to discipleship as autonomous human
effort – even when the later Kierkegaard polemicized against
Augustine and Luther, and, be it noted again, Paul – for lessening
the demand of the gospels and rendering Christianity into a matter

[80] *PC* 62 (*SV* xii 59).
[81] *Ibid.*
[82] *UG* 227, 228, 240 (*SV* xiv 283, 283–84, 294).

of "soothing and reassuring anguished consciences."[83] Theologically, Kierkegaard's concern is not with altering the doctrine, but with attacking its abuse; his concern is with *how* one relates to the "what," and his target is the shrewdness of the times. The real shift in Kierkegaard is not from grace to works, but, as Kirmmse identifies, from a "prioritarian" ethic (relate absolutely to the absolute, but relatively to relative ends) to a martyr-ideal. The martyr-ideal is still *imitatio Christi*, based ultimately upon grace, not in "radical human autonomy."

CONCLUSION

The later Kierkegaard's understanding of Christian existence as faith, hope, and love is profoundly social. This can be seen as either a radical break with his earlier thought, or as a development.[84] In either case, the elements of "inner and outer," "active and passive," "individual and social" come together in his last days, even within the tensiveness of his dialectical, dualistic thought. Approached from the standpoint of his reflections on "passions" and "virtues," Kierkegaard sees the religious individual as engaging the world of the finite.

Further, Kierkegaard's understanding of imitation of Christ develops extensively. Kierkegaard's deeper attention to the details of Christ's life, the extensive exegetical study of the gospels on "offense" and "suffering," provide the concrete image that lead him to an understanding of Christ as the absolute truth, and of discipleship as "following Christ" within the world. Christian pilgrimage is not a private gnostic flight of the soul to God, but is a call to discipleship in the social matrix. "As for the rigorously religious individual, his life is essentially action."[85]

Kierkegaard's concern with boundaries and priorities preserves the individual's relation to God over against communitarian interests. In a situation in which those boundaries are violated – as Kierkegaard believed them to be in his own day – the response of the Christian may well be one not of quietist resignation, but of vocal opposition to the established order. The "witness," who by definition faces the world's

[83] Rudd, *Kierkegaard on the Limits of the Ethical*, 169. *JP* III 2550 (*Pap.* XI¹ A 193, n.d., 1854); compare *JP* III 2551 (*Pap.* XI¹ A 297, n.d., 1854) and *JP* III 2554 (*Pap.* XI¹ A 572, n.d., 1854).
[84] Johannes Sløk sees the shift as a break, Merold Westphal as "symphonic development," indeed, in a Hegelian fashion. See Connell and Evans, *Foundations of Kierkegaard's Vision of Community*, xvii.
[85] *FSE* 11 (*SV* XII 303).

opposition, is accountable to God alone; the "witness" is the final and fullest expression of "the individual." While his or her stance will never be justified by the community, it is "transcendently" defensible as an exercise and expression of the Christian virtues of faith, hope, and love, in imitation of Christ, in service of the community while opposing the community.

Another way to put this is that the question of the individual and the social is a question of how one understands the First Commandment. Kierkegaard's strength is that he overcomes to a large extent the heritage of "hidden inwardness," culminating in his vision of the roles of citizen and finally witness as models for Christian character and action. The dualism of the "two-kingdoms" model is put to the service not of separation of the religious and public realms, but to the service of religious critique of the social world. The witness points to the independence and priority of the religious against the incursions of the political realm. Although an expression of "dying from the world," the witness is directed to God and to the world and neighbor. For this reason Kierkegaard's vision of the "witness" as expression of Christian existence embraces a concern for society, rather than a flight from existence. The passions and virtues of faith, hope, and love are requirements of personality and *praxis* necessary for the struggle of the individual in the world.

One question remains: is there a specifically Christian theological warrant for constructive work to *alter* political and social structures? On one hand, his vision of the religious witness stresses yet the "boundaries" preventing the encroachment of the secular. Kierkegaard continues to reject what he calls the "awakened" reforming zealot who reduces Christian faith to backroom politicking and self-righteousness. In maintaining the distinction between the religious and political realms, the dualism still at work in the later Kierkegaard is aimed not at reforming human institutions in the name of God's sovereignty, but at reclaiming the *boundary* between the two kingdoms that modern culture seeks to obliterate. Even when at the end in the "attack" he advocates change in the "objective" world in calling for the state to exercise its power to dispel the illusion of "Christendom," the goal is the assertion of the boundary.[86] Thus, despite Kierkegaard's abandonment of the earlier Lutheran two-kingdoms understanding in the interests of defining a public witness-martyr role for the Christian, the

---

[86]   Kirmmse, *Kierkegaard in Golden Age Denmark*, 467.

two-kingdoms conception is brought back in outlining the absolute good of the religious *in contrast* to the relative good of the political realm. As Kirmmse puts it, "there are no positive inferences of political *content* to be made from Christianity." This is hardly conservatism, Kirmmse maintains, but is rather classic liberalism, in embracing a purely secular understanding of the state. In contrast to Grundtvig's populism uniting Christianity with Danish folk culture, for Kierke-gaard, as a classic liberal (rather than a conservative), religion and politics must be kept separate. The state is secular; there can be no Christian state.[87] In Kierkegaard's own day, the Christian reformist option represented by Grundtvigian populism was so tainted by mixing Christian faith with romanticized Danish nationalism, political machi-nations, and its elevation of the "crowd," that Kierkegaard found it tantamount, crudely, to abandoning the absolute (Christianity) in pursuit of relative ends (votes). If Kierkegaard is a classic liberal suspicious for political and religious reasons of any attempt to sacralize the political realm, especially in the name of Christianity, he also runs the risk of classic liberals, allowing the political realm a *relative* independence.

Yet, on the other hand, there are resources for theologically motivated constructive political action aimed at altering the structures of society, beyond the "boundary ethic," without subordinating the priority of the individual's relation before God. Such resources, especially in *Works of Love*, can result in a more "world-affirming spirituality" that not only maintains the boundaries, but affirms the divine transcendence in creation and in Incarnational love; created by God, the world is fallen and therefore to be criticized – but with the object of redeeming it. In imitation of Christ, the world is the arena for prophetic faithfulness, courageous hope, and reconciling love. This vision is relatively "undeveloped" in Kierkegaard's later thought, given his stress on the witness role in the context of the attack, yet the resources are there.[88]

The great value of the later Kierkegaard's Christian social-political thought lies, however, finally in clarifying the peculiarly modern forces of idolatry and the subversion of Christianity to worldly norms. In probing the nature of idolatry, Kierkegaard reveals with clarity and passion the ways in which the "world," usually in the form of the

---

[87] Kirmmse, *Kierkegaard in Golden Age Denmark*, 448, 420, 421.

[88] See Michael Plekon's suggestive essays on the creational and Incarnational foundations of Kierkegaard's thought, as well as Kresten Nordentoft's work.

state, church, or group, and often in the name of Christianity, claims
to speak in the name of God, whereas it actually merely sacralizes
that group's self-interest, whether in the deathlike "silence" of Golden
Age Denmark's elitist amalgamation of Christianity and culture in
"Christendom," or in the subtle or horrific tyrannies of the modern
age. Kierkegaard knew, as surely as did Feuerbach, how "God"
becomes the mere projection of the group's identity and values, in
particular how the church sides with the crucifiers.[89] But, unlike
Feuerbach, Kierkegaard saw God as the Holy One who stands with
the outcast and crucified. Christ as Pattern for discipleship in this way
provides the transcendent revealed model for existence that offers the
standard for an individual to stand against her or his culture, to
embody and "do the truth." In outlining the stance of "witness to the
truth," Kierkegaard offers the imaginative conceptual tools to *recognize*
such worldliness when it arises and to *expect* such opposition; he
articulates and defends for the Christian community a stance of
opposition that the community itself may well not recognize; moreover, this vision of Christian existence as "witness to the truth" opens
to his readers the means for developing the personal virtues – the
patience, courage, and faith, hope, and love – that allow one to take
up the call to a discipleship of witness. Kierkegaard calls for human
beings to relate to none less than God, one by one, and calls too for
Christian existence in loyal discipleship to Jesus Christ, even unto
death. The alternative he points out is spiritual desolation, whether in
"spiritless" worldliness and mediocrity or the defiance that, because
the world hates the truth, demands the adoration due only to God –
or at least silence in face of its lies. In stating the standards, the ideal
of Christian existence, Christianity is not mere "belief," but is passion
and a shaping of the heart that beyond "hidden inwardness" is
"*praxis*, a character-task," the devotion of the entire self to God alone,
in which one seeks to live in faith, hope, and love.[90]

[89] On the themes of violence and despair, see Charles Bellinger, "Toward a Kierkegaardian
      Understanding of Hitler, Stalin, and the Cold War," in Connell and Evans, *Foundations of
      Kierkegaard's Vision of Community*, 218–30. Violence and the crucified, in relation to aesthetic
      image, is an important concern also in George Pattison, *Kierkegaard: The Aesthetic and the
      Religious*.
[90] *JP* IV 3864 (*Pap.* x^5 A 134, n.d., 1853).

Bibliography

For Kierkegaard's writings see abbreviations

Agacinski, Sylviane, *Aparté: Conceptions and Deaths of Søren Kierkegaard* (Tallahassee: Florida State University Press, 1988).

Althaus, Paul, *The Theology of Martin Luther*, trans. Robert C. Schultz (Philadelphia: Fortress Press, 1966).

Andic, Martin, "Confidence as a Work of Love," in George Pattison, ed., *Kierkegaard on Art and Communication* (New York: St. Martin's Press, 1992), 160–84.

Arbaugh, G. E., "Christian Virtues," in Niels Thulstrup and Marie Mikulová Thulstrup, eds., *The Sources and Depths of Faith in Kierkegaard, Bibliotheca Kierkegaardiana*, 16 vols. (Copenhagen: C. A. Reitzel, 1978), II, 100–04.

Arndt, Johann, *True Christianity*, trans. and Introduction Peter Erb. Preface by Heiko A. Oberman (New York, NY; Ramsey, NJ; Toronto, ON: Paulist Press, 1979).

Augustine, *Confessions*, trans. with an Introduction R. S. Pine-Coffin (Harmondsworth: Penguin Books, 1961).

Barrett, Cyril, *Wittgenstein on Ethics and Religious Belief* (Oxford and Cambridge, MA: Blackwell, 1991).

Barrett, Lee, "Kierkegaard's *Two Ages*: An Immediate Stage on the Way to the Religious Life," in Robert L. Perkins, ed., *International Kierkegaard Commentary, Volume 14:* Two Ages (Macon, GA: Mercer University Press, 1984), 53–71.

"Kierkegaard's 'Anxiety' and the Augustinian Doctrine of Original Sin," in Robert L. Perkins, ed., *International Kierkegaard Commentary, Volume 8:* The Concept of Anxiety (Macon, GA: Mercer University Press, 1985), 35–61.

Barth, Karl, *Church Dogmatics*, 4 vols. (Edinburgh: T. &. T. Clark, 1956–75).

Bell, Richard H., ed., *The Grammar of the Heart: Thinking with Kierkegaard and Wittgenstein: New Essays in Moral Philosophy and Theology* (San Francisco: Harper & Row, 1988).

Bell, Richard H., and Ronald E. Hustwit, eds., *Essays on Kierkegaard and Wittgenstein: On Understanding the Self* (Wooster, OH: The College of Wooster, 1978).

Bellinger, Charles, "Toward a Kierkegaardian Understanding of Hitler, Stalin, and the Cold War," in George B. Connell and C. Stephen Evans, eds., *Foundations of Kierkegaard's Vision of Community: Religion, Ethics, and Politics in Kierkegaard* (Atlantic Highlands, NJ, and London: Humanities Press, 1992), 218–30.

Bohlin, Torsten, *Kierkegaards dogmatiska åskådning* (*Kierkegaard's Dogmatic Views*) (Stockholm: Svenska Kyrkans Diakonistyrelses, 1925).

   Kierkegaards dogmatische Anschauung, trans. Ilse Meyer-Lüne (Gütersloh: Bertelsmann, 1927).

Bonhoeffer, Dietrich, *The Cost of Discipleship*, trans. R. H. Fuller, with some revision by Irmgard Booth (New York: Macmillan, 1963).

Bouwsma, O. K., "The Blue Book," in *Philosophical Essays* (Lincoln: The University of Nebraska Press, 1965), 175–201.

   "Notes on 'The Monstrous Illusion,'" *Perkins Journal* 24 (Spring 1971).

   Wittgenstein: Conversations 1949–1951, ed. with an Introduction by J. L. Craft and Ronald E. Hustwit. (Indianapolis: Hackett Publishing Company, 1986).

Bultmann, Rudolf, *Jesus Christ and Mythology* (New York: Charles Scribner's Sons, 1958).

   Kerygma and Myth: A Theological Debate, rev. trans. R. H. Fuller (New York: Harper & Row, 1961).

Cappelørn, N. J., "The Retrospective Understanding of Kierkegaard's Total Production," in Alastair McKinnon, ed. and Introduction, *Kierkegaard: Resources and Results* (Waterloo, ON: Wilfrid Laurier University Press, 1982), 18–38.

Caputo, John, *Radical Hermeneutics: Repetition, Deconstruction, and the Hermeneutic Project* (Bloomington: Indiana University Press, 1987).

Cavell, Stanley, "The Availability of Wittgenstein's Later Philosophy," in George Pitcher, ed., *Wittgenstein:* The Philosophical Investigations. *Modern Studies in Philosophy*, ed. Amelie Rorty. Anchor Books. (Garden City, NY: Doubleday & Co., 1966), 151–85.

   "Kierkegaard's *On Authority and Revelation*," in Josiah Thompson, ed., *Kierkegaard: A Collection of Critical Essays. Modern Studies in Philosophy*, ed. Amelie Oksenberg Rorty. (Garden City, NY: Doubleday-Anchor, 1972), 373–93.

Conant, James, "Kierkegaard, Wittgenstein, and Nonsense," in Ted Cohen, Paul Guyer, and Hilary Putnam, eds., *Pursuits of Reason: Essays in Honor of Stanley Cavell* (Lubbock, TX: Texas Tech University Press, 1993), 195–224.

Connell, George B., *To Be One Thing: Personal Unity in Kierkegaard's Thought* (Macon, GA: Mercer University Press, 1985).

   "Judge William's Theonomous Ethics," in George B. Connell and C. Stephen Evans, *Foundations of Kierkegaard's Vision of Community: Religion, Ethics, and Politics in Kierkegaard* (Atlantic Highlands, NJ; London: Humanities Press, 1992), 56–70.

Creegan, Charles L., *Wittgenstein and Kierkegaard: Religion, Individuality, and*

Philosophical Method (London and New York: Routledge & Kegan Paul, 1989).

Crites, Stephen D., *The Twilight of Christendom: Kierkegaard v. Hegel on Faith and History.* AAR Studies in Religion (Chambersburg, PA: American Academy of Religion, 1972).

Dewey, Bradley R., *The New Obedience: Kierkegaard on Imitating Christ.* Foreword by Paul L. Holmer (Washington, Cleveland: Corpus, 1968).

"Kierkegaard on Suffering: Promise and Lack of Fulfillment in Life's Stages," *Humanitas* 9:1 (February 1973): 21–45.

Diem, Hermann, *Kierkegaard's Dialectic of Existence*, trans. Harold Knight (London: Oliver & Boyd, 1959).

Drury, M. O'C., "Conversations with Wittgenstein," in Rush Rhees, ed., *Recollections of Wittgenstein* (Oxford University Press, 1984), 97–171.

"Some Notes on Conversations with Wittgenstein," in Rush Rhees, ed., *Recollections of Wittgenstein* (Oxford University Press, 1984), 76–96.

Dunning, Stephen N., *Kierkegaard's Dialectic of Inwardness* (Princeton University Press, 1985).

"Kierkegaard's 'Hegelian' Response to Hamann," *Thought* 55:218 (September 1980): 259–70.

"Kierkegaard's Systematic Analysis of Anxiety," in Robert L. Perkins, ed., *International Kierkegaard Commentary, Volume 8:* The Concept of Anxiety (Macon, GA: Mercer University Press, 1985), 7–33.

Dupré, Louis, *Kierkegaard as Theologian: The Dialectic of Christian Existence* (New York: Sheed and Ward, 1963).

Elrod, John W., *Being and Existence in Kierkegaard's Pseudonymous Works* (Princeton University Press, 1975).

Kierkegaard and Christendom (Princeton University Press, 1981).

"Climacus, Anti-Climacus and the Problem of Suffering," *Thought* 55:218 (September 1980): 306–19.

Emmanuel, Steven M., "Kierkegaard on Doctrine: A Post-Modern Interpretation," *Religious Studies* 25:3 (September 1989): 363–78.

Evans, C. Stephen, *Kierkegaard's* Fragments *and* Postscript: *The Religious Philosophy of Johannes Climacus* (Atlantic Highlands, NJ: Humanities Press International, 1983).

Søren Kierkegaard's Christian Psychology: Insight for Counseling and Pastoral Care (Grand Rapids, MI: Zondervan, 1990).

Passionate Reason: Making Sense of Kierkegaard's Philosophical Fragments. The Indiana Series in the Philosophy of Religion, general ed., Merold Westphal (Bloomington and Indianapolis: Indiana University Press, 1992).

Fenger, Henning, *Kierkegaard: The Myths and Their Origins: Studies in the Kierkegaardian Papers and Letters,* trans. George C. Schoolfield (New Haven: Yale University Press, 1980) .

Ferreira, M. Jamie, *Transforming Vision: Imagination and Will in Kierkegaardian Faith* (Oxford: Clarendon Press, 1992).

Fowler, James W., *Stages of Faith: The Psychology of Human Development and the Quest for Meaning* (San Francisco: Harper & Row, 1981).

Frei, Hans W., *Types of Christian Theology*, ed. George Hunsinger and William C. Placher (New Haven: Yale University Press, 1992).

Theology and Narrative: Selected Essays, ed. George Hunsinger and William C. Placher (New York: Oxford University Press, 1993).

"An Afterword: Eberhard Busch's Biography of Karl Barth," in H.-Martin Rumscheidt, ed., *Karl Barth in Re-View: Posthumous Works Reviewed and Assessed* (Pittsburgh, PA: The Pickwick Press, 1981).

Garff, Joakim, "The Eyes of Argus: The Point of View and Points of View with Respect to Kierkegaard's 'Activity as an Author,'" *Kierkegaardiana* 15 (1991): 29–54.

Goold, Patrick, "Reading Kierkegaard: Two Pitfalls and a Strategy for Avoiding Them," *Faith and Philosophy* 7:3 (July 1990): 304–15.

Gouwens, David J., *Kierkegaard's Dialectic of the Imagination* (New York: Peter Lang, 1989).

"Kierkegaard's Understanding of Doctrine," *Modern Theology* 5:1 (October 1988): 13–22.

"Understanding, Imagination, and Irony in Kierkegaard's *Repetition*," in Robert L. Perkins, ed., *International Kierkegaard Commentary: Volume 6: Fear and Trembling and Repetition* (Macon, GA: Mercer University Press, 1993), 283–308.

Green, Ronald M., *Kierkegaard and Kant: The Hidden Debt* (Albany: State University of New York Press, 1992).

Hall, Harrison, "Love and Death: Kierkegaard and Heidegger on Authentic and Inauthentic Human Existence," *Inquiry* 27 (1984): 179–97.

Hamann, Johann Georg, *Briefwechsel*, ed. Walther Ziesemer and Arthur Henkel, 6 vols. (Wiesbaden: Insel, 1955–75).

Hannay, Alastair, *Kierkegaard. The Arguments of the Philosophers*, ed. Ted Honderich (London and New York: Routledge & Kegan Paul, 1982).

"Refuge and Religion," in *Faith, Knowledge, and Action: Essays to Niels Thulstrup*, ed. George L. Stengren (Copenhagen: Reitzels Forlag, 1984).

"Reply to Roberts' Critique," *Kierkegaardiana* 14 (1988): 114–21.

Hauerwas, Stanley, "The Significance of Vision: Toward an Aesthetic Ethic," in *Vision and Virtue: Essays in Christian Ethical Reflection* (Notre Dame, IN: Fides Publishers, 1974), 30–47.

Heidegger, Martin, *Being and Time*, trans. John Macquarrie and Edward Robinson (New York and Evanston: Harper & Row, 1962).

Henriksen, Aage, *Kierkegaards Romaner* (Copenhagen: Gyldendal, 1954).

Hepburn, Ronald W., "Religious Imagination," in Michael McGhee, ed., *Philosophy, Religion and the Spiritual Life. Royal Institute of Philosophy Supplement: 32* (Cambridge University Press, 1992), 127–43.

Holmer, Paul L., *The Grammar of Faith* (San Francisco: Harper & Row, 1978).

"Kierkegaard and Logic," *Kierkegaardiana* 2 (1957): 25–42.

Hong, Howard, "*Tanke-Experiment* in Kierkegaard," in Alastair McKinnon, ed.

and Introduction, *Kierkegaard: Resources and Results* (Waterloo, ON: Wilfrid Laurier University Press, 1982), 39–51.

Hunsinger, George, *How to Read Karl Barth: The Shape of His Theology* (New York: Oxford University Press, 1991).

Johnson, Samuel, *The Rambler, No. 196*, in Samuel Johnson, *Essays from the Rambler, Adventurer, and Idler*, ed. W. J. Bate (New Haven; London: Yale University Press, 1968).

Keeley, Louise Carroll, "Subjectivity and World in *Works of Love*," in George B. Connell and C. Stephen Evans, eds., *Foundations of Kierkegaard's Vision of Community: Religion, Ethics, and Politics in Kierkegaard* (Atlantic Highlands, NJ, and London: Humanities Press, 1992), 96–108.

Kerr, Fergus, *Theology after Wittgenstein* (Oxford and New York: Basil Blackwell, 1986).

Khan, Abrahim H., *Salighed as Happiness? Kierkegaard on the Concept* Salighed (Waterloo, ON: Wilfrid Laurier University Press, 1985).

Kirmmse, Bruce H., *Kierkegaard in Golden Age Denmark* (Bloomington and Indianapolis: Indiana University Press, 1990).

Lash, Nicholas, *Easter in Ordinary: Reflections on Human Experience and the Knowledge of God* (Charlottesville: University Press of Virginia, 1986).

Law, David R., *Kierkegaard as Negative Theologian* (Oxford: Clarendon Press, 1993).

Lebowitz, Naomi, *Kierkegaard: A Life of Allegory* (Baton Rouge and London: Louisiana State University Press, 1985).

Lessing, G. E., "On the Proof of the Spirit and of Power," in Henry Chadwick, ed., *Lessing's Theological Writings* (Stanford University Press, 1956), 51–56.

Lewis, C. S., *Surprised by Joy: The Shape of My Early Life* (New York: Harcourt, Brace & World, 1955).

"The Language of Religion," in Walter Hooper, ed., *Christian Reflections* (Grand Rapids, MI: William B. Eerdmans, 1967), 129–41.

"Religion Without Dogma?," in Walter Hooper, ed., *God in the Dock: Essays on Theology and Ethics* (Grand Rapids, MI: William B. Eerdmans, 1970), 129–46.

Lindström, Valter, *Stadiernas Teologie, en Kierkegaard Studie* (Lund: Haakon Ohlsons, 1943).

Lovibond, Sabina, *Realism and Imagination in Ethics* (Minneapolis: University of Minnesota Press, 1983).

Lowe, Walter, "Christ and Salvation," in Peter C. Hodgson and Robert H. King, eds., *Christian Theology: An Introduction to Its Traditions and Tasks* (Philadelphia: Fortress Press, 1982), 196–222.

Lowrie, Walter, *Kierkegaard* (New York: Oxford University Press, 1938).

A Short Life of Kierkegaard (Princeton University Press, 1942; 1965).

Lønning, Per, "Kierkegaard as a Christian Thinker," in Niels Thulstrup and Marie Mikulová Thulstrup, eds., *Kierkegaard's View of Christianity, Bibliotheca Kierkegaardiana*, 16 vols. (Copenhagen: C. A. Reitzel, 1978), 1, 163–78.

McCarthy, Vincent A., *The Phenomenology of Moods in Kierkegaard* (The Hague; Boston: Martinus Nijhoff, 1978).

McCormack, Bruce L., *Karl Barth's Critically Realistic Dialectical Theology: Its Genesis and Development, 1909–36* (New York: Oxford University Press, 1995).

McKinnon, Alastair, "Søren Kierkegaard," in Ninian Smart, John Clayton, Steven Katz, and Patrick Sherry, eds., *Nineteenth Century Religious Thought in the West*, 3 vols. (Cambridge University Press, 1985), I, 181–213.

MacIntyre, Alasdair, *After Virtue* (University of Notre Dame Press, 1981).

Mackey, Louis, *Kierkegaard: A Kind of Poet* (Philadelphia: University of Pennsylvania Press, 1971).

  Points of View: Readings of Kierkegaard (Tallahassee: Florida State University Press, 1986).

  "The Loss of the World in Kierkegaard's Ethics," in Josiah Thompson, ed., *Kierkegaard: A Collection of Critical Essays. Modern Studies in Philosophy*, ed. Amelie Oksenberg Rorty. (Garden City, NY: Doubleday-Anchor, 1972), 266–88.

Malantschuk, Gregor, *Kierkegaard's Thought*, ed. and trans. Howard V. Hong and Edna H. Hong (Princeton University Press, 1971).

Marino, Gordon D., "Salvation: A Reply to Harrison Hall's Reading of Kierkegaard," *Inquiry* 28 (1985): 441–49.

Mehl, Peter J., "Kierkegaard and the Relativist Challenge to Practical Philosophy," *Journal of Religious Ethics* 14 (1987): 247–78.

Meilaender, Gilbert C., *The Theory and Practice of Virtue* (University of Notre Dame Press, 1984).

Michalson, Jr., Gordon E., "Kierkegaard's Debt to Lessing: Response to Whisenant," *Modern Theology* 6:4 (July 1990): 379–84.

Minear, Paul S., "Thanksgiving as a Synthesis of the Temporal and the Eternal," in Howard A. Johnson and Niels Thulstrup, eds., *A Kierkegaard Critique* (New York: Harper & Brothers, 1962), 297–311.

Minear, Paul, and Paul S. Morimoto, *Kierkegaard and the Bible: An Index* (Princeton Theological Seminary, 1953).

Mooney, Edward F., *Knights of Faith and Resignation: Reading Kierkegaard's* Fear and Trembling (Albany, NY: State University of New York Press, 1991).

  "Kierkegaard Our Contemporary: Reason, Subjectivity and the Self," *Southern Journal of Philosophy* (Fall 1989): 381–97.

Murdoch, Iris, *The Sovereignty of Good* (New York: Schocken Books, 1971).

  "Against Dryness: A Polemical Sketch," in Stanley Hauerwas and Alasdair MacIntyre, eds., *Revisions: Changing Perspectives in Moral Philosophy* (Notre Dame and London: University of Notre Dame Press, 1983), 43–50.

Müller, Paul, *Kristendom, etik og majeutik i Søren Kierkegaard's "Kjerlighedens Gjerninger,"* 2. oplag. (Viborg: C. A. Reitzels Forlag, 1983).

  Kierkegaard's Works of Love: Christian Ethics and the Maieutic Ideal, trans. C. Stephen Evans and Jan Evans (Copenhagen: C. A. Reitzel, 1993).

  "The God's Poem – The God's History," in Birgit Bertung, ed., *Kierkegaard*

– *Poet of Existence. Kierkegaard Conferences 1.* (Copenhagen: C.A. Reitzel, 1989), 83–88.

Nagley, Winfield E., "Kierkegaard's Early and Later View of Socratic Irony," *Thought* 55:218 (September 1980): 271–82.

Nicoletti, Michele, "Politics and Religion in Kierkegaard's Thought: Secularization and the Martyr," in George B. Connell and C. Stephen Evans, eds., *Foundations of Kierkegaard's Vision of Community: Religion, Ethics, and Politics in Kierkegaard* (Atlantic Highlands, NJ, and London: Humanities Press, 1992), 183–95.

Nielsen, H. A., *Where the Passion Is: A Reading of Kierkegaard's* Philosophical Fragments (Tallahassee: University Presses of Florida, 1983).

Nordentoft, Kresten, *Hvad Siger Brand Majoren?: Kierkegaards Opgør med sin Samtid* (*What Says the Fire-Chief?: Kierkegaard's Settling-Up with His Times*) (Copenhagen: G. E. C. Gad, 1973).

Kierkegaard's Psychology, trans. Bruce Kirmmse (Pittsburgh: Duquesne University Press, 1978).

Norris, Christopher, *The Deconstructive Turn: Essays in the Rhetoric of Philosophy* (London and New York: Methuen, 1983).

"De Man Unfair to Kierkegaard?: An Allegory of (Non)-Reading," in Birgit Bertung, ed., *Kierkegaard – Poet of Existence. Kierkegaard Conferences 1* (Copenhagen: C. A. Reitzel, 1989), 89–107.

"The Ethics of Reading and the Limits of Irony: Kierkegaard Among the Postmodernists," *Southern Humanities Review* 23:1 (Winter 1989): 1–35.

Nygren, Anders, *Agape and Eros*, trans. Philip S. Watson (New York: Harper & Row, 1969).

O'Flaherty, James C., *Johann Georg Hamann* (Boston: Twayne, 1979).

Outka, Gene, *Agape: An Ethical Analysis* (New Haven; London: Yale University Press, 1972).

"Equality and Individuality: Thoughts on Two Themes in Kierkegaard," *The Journal of Religious Ethics* 10:2 (Fall 1982): 171–203.

Pattison, George, *Kierkegaard: The Aesthetic and the Religious: From the Magic Theatre to the Crucifixion of the Image* (New York: St. Martin's Press, 1992).

Perkins, Robert L., ed., *International Kierkegaard Commentary: Volume 13: The Corsair Affair* (Macon, GA: Mercer University Press, 1990).

"Comment on Hong," in Alastair McKinnon, ed. and Introduction, *Kierkegaard: Resources and Results* (Waterloo, ON: Wilfrid Laurier University Press, 1982), 52–55.

"Kierkegaard, A Kind of Epistemologist," *Journal of the History of European Ideas* 12:1 (1990): 7–18.

Phillips, D. Z., *Belief, Change and Forms of Life* (Atlantic Highlands, NJ: Humanities Press International, 1986).

Wittgenstein and Religion (New York: St. Martin's Press, 1993).

Placher, William C., *Unapologetic Theology: A Christian Voice in a Pluralistic Conversation* (Louisville, KY: Westminster/John Knox Press, 1989).

Plekon, Michael, "'Anthropological Contemplation': Kierkegaard and Modern Social Theory," *Thought* 55 (1980): 346–69.

"Towards Apocalypse: Kierkegaard's *Two Ages* in Golden Age Denmark," in Robert L. Perkins, ed., *International Kierkegaard Commentary, Volume 14: Two Ages* (Macon, GA: Mercer University Press, 1984), 19–52.

"Kierkegaard the Theologian: The Roots of His Theology in *Works of Love*," in George B. Connell and C. Stephen Evans, eds., *Foundations of Kierkegaard's Vision of Community: Religion, Ethics, and Politics in Kierkegaard* (Atlantic Highlands, NJ, and London: Humanities Press, 1992), 2–17.

Pojman, Louis, *The Logic of Subjectivity: Kierkegaard's Philosophy of Religion* (University of Alabama Press, 1984).

Polk, Timothy, "'Heart Enough To Be Confident': Kierkegaard on Reading James," in Richard H. Bell, ed., *The Grammar of the Heart: Thinking with Kierkegaard and Wittgenstein: New Essays in Moral Philosophy and Theology* (San Francisco: Harper & Row, 1988), 206–33.

Popkin, Richard H., "Kierkegaard and Scepticism," in Josiah Thompson, ed., *Kierkegaard: A Collection of Critical Essays. Modern Studies in Philosophy*, ed. Amelie Oksenberg Rorty (Garden City, NY: Doubleday-Anchor, 1972), 342–72.

Proudfoot, Wayne, *Religious Experience* (Berkeley: University of California Press, 1985).

Putnam, Hilary, *Renewing Philosophy* (Cambridge, MA; London: Harvard University Press, 1992).

Roberts, Robert C., *Rudolf Bultmann's Theology: A Critical Interpretation* (Grand Rapids, MI: William B. Eerdmans, 1976).

Spirituality and Human Emotion (Grand Rapids, MI: William B. Eerdmans, 1982).

Faith, Reason, and History: Rethinking Kierkegaard's Philosophical Fragments (Macon, GA: Mercer University Press, 1986).

"A Critique of Alastair Hannay's Interpretation of the *Philosophical Fragments*," *Kierkegaardiana* 13 (1984): 149–54.

"Will Power and the Virtues," *The Philosophical Review* 93 (April 1984): 227–47.

"The Socratic Knowledge of God," in Robert L. Perkins, ed., *International Kierkegaard Commentary, Volume 8:* The Concept of Anxiety (Macon, GA: Mercer University Press, 1985), 133–52.

"Therapies and the Grammar of a Virtue," in Richard H. Bell, ed., *The Grammar of the Heart: Thinking with Kierkegaard and Wittgenstein: New Essays in Moral Philosophy and Theology* (San Francisco: Harper & Row, 1988), 149–70.

"What Is an Emotion? A Sketch," *The Philosophical Review* 97 (April 1988): 183–209.

Roos, H., "Søren Kierkegaard und die Kenosis-Lehre," *Kierkegaardiana* 2 (1957): 54–60.

Rosas, III, L. Joseph, *Scripture in the Thought of Søren Kierkegaard* (Nashville: Broadman and Holman, 1994).

Rudd, Anthony, *Kierkegaard and the Limits of the Ethical* (Oxford: Clarendon Press, 1993).

Ryle, Gilbert, *The Concept of Mind* (London: Hutchinson, 1949).

Saliers, Don E., *Worship as Theology: Foretaste of Glory Divine* (Nashville: Abingdon, 1994).

"Religious Affections and the Grammar of Prayer," in Richard H. Bell, ed., *The Grammar of the Heart: Thinking with Kierkegaard and Wittgenstein: New Essays in Moral Philosophy and Theology* (San Francisco: Harper & Row, 1988), 188–205.

Schleiermacher, Friedrich, *The Christian Faith*, ed. H. R. Mackintosh and J. S. Stewart (Edinburgh: T. & T. Clark, 1928).

Schmid, Heinrich, *Doctrinal Theology of the Evangelical Lutheran Church*, trans. Charles A. Hay and Henry E. Jacobs (Minneapolis: Augsburg, 1899).

Sherry, Patrick, *Religion, Truth and Language-Games* (London: Macmillan, 1977).

Sløk, Johannes, *Da Kierkegaard Tav: Fra Forfatterskab til Kirkestorm* (*When Kierkegaard Remained Silent: From the Authorship to the Attack on the Church*) (Copenhagen: Reitzel, 1980).

Smyth, John Vignaux, *A Question of Eros: Irony in Sterne, Kierkegaard, and Barthes* (Tallahassee: Florida State University Press, 1986).

Swenson, David F., "The Anti-Intellectualism of Kierkegaard," in *Something About Kierkegaard* (Minneapolis: Augsburg, 1941), 95–118.

Taylor, Charles, *Sources of the Self: The Making of the Modern Identity* (Cambridge, MA: Harvard University Press, 1989).

Taylor, Mark C., *Kierkegaard's Pseudonymous Authorship: A Study of Time and the Self* (Princeton University Press, 1975).

Journeys to Selfhood: Hegel and Kierkegaard (Berkeley: University of California Press, 1980).

Taylor, Mark Lloyd, "Ordeal and Repetition in Kierkegaard's Treatment of Abraham and Job," in George B. Connell and C. Stephen Evans, eds., *Foundations of Kierkegaard's Vision of Community: Religion, Ethics, and Politics in Kierkegaard* (Atlantic Highlands, NJ, and London: Humanities Press, 1992), 33–53.

Thomas, J. Heywood, *Subjectivity and Paradox* (Oxford: Basil Blackwell, 1957).

Thompson, Josiah, *The Lonely Labyrinth: Kierkegaard's Pseudonymous Works* (Carbondale, IL: Southern Illinois University Press, 1967).

Kierkegaard (New York: Alfred A. Knopf, 1973).

Thulstrup, Marie Mikulová, "Studies of Pietists, Mystics, and Church Fathers," in Niels Thulstrup and Marie Mikulová Thulstrup, eds., *Kierkegaard's View of Christianity*, Bibliotheca Kierkegaardiana, 16 vols. (Copenhagen: C. A. Reitzel, 1978), 1, 60–80.

Thulstrup, Niels, *Kierkegaard's Relation to Hegel*, trans. George L. Stengren (Princeton University Press, 1980).

Commentary on Kierkegaard's Concluding Unscientific Postscript, *with a New Introduction*, trans. Robert J. Widenmann (Princeton University Press, 1984).

"Theological and Philosophical Studies," in Niels Thulstrup and Marie Mikulová Thulstrup, eds., *Kierkegaard's View of Christianity, Bibliotheca Kierkegaardiana*, 16 vols. (Copenhagen: C. A. Reitzel, 1978), 1, 38–60.

Tillich, Paul, *Biblical Religion and the Search for Ultimate Reality* (University of Chicago Press, 1955).

Systematic Theology. Three volumes in one. (University of Chicago Press; New York and Evanston: Harper & Row, 1967).

Viallaneix, Nelly, "The Law of 'Gjentagelse,'" in Birgit Bertung, ed., *Kierkegaard – Poet of Existence. Kierkegaard Conferences 1* (Copenhagen: C. A. Reitzel, 1989), 120–31.

Walker, Jeremy, *Kierkegaard: The Descent into God* (Kingston and Montreal: McGill-Queen's University Press, 1985).

"The Idea of Reward in Morality," *Kierkegaardiana* 8: 30–52.

Walsh, Sylvia, *Living Poetically: Kierkegaard's Existential Aesthetics* (University Park, PA: The Pennsylvania State University Press, 1994).

"Kierkegaard: Poet of the Religious," in George Pattison, ed., *Kierkegaard on Art and Communication* (New York: St. Martin's Press, 1992), 1–22.

"Forming the Heart: The Role of Love in Kierkegaard," in Richard H. Bell, ed., *The Grammar of the Heart: Thinking with Kierkegaard and Wittgenstein: New Essays in Moral Philosophy and Theology* (San Francisco: Harper & Row, 1988), 234–56.

Weil, Simone, *Waiting for God*, trans. Emma Craufurd, Introduction Leslie A. Fiedler (New York: G. P. Putnam's Sons, 1951).

Gravity and Grace, trans. Arthur Wills, Introduction Gustave Thibon (New York: G. P. Putnam's Sons, 1952).

First and Last Notebooks, trans. Richard Rees (Oxford University Press, 1970).

Welch, Claude, ed. and trans., *God and Incarnation in Mid-Nineteenth Century German Theology* (New York: Oxford University Press, 1965).

Westphal, Merold, *God, Guilt, and Death: An Existential Phenomenology of Religion* (Bloomington: Indiana University Press, 1984).

Kierkegaard's Critique of Reason and Society (Macon, GA: Mercer University Press, 1987).

"Kierkegaard's Phenomenology of Faith as Suffering," in Hugh J. Silverman, ed., *Writing the Politics of Difference, Selected Studies in Phenomenology and Existential Philosophy* 14 (Albany: State University of New York Press, 1991), 55–71.

"Kierkegaard's Teleological Suspension of Religiousness B," in George B. Connell and C. Stephen Evans, eds., *Foundations of Kierkegaard's Vision of Community: Religion, Ethics, and Politics in Kierkegaard* (Atlantic Highlands, NJ, and London: Humanities Press, 1992), 110–29.

Whittaker, John H., "Christianity Is Not a Doctrine," in Richard H. Bell, ed., *The Grammar of the Heart: Thinking with Kierkegaard and Wittgenstein: New*

Essays in Moral Philosophy and Theology (San Francisco: Harper & Row, 1988), 54–74.

Williams, Rowan, " 'Religious Realism': On Not Quite Agreeing with Don Cupitt," *Modern Theology* 1:1 (1984): 3–24.

Winch, Peter, *Simone Weil: "The Just Balance"* (Cambridge University Press, 1989).

Wisdo, David, "Kierkegaard on Belief, Faith, and Explanation," *International Journal for Philosophy of Religion* 21 (1987): 95–114.

Wittgenstein, Ludwig, *Philosophical Investigations*, trans. G. E. M. Anscombe (New York: The Macmillan Company, 1953).

Zettel, ed. G. E. M. Anscombe and G. H. von Wright, with English translation, G. E. M. Anscombe (Oxford: Basil Blackwell, 1967).

Lectures and Conversations on Aesthetics, Psychology and Religious Belief, ed. Cyril Barrett (Berkeley and Los Angeles: University of California Press, 1972).

Wittgenstein's Lectures Cambridge 1932–1935, ed. Alice Ambrose (Oxford: Basil Blackwell, 1979).

Culture and Value, trans. Peter Winch, ed., G. H. von Wright (Oxford: Basil Blackwell, 1980).

Index

GENERAL THEOLOGICAL SEMINARY
NEW YORK

DATE